6/05

THE
TRUTH
ABOUT
TOLERANCE

 Pluralism, Diversity and the Culture Wars

BRAD STETSON
AND JOSEPH G. CONTI

InterVarsity Press
Downers Grove, Illinois

InterVarsity Press
P.O. Box 1400, Downers Grove, IL 60515-1426
World Wide Web: www.ivpress.com
E-mail: mail@ivpress.com

InterVarsity Press® is the book-publishing division of InterVarsity Christian Fellowship/USA®, a student movement active on campus at hundreds of universities, colleges and schools of nursing in the United States of America, and a member movement of the International Fellowship of Evangelical Students. For information about local and regional activities, write Public Relations Dept., InterVarsity Christian Fellowship/USA, 6400 Schroeder Rd., P.O. Box 7895, Madison, WI 53707-7895, or visit the IVCF website at <www.intervarsity.org>.

All Scripture quotations, unless otherwise indicated, are taken from the Holy Bible, New International Version®. NIV®. *Copyright ©1973, 1978, 1984 by International Bible Society. Used by permission of Zondervan Publishing House. All rights reserved.*

The Prayer by Carole Bayer Sager and David Foster ©1998 Warner-Tamerlane Publishing Corp. (BMI). All rights reserved. Used by permission of Warner Bros. Publications U.S. Inc., Miami, FL. 33014.

Design: Cindy Kiple

ISBN 0-8308-2787-0

Printed in the United States of America ∞

Library of Congress Cataloging-in-Publication Data

Stetson, Brad.
  The truth about intolerance: pluralism, diversity, and the culture
wars / Brad Stetson and Joseph G. Conti.
    p. cm.
Includes bibliographical references and index.
ISBN 0-8308-2787-0 (alk. paper)
1. Toleration. 2. Religious tolerance—Christianity. 3.
Truth—Religious aspects—Christianity. 4. Christianity and
culture—United States. 5. Evangelicalism—United States. I. Conti,
Joseph G. II. Title.
BJ1431.S74 2005
179'.9—dc22

                                                                    2004025820

| **P** | 18 | 17 | 16 | 15 | 14 | 13 | 12 | 11 | 10 | 9 | 8 | 7 | 6 | 5 | 4 | 3 | 2 | 1 |
| **Y** | 18 | 17 | 16 | 15 | 14 | 13 | 12 | 11 | 10 | 09 | 08 | 07 | 06 | 05 | | | | |

In remembrance

Matthew David Wise

1985-2002

Inquisitive, kind, always gentle

CONTENTS

ACKNOWLEDGMENTS

Several people have assisted us, in various ways, in the production of this book. We would like to thank professor Peter Lowentrout of the department of religious studies at Cal State Long Beach and professor Ben Hubbard of the department of comparative religion at Cal State Fullerton.

We would also like to express appreciation to professor Steve Wilkens of the philosophy deptartment at Azusa Pacific University, and to Ms. Houri Hagopian, as well as professors Chris Flannery, Dan Palm and Bryan Lamkin, all of the department of history and political science at Azusa Pacific University. We are also grateful to Dr. David Weeks, dean of the college of letters, arts and sciences at Azusa Pacific University.

Thanks are also due to Andrew Paslovsky, Dr. Muazzam Gill, Dr. Charles Folcke, Frank Montejano, Steve Bivens, Ed Trenner, Hannah, Sam and Sophie Stetson, and Nina Stetson.

We are especially grateful to Dr. Gary Deddo and his colleagues at InterVarsity Press for their great patience and help.

The authors of this book are solely responsible for any of its errors or omissions.

PREFACE

Absolute tolerance is altogether impossible; the allegedly absolute tolerance turns into ferocious hatred of those who have stated clearly and most forcefully that there are unchangeable standards founded in the nature of man and the nature of things.

LEO STRAUSS

There is widespread feeling today that something is very wrong with the way we think about tolerance. We have an intuition that in our diverse society tolerance is very important to practice, but at the same time we are unable to agree on what exactly it means to be tolerant. Does tolerance require the acceptance of all views on a given subject as equally true? Does it mean that I must not believe too strongly that my views are right about a given subject? Can I be tolerant and still believe in objective truth about religion, ethics and politics?

These are just three of the broad questions that any consideration of tolerance immediately places before us. But reflection on tolerance, like any topic of moment, leads very quickly into other topics, such as the nature of truth, the nature of human beings and the possibility of moral knowledge. Any study of tolerance will inevitably be broad in scope and interdisciplinary in focus, and this one is no exception. This book is not intended to be a technical philosophical or political tome on tolerance; nor does it have any pretensions of being a comprehensive study detailed in every respect. Rather the style and method of this work is impressionistic and panoramic; it seeks mainly to give to readers, in the worldview context of evangelical Christianity, an overview of the intersection of truth and tolerance in contemporary American social life.

The importance of this topic cannot be overestimated. The deep diversity of American life, and many other societies across the globe, demands a vigorous and proper understanding and practice of tolerance as a value. Without tolerance, pluralism and diversity dissolve into nothing more than tyranny and chaos.

It is perhaps one of the more disconcerting features of contemporary intellectual life that given the current prominence of social debates about tolerance, and given its obviously crucial standing as a social virtue today, comparatively few book-length studies of it have been published. This work's selected bibliography lists useful and sound reflections on tolerance, including those from a Christian perspective.

The fundamental aim of this book is to stimulate reflection and writing on tolerance (both social and personal), particularly from a Christian point of view, and to affirm that personal and political commitments to truth are not averse to genuine tolerance. Indeed, truth and tolerance are inseparable. In their symbiosis tolerance gives to truth the cognitive freedom it needs to be authentically recognized, and truth gives to tolerance the parameters and purpose it needs to function as it is intended—to serve people and communities in their quest for meaning and ultimately the knowledge of the One in whom alone lies their fulfillment.

PART ONE

FLASHPOINTS IN THE DEVELOPMENT OF TOLERANCE

Ideas don't simply fall out of heaven, someone once said. Under God's providence the concepts that shape our lives today have a history and intellectual pedigree. They have descended from the clash of cultures and values, the pressures of time and civilization.

Modern principles of toleration are no different. They have an extensive history, changing and developing in different directions at different times. As with all great ideas, tolerance has had its martyrs, its colorful provocateurs, its systematic theorists and its demagogues who, glibly waving its banner, have promulgated caricatures of it.

Still, God's hand has been at work catalyzing it—sometimes with stunning clarity and decisiveness (as with that most significant energizer of toleration, the incarnation)—but more often with invisible yet potent ferment in the minds of citizens and philosophers struggling for liberty and understanding. Out of this crucible of thought, blood and spirit has emerged an ensemble of principles, habits, laws and institutions that advance true toleration, a virtue essential to any just and free society.

In this first section we will examine the general procession of ideas and events that have significantly contributed to the development of toleration as it has evolved in Western society. After preliminary observations about the unfortunate ubiquity of intolerance in human cultures and the essentiality of self-government to toleration rightly understood, we will then turn to a historical overview of some philosophically significant contributions to the West's construction of toleration as a value.

1

TWO PRELIMINARY OBSERVATIONS

False words are not only evil . . .

but they infect the soul with evil.

PLATO

Because the survey we are about to undertake focuses specifically on the development of tolerance in the Western world, a word is in order about tolerance in the non-Western world. A systematic study of tolerance in the non-Western world is, of course, a difficult and complex subject, and one well beyond our scope. Our intent is not to systematically broach it here but simply to make a few historical and sociological points to put the Western development of toleration in a larger context. Our remarks will serve a practical purpose as well: to demonstrate that the charge of intolerance—a charge now regularly leveled at the Judeo-Christian tradition at the core of Western culture—even if true (and we believe it is largely false) is not unique to the West. Intolerance has always been and will always be a *human* problem, not a peculiarly Western or Christian one.

Today this is an extremely important point to make. Toleration, a hard-won principle in the West, in its true sense is directly and indirectly belittled by ideologues of an anti-Western bias. To demonstrate the tawdry and unjust character of what they assert to be the globe-threatening West, they insist its so-called achievements—including toleration itself—are largely empty and hypocritical chimeras. They then typically contrast these Western illusions and failures to an idealized vision of the non-Western world. While they shout from the rooftops instances of Western intolerance, they are curiously silent regarding the record of the non-Western world on this count.

So we will begin our survey by examining a little further the sociology of the anti-Western bias that posits intolerance as a distinctively Western malaise. We then will examine the charge itself: Is the West uniquely intolerant?

Among contemporary documentarians of anti-Western bias, Dinesh D'Souza has made a vital contribution. D'Souza's opening salvo in his bestselling study *Illiberal Education* exposed the blatant leftist propagandizing that had become common on America's university classrooms by the early 1990s.[1] *Illiberal Education* cited a hitherto obscure term from Marxist theory—*political correctness*—and is the book most responsible for making that term a household word and powerful concept in political debates today. The politically correct leftist agenda of the university includes the axiom that Western civilization was and is incorrigibly intolerant and ethnocentric, and this cruelty was manifested as slavery and colonialism in the past and is manifest today in continued virulent racism, sexism and homophobia.

D'Souza continued these themes in the later work *What's So Great About America?*, written as a defense of Western culture against the genocidal indictments of it from Islamic terrorists like Osama bin Laden. D'Souza notes that university professors as well as high school teachers routinely accuse the United States of egregious intolerance and typically present American history as "an uninterrupted series of crimes visited on blacks, American Indians, Hispanics, women, and natives of the Third World."[2] While hardly denying the West's legacy of ethnocentrism and intolerance, D'Souza makes two important clarifications. First, when we honestly consider other world cultures, we decisively notice that there is nothing distinctively Western about ethnocentrism and bigotry, and second, what "is distinctively Western is not ethnocentrism but a profound and highly beneficial effort to transcend ethnocentrism."[3] The self-correcting quality to Western culture and American society in particular is a great but often overlooked virtue of the American nation. For example, nearly four hundred thousand Americans gave their lives to end the vile practice of black slavery, but this fact is seldom dwelled on as a historically unprecedented example of an entire country reforming itself.[4]

Non-Western Intolerance: India

D'Souza's view that there is nothing distinctively Western about ethnocentrism and intolerance is as true as it is overlooked today. The ancient civilization of India, for example, practiced an acute form of intolerance in its rigid caste system, into which people were born and destined to always remain. Influential ancient scriptures of India had dogmatized a four-caste system of society: Brahmins (priests), Kshatriya (warriors), Vaisya (farmers and merchants) and Sudras (laborers and servants). This social framework was inviolable. The privileged Brahmins—who derived their status by virtue of the good karma they had accrued in their former lives and which prompted their present incarnation into this favored class—enforced strict laws against any contact with untouchables (Chandalas), whose social standing was so low (due to terrible karma from a past life), that they existed in a no-man's land beneath even the lowest caste. (Of course, the lifestyle of the fourth class, the Sudras, was no cakewalk.) The unfortunate Chandalas were one-fifth of India's population, and their brutal rejection by Indian society must be considered infamous, even in the hideous annals of humankind's cruelty. Writes Klaus K. Klostermaier in his masterful study, *A Survey of Hinduism:*

> A notorious example of the distance that Brahmins put between themselves and the outcastes was offered by the Nambudiris. Whenever a Nambudiri [Brahmin] left his house, [someone] had to precede him to proclaim that the great Lord was about to come. All outcastes had to hide, the mere sight of them would make a Nambudiri unclean. If by any accident the shadow of a pariah fell upon a Nambudiri, he had to undergo a lengthy purificatory ceremonies.[5]

Even today, writes Klostermaier, though the Indian constitution has outlawed untouchability, it continues to be the reality for many Hindus.[6] In addition to the systematic intolerance and suppression practiced in India for millennia against the outcastes, the degradation of women evinced in the conventional Hindu practice of *suttee*—the burning of widows, whose lives on earth, it was assumed, were meaningless without their husbands—demonstrates that violent, arbitrary intolerance is hardly an exclusively Western phenomenon in history.

Intertribal Intolerance in Africa

Did Africa escape the blight of intolerance? Ethnic warfare, intertribal enslavement and the physical mutilation of women—the hideous ritual of
clitorectomy—have afflicted this continent since ancient days. A contemporary manifestation of intolerance in Africa that began four centuries
ago is the haughty bigotry of the Tutsi people against the Hutus. After
their conquest of Rwanda, the Tutsi—though about 15 percent of the
population—elaborated an ethnocentric doctrine espousing the essential
inequality of human beings—and of course the natural preeminence of
the Tutsi among humans. Through this ethnic ruse and by force, the Tutsis dominated and exploited the Hutu for centuries.

Tutsi intolerance and Hutu reaction has continued into our time. In
the 1970s ethnic violence between them manifested in a Tutsi genocide
of one hundred thousand Hutus. In 1994 the Hutus avenged this by killing up to a million Tutsis.[7] From Liberia to Somalia to South Africa, brutality continues to define much of African life.

Intolerance Among the Mesoamerican Natives

The record of the early people of Mesoamerica—the subject of myriad
New Age panegyrics as a race of untainted spirituality and nobility—is
hardly one of sterling toleration. Gender, ethnic and class intolerance
and oppression were widespread, routine and brutal. The bloodbath of
Mayan intolerance was typically whitewashed by New Age champion
James Redfield, whose religious novel *The Celestine Prophecy* was a
megabestseller, to the tune of about five million copies.[8] Redfield's nar-
rative displays its bona fides to the contemporary American mind by
condemning "organized religion," but he mentions nary a corpuscle of
sacrificial blood while praising a Mayan culture in which ritual sacrifice
(e.g., cardiectomy, the removal of the human heart from living victims)
was a sacred commitment and the chief means of imperial power. The
imperial Mayan hierarchy enforced a rigid caste system and a system of
blood sacrifice to establish cosmic balance. The victims—children,
women, captives, enemies—were drugged before the bloodletting to
perversely induce smiles on their faces as their life-blood drained down
slave-built pyramids.[9] The blood of children was especially relished by
the gods.

Yes, the Mayans did innovate a remarkable calendar based on subtle celestial movements—as contemporary apologists for Mayan culture continually remind us, apparently finding scientific progress trumping moral decency as an index to civilization. No such standard is usually applied to the West though, as its historical shortcomings are continually played over and over in academic, entertainment and media culture, a never-ending indictment of Western civilization and its Judeo-Christian heritage.

Intolerance in Contemporary Islam

Curiously, though, these same critical voices say comparatively little about the flagrant and often violent intolerance seen in some Islamic regions today. For example:

- During a televised fundraiser for Palestinians an official Saudi Arabian government Islamic cleric urged Palestinians to kill and enslave their Jewish neighbors, saying "Muslim brothers in Palestine, do not have any mercy, neither compassion on the Jews, their blood, their money, their flesh. Their women are yours to take, legitimately. God made them yours. Why don't you enslave their women? Why don't you wage *jihad?* Why don't you pillage them?"[10]

- Following a Nigerian reporter's innocent remark that the women in a local beauty contest were so attractive that even the prophet Muhammad might desire one for a wife, enraged Muslim mobs burned down the newspaper's offices, and a local Muslim cleric issued a fatwa (command for assassination) on the reporter.[11]

- A Sudanese writer, Kola Boof, who has written of the enslavement and murder of Christians—crimes which have been officially condoned by the Muslim government of the Sudan—fled to the United States after a fatwa was issued on her for her condemnations of the government.[12] Reports continue to come from the African nation of the forced conversions of Sudanese Christians to Islam and the slaughtering of Christians and others who refuse to convert.[13]

- In Saudi Arabia, where Christianity and other non-Islamic religions are illegal, several Philippino workers were arrested by the Saudi religious police after their Christian prayer meeting was raided. A British television station reported the arrest and subsequent torture of the men.[14]

- In the Malaku province of eastern Indonesia, an Al-Qaeda-linked terrorist group called Laskar Jihad has operated with impunity, burning the churches and homes of Christians and other non-Muslims, and seeking either to rid the area of all non-Muslims or compel their conversion to Islam.[15]

Unquestionably, it is non-Western cultures and religious traditions that are in the vanguard of intolerance and the repression of pluralism today. D'Souza is patently right: there is "nothing essentially Western" about intolerance. As to his second thesis—that what "is distinctively Western is not ethnocentrism but a profound and highly beneficial effort to transcend ethnocentrism"[16]—we will view selected milestones in that effort.

Self-government

First, though, a word about self-government is needed. The concept of self-government, which is based on a Judeo-Christian understanding of the person as a free moral agent with natural rights *and* responsibilities, is a thread interwoven throughout the various philosophical, religious and political themes that have delivered to us the concept of tolerance we have today.

The practice of tolerance is both a personal and social challenge. That is, we practice it personally, but we also expect it interpersonally or as a matter of social convention. Thus toleration is supported—or undermined—by a nation's laws, culture, institutions and the quality of its people's moral habits. That is because all these elements contribute to or work against what political philosopher Russell Kirk calls "inner" and "outer" order. These complementary forms of order are the two components of self-government in the overall sense, and they make or break a democracy (and, we would add, therefore, the practice of toleration).

Indeed, self-government, rightly understood and practiced, is an essential foundation for any society to manifest and practice true tolerance. Without a soundly functioning moral order, personal and social, the moral machinations of tolerance will not properly interrelate. Without responsible self-governing individuals and a body politic able to manage its own social and political life, the personal and corporate temperament and capacities for moral deliberation that allow for toleration will never flower. Russel Kirk explains the direct relationship between the interior life of the citizen and the order of society:

> The "inner order" of the soul and the "outer order" of society [are] . . . intimately linked. . . . Without a high degree of private moral order among the American people, the reign of law could not have prevailed in this country. Without an orderly pattern of politics, American character would have sunk into ruinous egoism.[17]

Philosopher Michael Novak has written in parallel ways about the indispensable role of self-government in both the personal and civil sense. He too is worth quoting:

> This distinctive concept of natural rights embodied a national moral project that can be expressed through the two-sided meaning of "self-government." A republican experiment is an experiment in public self-government through public institutions on the part of the whole people. At the same time, such public self-government can only succeed if its citizens also practice self-government in their personal lives. The citizens of a republic must comport themselves with capacities for sober reflection and deliberate choice at the ready. It is not necessary for all or even most to be saints. Nonetheless, to suppose that a republican government could succeed without at least a modicum of virtue in its citizens would be a pipe dream.[18]

The following flashpoints in the history of tolerance then take place in the context of developing both the inner and outer order—or the twofold self-government—that, as Kirk and Novak explain, is essential for stable government and society, and a healthy social institution of toleration.

PRE-CHRISTIAN
CONTRIBUTIONS

*The West [has drawn] from a tradition of toleration much deeper and
older than is apparent [from toleration's] sudden appearance in the
seventeenth century.*

A. J. CONYERS

I t comes as something of a shock to Americans who have often heard
civil libertarians remind us that Thomas Jefferson wrote of a "wall of separation between church and state" to discover that Jefferson proposed
for the official seal of the new United States a design representing the
people of Israel being led through the wilderness by a cloud by day and
a pillar of fire by night. To understate it, Jefferson's proposal that the
Shekinah—for the Hebrews, the glory light of God—appear on the
American emblem is highly ironic. But there it is: Jefferson's explicit acknowledgment of the biblical heritage of American democracy, a view
he shared with all the founders.[1]

Viewing this irony as symptomatic of the contemporary disregard of
America's biblical heritage, Michael Novak sees most contemporary history of America as skewed, having amputated the wing of faith from the
two wings of the American eagle: faith and reason. The founders, in the
main, believed deeply in the God of the Judeo-Christian tradition. They
were steeped in the Old and New Testaments, and intellectually relied on
the understanding of God and humanity they gleaned from what to them
(and to Christians throughout the history of the church) was sacred writ.[2]

Though toleration has important developments far before the American founding, of course, the vital maturation of the idea of toleration in
American democracy—and the Judeo-Christian heritage that spawned

and nurtured the new nation and its aspirations—should not be diminished. Any accurate consideration of the pedigree of true tolerance must acknowledge this point. Professor A. J. Conyers does so in his study of the history of toleration as an idea, writing, "If, by toleration, we mean a willingness to hear other traditions and to learn from them, then we find much in both the Old Testament and the New Testament to encourage such an attitude."[3] What elements in Jewish thought specifically contribute to toleration?

Judaism and Toleration

God revealed to the Hebrews, a humble and struggling people, a way of living, a vision of life, an order of things, that would eventually have incalculable effect in Western civilization. Jewish ethicist Dennis Prager and Rabbi Joseph Telushkin capture the improbability and magnitude of this history: "A tiny group of uncultured and homeless slaves gave the world God, ethical monotheism, the concept of universal moral responsibility, the notion of human sanctity (human creation in the 'image of God'), messianism, the Prophets, the Bible, and the Ten Commandments."[4]

Many of these concepts, working their energies through Western culture, have shaped the practice and doctrine of tolerance. In particular the emphasis on personal moral behavior, which is the essence of Judaism, is directly relevant to tolerance.[5] Tyranny, the absence of civil toleration, is inevitable if objective moral values for human conduct—a core meaning of ethical monotheism—do not exist. The unceasingly moral texture of Jewish life and law gives a moral framework in which immoral conduct can be named and denounced, whether perpetrated by a person or a government.

Prager and Telushkin would have us never dissociate the modifier *ethical* from monotheism as it was revealed to the Jews. The very essence of the Jews' relationship to God was ethical, they insist. Even the rituals of Judaism, including kosher food laws, which would seem only complementary to Jewish ethics in the totality of Jewish life, is suffused with "ethical meaning."[6] Since true tolerance can never be based on moral relativism but implies a vision of the good, Judaism's ethical monotheism helpfully points us back to an important aspect of any authentic conception of tolerance.

A further gift to toleration from the Jews is the prophets, who ever warned Israel of the danger of neglecting goodness and moral responsibility while ritualistically worshiping God:

> Does the LORD delight in burnt offering and sacrifices
>   as much as in obeying the voice of the LORD?
> To obey is better than sacrifice,
>   and to heed is better than the fat of rams. (1 Sam 15:22)

So distinctive was this phenomenon that it has come to be called "prophetic criticism." Prophetic criticism reversed the conventional collusion in the ancient world between the spiritual power of the priesthood and regal power. The voice of the prophets, through whom God spoke, was no respecter of persons, whether priests or kings. Characteristically, the prophets took Hebrew kings to task for personal and political immorality, that is, idol worship, oppressive statutes, inconsistent justice, arrogance, indifference to the poor, the orphaned, the widowed. As Russel Kirk observes, the Israelites uniquely had their priests and kings but not priest-kings.[7] Indeed, the Hebrew prophetic tradition reversed the rampant ancient model of the priest-king: prophets forthrightly and regularly rebuked kings, with expected results such as dishonor, disapproval and even dismemberment.

Given the magnitude of its charge to distinguish good from evil and craft fair laws for the common good, a tolerant society requires self-criticism. The tolerant society is not morally neutral, and therein lies its nobility, stability and survival. But therein also lies the danger of inappropriate nontoleration. The prophetic criticism of government by religious voices is a necessary hedge against the state's greedy embrace of over-wide authority and the institutionalization of evil. Needless to say, totalitarian and autocratic governments and robust criticism from people of conscience do not often coincide.

Although rarely recognized as such in history textbooks, the Reverend Martin Luther King Jr.'s criticism of segregation was squarely and even consciously in the biblical tradition of prophetic criticism. A Baptist minister, King's passionate rebukes against the twentieth-century pharaohs of racism resolutely rang with quotations from the implacable Hebrew prophets. Following the example of the prophet Nathan (who spoke condemning truth to King David, who had committed profound injustices), Dr. King said, "You are the man!"[8]

But what of the Hebrew prophets' condemnation of polytheism and the worship of gods other than Yahweh? While in one sense this act of religious delineation obviously rules a lot of cherished deities out of bounds, it would be quite mistaken to see this prophetic assertion as somehow mean or intolerant. For in asserting the personal, infinite and exclusively real character of the one God, the prophets embrace all of humanity and burden (or perhaps liberate) all of humanity with the ethical treatment of one another. Truth can never be oppressive.

Yet, argues Conyers, there is a paradox here:

> The moment someone confesses the belief in one God, that person excludes all other gods; but necessarily he is saying that all people belong in some fashion to that same God. To reject the god of the foreigner on monotheistic and exclusive grounds is to accept the foreigner himself as a fellow human being tied in kinship by the fact of their both being created by the same God. In one and the same gesture, one rejects the foreign gods and embraces the foreigner.[9]

The following verses from Leviticus have been especially famous and influential in this regard: "When an alien lives with you in your land, do not mistreat him. The alien living with you must be treated as one of your native-born. Love him as yourself, for you were aliens in Egypt" (Lev 19:33-34). The very embrace of other people entailed by universal monotheism creates a framework for human rights and reciprocal responsibilities that generates an ethos of concern for the will and autonomy of the other, and this of course is an important prerequisite for any morally serious ethic of toleration.

Another way Jewish thought has contributed to the foundations of toleration is through its nascent development of the natural law—an unwritten but discernible law of morality built into human nature and which speaks through conscience and inclination.[10] Though Judaism is most famous for its "revealed law" (e.g., the Ten Commandments) and ceremonial requirements, in the Hebrew Scriptures we see the seeds of a natural-law understanding as well. Though the natural law is not inscripturated like the revealed law, it corresponds, as far as it goes, with revealed law, for God the Revealer is also the Creator who has fashioned human nature in his image (Gen 1:27; Rom 1:20). His whispers of the good still sound (and always will) in our conscience.[11]

C. S. Lewis thought so highly of the natural law as at least a provisional basis for transcultural toleration and order that in his book *The Abolition of Man* he devoted an appendix to examples of its consistent expression across epochs and civilizations.[12] Lewis's work clearly illustrates the existence of a universally recognized natural law. The multiculturalist who so facilely assumes all cultures have had their own distinctive ethical code, each relativizing one another, is quite mistaken. Lewis sees a common acceptance with varied expression of, among other moral principles, a law of general beneficence; a law of special beneficence; duties to parents, elders, ancestors; a law of justice; and a law of magnanimity.

So while this natural moral knowledge "written on the heart" (Rom 2:15) is to a degree manifested in the Old Testament and Jewish tradition too, it is the explicit moral character of Judaism that not only informs so much thinking about toleration throughout history but also serves as the bedrock of Western life today. In their delineation of the ethical calling and meaning of human existence, Jewish ethics, the law, the prophets and the common creation of all people provide a critical foundation for the civil life of modern Western culture.[13]

The Teaching of Socrates

An unforgettable exemplar of tolerance—and nearly archetypal as a victim of intolerance—was the Greek philosopher Socrates, teacher of Plato and the most famous practitioner of truth-seeking through systematic conversation (the dialectic method). On the pathways of Athens he would casually accost some of the city's leading figures, engaging them in conversations regarding their areas of expertise. He listened carefully to their responses, delighting in whatever truth their doctrines held but also gently, civilly and persistently challenging whatever he found to be false. What is law? Goodness? Truth? Love?

Some have suggested that Socrates' humility was feigned, that his ignorance was mere dissembling—he knew full well the end to which he was directing his conversation. There may be some truth in that charge—that he knew before his first question the conclusion he wished to lead his conversation partner to. Still, there is nothing insidious in this, and its pedagogical value is obvious. The dialectic method of question and answer implicitly affirms the values significant to true tolerance. It affirms, for example, the quest for the truth in community, the importance of patience and self-criticism in truth-seeking, and the very possibility of knowing the true and the good.

A darker accusation (that the sage pretended ignorance while knowing the truth) has been lodged against Socrates.[14] The most famous leveler of this accusation was a young Søren Kierkegaard. Kierkegaard insisted that Socrates' method was ironic: rather than intending to finally demonstrate the truth, he was trying to show the impossibility of certainty by showing the inconsistency and superficiality of expert opinion.[15] In other words Kierkegaard thought that Socrates' doctrine was nihilistic and agnostic. By picking apart the arguments of the experts Socrates tried to show the futility of striving for positive knowledge of reality.

Moreover, according to Kierkegaard, Socrates relished for its own sake the irony of making everything problematic. It is no surprise, given the nihilistic milieu of the university today, that this reading of Socrates has been promoted by many university philosophy teachers. The gadfly of Athens, they say, was wise insofar as he admitted he knew nothing, and his mission was to invite others to this radical "humility" before reality. Professors often hold that this reading of Socrates invites civil tolerance: a tolerance based on skepticism. If no one knows what is true or false, good or evil, then we must be tolerant of all. But skepticism cannot be the basis of true tolerance. Rather, the cynicism of wholesale skepticism invites only the brutality of subjectivity and power (might makes right). Such a reading of Socrates makes him a foe of true tolerance, not its champion.

Those who read the mission of Socrates in this way often point to a milestone in his truth quest: his hearing the oracle of Delphi's tribute to him. The farseeing oracle had pronounced Socrates the wisest man in the world. Socrates took this as cryptic. He finally interpreted it to mean that his wisdom must consist in a frank acknowledgment of his ignorance. Others were ignorant but unaware of their lack of understanding. Socrates, though, was aware of what he did not know. Advocates of radical skepticism point to this moment in Socrates' life as evidence of—paradoxically—the truth of skepticism. This is of course often suggested as evidence for the wisdom of affirming no truth other than the truth of human ignorance.

But this event is nothing of the sort. All it suggests is a proper spirit of intellectual humility and rejection of presumption. To clear the decks, as it were, of falsehood and delusion, what we do not know we must admit so we may approach the truth unobstructed. This is Socrates' method: he does not despair of knowing the truth but is properly self-critical and skeptical of conventional wisdom when approaching it, thereby insuring that when truth is affirmed, it is genuine and has been tried by the fire of examination and reexamination. When the message of Delphi is set properly in context within the full philosophical career of this sage, it becomes clear that Socrates' initial confession of ignorance was not the first and last step but a beginning down the road to understanding. Socrates' dialogic journeys ended in additional clarity, not in agnostic opacity or a celebration of debate for its own sake.

An indispensable attitude of true tolerance is illustrated by the Socratic method. For it is rightly humble, but not agnostic, in truth-seeking. What it knows does not lead to the suppression of other viewpoints but rather acts as a spur to continuing personal dialogue, consistently civil in tone, with the knowledge of the truth as it is in itself an abiding goal.

Of course the trial and punishment of Socrates is a most infamous case of intolerance. Found guilty by the Athenian Senate of corrupting the youth of Athens, Socrates is given two choices: exile or suicide. He chooses the hemlock because exile to a place where he cannot teach is unthinkable to a man so devoted to the pursuit of truth. In Socrates' commitment to the examined life we find a model of the personal attitude most conducive to the practice of toleration.

Aristotle's Influence

Plato's student Aristotle imitated his teacher's humility and commitment to truth-seeking, and is arguably the greatest philosopher of all time. In the Middle Ages he was simply called "the Philosopher," and his panoramic thought—from the natural sciences to metaphysics, aesthetics, politics, ethics and logic—framed much of the development of the Western tradition. Still, though, certain particulars of Aristotle's thought were encrusted with intolerance: for example, his reluctance to acknowledge the full humanity of women and his arguments in favor of the natural basis of slavery.

Taken as a whole, though, Aristotle's thought made indirect but foundational contributions to the development of true tolerance. We will consider in brief five of these: his elaboration of the principle of essence; the doctrine of transculturalism, latent in his thought; the natural law; human beings as "social animals" whose ideal government concerns the common good; and virtue as habit, not simply knowledge.

Great philosophers before Aristotle typically promulgated opposite errors regarding the nature of things. Parmenides insisted that there was only one reality, one Being—and that the seeming particularity of each thing was an illusion. This view discounted individuality as illusory: a rock was essentially no different from a human being because, seen rightly, they are both one Being. Such a view obviously can provide no proper starting point for an ethic that recognizes individuality and so, finally, human rights.

The opposite view was advanced by Heraclitus: there is no common nature to all, no illusion transcending the stable One because there is nothing but change. All is in flux, said Heraclitus. His most famous framing of this principle was illustrative: "You cannot step into the same river twice."

Aristotle saw partial truth in each of these views: the world was characterized by a continuing unity of existence (Parmenides) and change (Heraclitus). But daily experience showed that despite Parmenides' assertion, particularity did exist, and despite Heraclitus's contention, each particular thing continued to exist as itself while changing in some of its properties.

His attempt to unite these partial truths led Aristotle to conceive of the principle of essence—*what* a thing is, categorically—as related to the principle of potency and act (what a thing *can* and may actually *do*). Aristotle saved Parmenides' true intuition of the grand actuality (the shared beingness of things) while holding fast to our direct experience of difference and change. Likewise, while retaining Heraclitus's grasp of change, Aristotle rejected Heraclitus's counterintuitive claim that nothing of the original existing thing (say, an emerald) continued from moment to moment.

In this vein Aristotle posited a human essence. This essence, he held, is the same for each human being *as* a human being. Each human being actualizes or realizes to a greater or lesser degree peculiarly human potencies or capacities (say, that of speech). What makes us human is our essence, not the degree to which the potential expressions of that essence are realized. Thus Aristotle accommodated what Parmenides and Heraclitus could not: continuing being (in this case, human being) and change (human potencies actualized). Hence Aristotle's elaboration of essence—particularly human essence—is not only vague metaphysics but the basis of such important principles as the universal nature of the human person.

We are human not because of the tribe we belong to, the ideology we follow or even the God we worship. But we are human by virtue of our essence, our essential nature which is transcultural and transhistorical. It is unchanged by time and place. This implication of essence was not fully grasped by Aristotle himself and was left up to his disciples in later generations to uncover what was virtually present in his system. This matches well with Aristotle's own view of potency and act: his greater vision of human essence, latent as potency in his written work, was actualized by the insights of his philosophical posterity.

Contemporary Aristotelians such as the twentieth-century thinker Mortimer Adler have shown how Aristotle's thought drives toward transculturalism, the view that basic morality and the good are not determined by race, culture or nationality but transcend these and remain as they are irrespective of cultural context. This idea is essentially humanism and is fully compatible, indeed mandated by, Christian theism.* The transcultural principle in Aristotle's thought is highly significant for a doctrine of tolerance. While pseudotolerance forbids a society from making laws that infringe on persons claiming cultural or ethnic immunity from those laws, true tolerance—while respecting cultural differences prudently and to a degree—empowers society to make truly *hu-*

---

*Unfortunately, during the twentieth century the term *humanism* has gradually been taken over by secularists, and so the phrase *secular humanism* is often heard. But humanism, an emphasis on the worth and value of the human, is a Christian idea, not a secular one. The incarnation and the cross of Christ testify to this more profoundly than any secular reading of world history ever could. For full scale delineation of this see J. I. Packer and Thomas Howard, *Christianity: The True Humanism* (Waco, Tex.: Word, 1985).

man laws applicable to all. That is, the social order recognizes the reality and universality of human nature, and the fact that people—given human nature—respond better to some social-legal arrangements than to others. No one yet has testified to the glory of being repressed by a brutal dictator or fascist racist. The fall of Soviet communism and German National Socialism (Nazism), still testify loudly to this truth.

Such truly human laws that recognize the continuity of human nature silently acknowledge what Aristotle posited as the natural law—the invisible law of living well present in the consciousness of every rational being.

The basic prescription of the natural law has been admirably summed by Adler: "We ought to seek only that which is really good for us" and nothing else.[16] But what is "good" for us? Aristotle asks us to examine our functions as human beings and discern what true human needs they suggest. For example, one need of human beings is knowledge, for we function as rational beings. And from the human need for knowledge we can further discern the need for intellectual and political freedom. This suggests the need for the ordered liberty of democracy, which allows for, among other human endeavors, freedom of intellectual exploration, and it therefore meets the natural human need for knowledge. A good government then is structured by laws that do not contradict the unwritten natural law, the realities of human nature and its implications.

Before developing the significance of the natural law for tolerance, it will be helpful to develop some insight into what has happened in more recent times to Aristotle's view that human beings possess a vital yet definite nature.

Let's leap forward nearly two-and-a-half millennia from Aristotle's time to that of Jean Paul Sartre, who in the twentieth century proposed a view opposite to Aristotle's position that human nature consists of a stable, unchanging structure. The iconoclastic battle cry of Sartre was "existence precedes essence." Sartre characteristically was ambivalent about what he meant by *existence*. Some take it to mean choice and lived experience, and agree with Sartre: what human beings choose as their way of life, as their nature, is prior to any structured "essence" we would posit of them. Others agree with Sartre on a different basis, understanding *existence* to mean life itself, prior to any structure. Human beings, these followers of Sartre contend, have life—"existence"—before choice, and therefore their choice of how to live and the being they construct through that choice precedes essence, or human nature. But both Sartrean camps agree that Aristotle is wrong: there is no constant "human essence" or "human nature." Existence precedes essence.

But as we have seen, Aristotle would disagree: he held that the kind of existence a person lived flowed from what a person is. Human beings live from a human essence, an unchanging substance, that endures from age to age. Aristotle recognized individual inclination and development but said that human nature outshone these: it is one, despite inclination and development.

The Sartreans blast back: there is no such structure as human nature or human essence. Each individual willfully determines his or her own essence.

This Aristotelian-Sartrean dichotomy is meaningful historically in that it sifts opinion. A portion of the populace recognizes, with Aristotle, a distinct human nature as real; another portion does not recognize a distinctive human nature as real. Aristotle would see human nature as like a crystal with variations; Sartreans would dissolve this crystal into the mist and recognize nothing as distinctively human. Followers of Aristotle protest this as making no distinction between the human and the purely animal; followers of Sartre see such an equation as a victory for freedom, allowing each human person to be what he or she will be.

To employ a phrase from the contemporary economist Thomas Sowell, this is indeed a "conflict of visions." In his book *A Conflict of Visions* Sowell explores the many dimensions of these opposing visions of humanity and society. He calls these perennial visions "constrained" and "unconstrained." He notes something we have all experienced, that people tend to line up on opposite sides of issues, that is, if two people have an opposing view on abortion, for example, they will have opposite views on many other issues as well.[17]

In Aristotle's claim that there is a structure to human nature, we have an early instance of what Thomas Sowell calls the "constrained vision." Each of the two visions flows from a conception of human nature. One philosopher who agreed with Aristotle's positing of a definite human nature was the English philosopher Edmund Burke (1729-1797), who was a great influence on the American founders. Burke expressed his conviction of a static, unchanging human nature and the need to structure social life accordingly, writing, "We cannot change the Nature of things and of men—but must act upon them the best we can."[18]

In contrast the "unconstrained vision"—exemplified by Sartre and so many contemporary progressives—insists on the infinite plasticity of human nature: the view that human beings may be radically transformed for the better in the future. This general view was expressed in the eighteenth century by William Godwin, writing in *An Enquiry Concerning Political Justice:* "Men are capable, no doubt, of preferring an inferior interest of their own to a superior interest of others; but this preference arises from a combination of circumstances and is not the invariable law of our nature."[19] So people are not selfish or even imperfect but changeable, according to the quality of the social institutions they are a part of.

The natural law theory of Aristotle (and Burke) at once agrees in part with this objection and dissents from it. The natural law both concedes human limitation and humbly seeks to work within it toward a distinctively human good—finding irrelevant the Sartrean obliteration of the human.

An example from contemporary history should clarify the importance of the idea of human nature in political life. The setting: the American South in the 1950s and 1960s. The Civil Rights Movement is in full swing, two-and-a-half millennia after Aristotle—but still harking to the natural law principles he helped develop. In these years Martin Luther King Jr. founded his quest for racial toleration on natural law in his *Letter From Birmingham Jail.* Dr. King famously wrote:

> How does one determine whether a law is just or unjust? A just law is a man-made code that squares with the moral law or the law of God. An unjust law is a code that is out of harmony with the moral law. To put it in the terms of St. Thomas Aquinas: An unjust law is a human law that is not rooted in eternal law and natural law. Any law that uplifts human personality is just. Any law that degrades human personality is unjust. All segregation statutes are unjust because segregation distorts the soul and damages the personality. It gives the segregator a false sense of superiority and the segregated a false sense of inferiority.[20]

So: one of the great landmarks of toleration—the Civil Rights Movement of the 1960s—is indebted to natural law theory. As noted, the natural law is part of the "constrained vision," a vision that recognizes an enduring human essence and rights and duties derived therefrom. We will meet this vision again in the thought of early Christian thinkers who balanced the human capacity for good with a sharp awareness of the innate and entrenched human egoism and sin, in the Reformers' cry for freedom of conscience, and in Edmund Burke's appreciation of human tradition.

There are two further Aristotelian insights into the natural law that have enriched the concept of toleration: Aristotle held that (1) human beings are essentially "social animals," and (2) they can be trained in virtue and good character.

Concerning the first point, Aristotle held that the person who does not live in society is either a beast or a god. Aristotle derives the social and political character of human nature mainly from an examination of innate human needs and inclinations. Society is not artificial and merely contractual (as some later philosophers will argue). Rather, society— beginning with the family—meets distinctive human needs and plays an indispensable role in actualizing rational human potential—that is, in making the human person truly human.

Aristotle's idea of the "social animal" significantly builds up the social aspect of true toleration. It implies that the family merits the state's special consideration and protection as a value-inculcating microsociety that is uniquely equipped to develop good and valuable human abilities in the young, whose awakening of potential, like that of Sleeping Beauty, requires the kiss of affectionate, personal attention.

Today's profamily political lobbying groups like Focus on the Family instinctively draw on Aristotle's view here. For example, in 2003 many profamily groups favored the installation of pornography-blocking software in public library computers to protect the innocence and decency of children—a family responsibility that, they insisted, the state should not implicitly thwart by allowing the young public access to Internet pornography. Civil libertarians opposed the blocking devices, insisting that a policy of blocking computer software was unduly intolerant toward those who want full freedom of Internet access. The Supreme Court voted to allow the installation of the blocking devices in library computers, and profamily groups declared a victory.

The support of virtue by a good society is connected with yet another Aristotelian idea, the axiom that virtue can be learned and is a function of habit; it is not simply identical with knowledge. Socrates and Plato had equated knowledge with virtue: to know the good is to do it. (Socrates' high valuation of knowledge in ethics is of a piece with his trust in knowledge—as noted, he was not dogmatically skeptical.) While Aristotle agreed with Socrates and Plato that knowledge undergirds the good act, Aristotle found knowledge was ethically insufficient. Given human nature, wise habit, not mere knowledge, was the true principle of virtue.

This ancient argument continues today in the culture-war skirmishes. Virtue in the young—affirm the Aristotelians of today—is best developed in families and small communities of meaning like churches, whose instruction and structured discipline can form wise habits in children. The Platonists of today trust knowledge imparted by schools (e.g., peace studies, sex education and self-esteem workshops) to result in virtue. The Aristotelians are concerned that secularized tolerance siphons power from families and gives it to government and schools, the "experts." A. J. Conyers notes that in recent American culture the lessening of family authority and the increase of governmental authority in its place has been substantial. Conyers writes:

> Recently Texas, along with a few other states, passed laws over stiff opposition to ensure that parents are informed if their minor child, shepherded usually by school counselors and Planned Parenthood operatives, plans to have an abortion. Never mind permission, this was only to ensure that parents *know* what is happening to their teenage daughters. Authority in such a case was once, not so long ago assumed to belong to the family and only by default to a public agency.[21]

Presumably, a Platonic perspective (albeit a hideously decadent one) that equates knowledge with virtue finds these teens—enlightened by academic instruction in sex education and so-called values clarification—competent to wisely choose in these matters. From an Aristotelian perspective unseasoned youth—even those with A's in sex education and values clarification—naturally have not yet developed the stable *habitus* of virtue any person needs for such momentous decisions.

The Stoic Contribution

In addition to enriching the concept of the natural law, the Greek and Roman Stoics, who came after Aristotle, would add to the concept of true tolerance in two ways: by developing a vision of cosmic reason or Logos and refining to a state of ethical art the practice of patient forbearance or toleration of certain evils.

The key to pantheistic Stoic thought is the recognition that the cosmos is superintended by a pervasive divine Mind—a universal Reason that is creative, organizing, benevolent: the Logos. The divine in Stoicism is shorn of mythology and tribal partiality. The divine, in their view, is approached through ethical excellence and hence bears a partial likeness to the God of ethical monotheism.

Of course, in the New Testament the Logos was clearly and specifically identified with the incarnation of Jesus Christ—enriched and expanded beyond any conceptions of the Stoics. The most famous Christian expression of the Greek word *logos* ("the Word" in English) occurs in the prologue to the Gospel of John. (Though John the apostle lived in Judea, he wrote his Gospel in Greek, the international language of the day.) John wrote, "In the beginning was the Word, and the Word was with God, and the Word was God. He was with God in the beginning. Through him all things were made; without him nothing was made that has been made" (Jn 1:1-3).

Stoicism's vision of human nature and ethics flows from its pre-Christian doctrine of the Logos. While Aristotle had limited the concept of humanity to civilized Greeks, the Stoics enlarged the concept to compass all of humanity, including the slave, the alien and the barbarian. All received their life and the laws of their existence equally from the universal Logos. Conceiving every human being as a citizen of this world, Stoicism helped advanced toleration as a universal principle.

Further, the Stoics held that the Logos is present in human beings in reason and virtue; after all, the Logos is reason and goodness. Thus the Stoics definitively linked the natural law and the divine: virtue is adherence to the natural law, which mirrors the universal law of the Logos. Because the Stoics held such a high vision of the human capacity for reason and the divine rationality of the law, they applied great energy to the task of conceiving a rationally ordered civilization, an effort that is in some sense a prologue to the maturation of toleration as a civil ideal that would come centuries later. Stoicism produced great statesmen such as Cicero, who wrote in his *Republic:* "True law is right reason in agreement with Nature, . . . it is of universal application, unchanging and universal."[22]

It followed then that since the natural law is higher than any written law or kingly decree, the true Stoic was willing to defy unjust civil statutes to fulfill the requirements of the natural law and accept with patience the evil penalty this incurred. This is but one application of a chief virtue of Stoicism, patient forbearance—in other words, toleration in personal and civil life of what one believes to be wrong. Of course, so exemplary was the Stoic sages' practice of this virtue that the term *stoic* became an adjective. Though depleted as a living religio-philosophical system millennia ago, we still speak admirably of a stoical attitude in the face of hardship or grievance.

Though its contributions to toleration were noble, Stoicism would not be the chief agent of toleration's vivification in Western civilization. Its metaphysics was too abstract, and its moral athleticism too rigid. Russell Kirk, after summarizing Stoicism's limitation in this regard, proposes alternative wisdom through which liberty and toleration did finally flower:

> The Stoic philosophy, and the integrity of the Good Emperors, could not regenerate Roman masses. Stoicism was a high and austere creed, too abstract and intellectual for popular acceptance. . . . In the long run, the Christian faith which Saint Peter and Saint Paul brought to Rome would renew the moral order. . . . Christianity was a revealed religion, the worship of a crucified God, and it would touch the heart.[23]

CHRISTIAN CONTRIBUTIONS

The true basis for tolerance is a religious view of mankind that re-quires tolerance because it teaches that every kind of authority has the potential to become abusive.

PHILLIP E. JOHNSON

Being a disciple of Jesus alerts us to the grand themes of God's story and the unfolding of his eternal plan of creation, fall and redemp-tion. Christians live, as Kierkegaard put it, "under the audit of eter-nity" and within the vicissitudes of the divine drama. Everything mat-ters, when viewed under the audit of eternity.

DOUGLAS GROOTHUIS

There are many themes of the Christian worldview that coincide with an understanding of people and society that places a high value on tol-erance. But in a very real sense, key events and doctrines of Christianity have also contributed to the evolution of tolerance as an idea important for human societies to pursue and uphold. We will now take a brief look at these Christian themes.

The Incarnation and Tolerance

"I have come that they may have life, and have it to the full," said Jesus of his mission (Jn 10:10). There is not an aspect of life—the interior life, familial life, the common life of society—that would be untouched by the incarnation. Of course, owing to our hardness of heart and sluggish-ness of human understanding, the new life offered by the person and work of Christ has been opposed by humanity in a variety of ways, personal and collective. Yet when God's grace and the implications of his Word have been permitted to exercise their liberating vitality in human affairs, the results indeed have been life and abundance.

The development of true toleration, as a practice and doctrine, has been an expression of that vitality. Christian philosopher J. Budziszewski puts this directly:

> The popular view is that tolerance is a secular innovation, against which Christianity held out for centuries until "converted" by secular thinkers like John Locke. I maintain that tolerance is a Christian innovation. Though Christians through the centuries have often, and notoriously, forgotten it, their own tradition was the source of the very standard by which their intolerant acts could be judged wrong.[1]

It would seem that the nativity itself—the Absolute coming to us as the baby Jesus in a straw-strewn stable—would stamp into the consciousness of humanity once and for all the imagery of toleration. It is an object lesson in care for the weak and regard for the other, the very spirit of true toleration. We are astonished by the paradox here—that God Almighty would give himself to us in weakness, to melt our indifferent hearts—but we are not scandalized by it, for it is of a piece with the miraculous paradoxes of God's life among us: the Healer comes as the "suffering servant," the Lover as the scorned, Life dying on a cross. In the imagery of the nativity the archetype of tolerance has colored human consciousness, working within it as a silent and hidden but powerful ferment. Two principal aspects of toleration—responsibility and humility—are envisioned in this historical but also archetypal imagery, coming at two poles of Christ's preresurrection life. Jesus shocks awake our responsibility for the weak in the nativity manger, and he astonishes us awake to the sublime beauty and efficacy of humility on the cross.

Kingdom Living and Toleration

Jesus' teaching as it touches on toleration is subtle but complex. He teaches a radical empathy, complementing responsibility and humility as kingdom dispositions that undergird empathy: "Love your neighbor as yourself" (Mt 22:39), he urges his listeners, and "Whatever you did for one of the least of these brothers of mine, you did for me" (Mt 25:40).

Conyers writes on empathy and humility as integral features of a Christian doctrine of toleration. He relates these to contemporary issues of toleration—and today's distortion of the doctrine of toleration:

> Because authentic toleration is a reflection of humility, it militates against the egoistic tendencies of the individual and makes the formation of groups possible and meaningful. . . . It endures assaults upon its most long-lasting dogmas for the sake of making dialogue possible. . . . By contrast, pseudo-toleration wants to make dialogue possible only so long as it conforms to certain "rules" that preordain its result. Thus do universities impose strictures on the speech of both faculty and students that do not conform to ever-changing notions about gender, "sexual orientation," minorities and an anti-Western bias."[2]

Certainly the teaching and grace of Jesus Christ work against the "egoistic tendencies," the relentless human capacity for selfishness, to which Conyers alludes. Liberty from narrow egoism through Christ-centeredness has been exemplified in diverse figures in Christian history, from Francis of Assisi to Martin Luther to Dietrich Bonhoeffer to Jim Elliot. Such liberty goes hand in hand with the virtue of self-criticism: the ability to look objectively at ourselves—our errors, evasions, shortcomings— and criticize ourselves in light of biblical truth. What Christian, reading Jesus' rebuke of the scribes and Pharisees as "whitewashed tombs, which look beautiful on the outside but on the inside are full of dead men's bones and everything unclean" (Mt 23:27), has not painfully if silently recognized such hypocrisy within him- or herself? Such self-awareness and self-criticism have amounted to important Christian contributions to toleration. When Martin Luther King Jr. observed that it was not a sign of weakness but of high maturity to rise to a level of self-criticism, he was not speaking as a political protestor but as a Christian minister. His campaign for racial toleration turned on the tactic of inviting socially indifferent Christians, inured to the habits of blinding bigotry, to self-criticism in light of the gospel.

Mature Christian dispositions such as self-awareness, humility and empathy manifested throughout society make possible sound, personal self-government, what Russel Kirk termed the "inner order." A society significantly leavened by Christians who earnestly aspire to the kingdom heart will reflect a robust "outer order," or vigorous political self-government. In such a government, authentic toleration will flourish.

Early Christian history is rife with examples of how the "kingdom heart" benefited civil order. In the third century, for example, a dreadful epidemic killed as many as five thousand persons a day in Rome and finally killed as much as two-thirds of Alexandria's population.[3] Vincent Carroll and David Shiflett note:

> Not unreasonably, any pagan who could leave town when major epidem-
> ics struck quickly did so. . . . The Christian's response was different from
> their neighbors'. They tended to stand fast in the cities and nurse the
> stricken. Providing food, water, and basic sanitation was not enough to
> save all the diseased, by any means, and [this] cost many Christians their
> lives. . . . [T]his rudimentary care may have cut the mortality rate by two-
> thirds or more.[4]

Dionysius, the bishop of Alexandria at the time of the plague, addressed this ethic of self-sacrifice in an Easter letter: "Most of our brother Christians showed unbounded love and loyalty, never sparing themselves. . . . Heedless of danger, they took charge of the sick, attending to their every need and ministering to them in Christ."[5]

The interior order of the kingdom heart, then, immeasurably benefits civil order, promoting a moral ethos conducive to toleration.

The Universality of the Christian Message

Christianity, importantly, has never represented itself as a faith only for *some* people. In its essence it is for and open to all. From Jesus' death on the cross to the disciples' charge to globally proclaim his death and subsequent resurrection, Christianity's message is inclusive of humanity and radically nondiscriminatory. Artificial boundaries of culture, class, ethnicity and sex are transcended by the truth claims of Christianity. This is unique, as Nick Fotion and Gerard Elfstrom note: "Christianity differed from previous religions in purporting to be the religion of all human beings rather than of a particular tribe, state, or people"[6]

And of course as Christianity spread throughout the Roman Empire and ultimately the world, its concepts became more and more influential. One of these, the recognition of spheres of authority, that is, the sacred and the secular (though the authority of the secular, for example human government, is always only provisional), was especially influential as a theory of toleration coalesced through the centuries. Fotion and Elfstrom write: "The universality of the Christian church paved the way for a . . . feature of Christianity that had a major impact on the issue of religious toleration. This is the distinction between spiritual and secular authority, as encapsulated in Christ's teaching, 'Render unto Caesar that which is Caesar's, and render unto God that which is God's.' "[7]

Though this principle has hardly had a peaceful history, and it has not always been observed by Christians, it did spur thought and practice toward solving the problem of pluralism and conflicting claims to authority rendered by state and church. Arguably, in asserting the distinction between Caesar and God, Jesus laid the foundation for religious toleration in the civil order as well as what would come to be called—and pathetically misunderstood in our time—the separation of church and state.

Sin and Toleration

The Christian doctrine of the Fall and the resultant sinfulness of humanity, which speaks to the innate fallibility of human reason and the egocentricity of human will, assisted the development of the doctrine of toleration in a number of ways.

First, it supplies a rationale for the democratic principle—which fosters free expression and is itself so well-expressed in the American order—of checks and balances. C. S. Lewis puts it sardonically: "I am a democrat because I believe in the Fall of Man. . . . Mankind is so fallen that no man can be trusted with unchecked power over his fellows."[8]

Intolerance is the wrongful arrogation of power to force conformity. The doctrine of original sin is a caution against such arrogation. The "democratic" intolerance notoriously exercised by a few in the name of the people by the leaders of the French Revolution, for example, exemplifies this arrogance. In the name of liberty, equality, fraternity—and yes, in the name of a misconceived toleration itself—the French revolutionaries of 1789 and the early 1790s prosecuted a dictatorial Reign of Terror, sans any checks and balances, against whomever it deemed enemies of the Republic. These guardians of this "new toleration" kept the guillotine blade sharp for those deemed intolerant of their utopia. Writes Jacques Barzun in his panoramic study of Western civilization since 1500, *From Dawn to Decadence:* "The roster of victims was distinguished. . . . Mme. Roland, also an intellectual and known as the 'Muse of the Girondists,' because that entire party was accused and sent to its doom. On the scaffold, she cried, 'Oh Liberty, what crimes are committed in thy name!'"[9]

The patent hypocrisy of the Reign's perverse conception of toleration astonished the French philosophe Voltaire, who initially supported the revolution's aims but then despaired at its vicious turn. Voltaire wrote, specifically about the anticlerical focus of the revolutionaries, "Is not the fanaticism of your irreligion more absurd and dangerous than the fanaticism of superstition? Begin by tolerating the faith of your fathers. You talk of nothing but tolerance, and never was a sect more intolerant."[10]

In contrast, the conduct of the American Revolution and the ideology of the American founders show a marked awareness of human fallibility, that is, a recognition of human fallenness. Russell Kirk comments on this very distinction:

> A principle difference between the American Revolution and the French Revolution was this: the American revolutionaries in general held a biblical view of man and his bent toward sin, while the French revolutionaries in general attempted to substitute for the biblical understanding an optimistic doctrine of human goodness advanced by the philosophes of the rationalistic Enlightenment.[11]

Thus the structure of American government takes into account human sinfulness and adopts governmental controls like checks and balances and the separation of powers to rein in the inevitable malevolent expressions of it. James Madison, in the *Federalist Papers*, essay 51, arguing for the people of New York state to adopt the new Constitution of 1789, explicitly assumes this low view of human nature, famously writing, "It may be a reflection on human nature that such devices [the separation of powers and checks and balances] should be necessary to control the abuses of government. But what is government itself but the greatest of all reflections on human nature? If men were angels, no government would be necessary."[12]

In Madison's writings and American order we see an explicit embrace of the biblical view of humans as flawed and fallen. The realism and caution this idea inculcates in governments that make use of it aids the development of an ethic of toleration since it puts us on notice that, at the very least, people will try our patience. In addition, the government predicated on a Judeo-Christian anthropology can partly counteract the selfishness of human beings by building into its foundations devices that can control it and thereby foster a social order of greater stability.

The Lesser of Two Evils

A related way the doctrine of original sin has affected the development of toleration is that through affirming the fallenness of the world, it cautions us against perfectionism. Sometimes, according to a realistic understanding of humanity and the world, even the best a person can do is imperfect. We might think of this as the principle of the lesser-evil approach. This principle was summed up in the old motto: "The perfect is the enemy of the good."

Recall our earlier reference to Thomas Sowell's "conflict of visions" and his contrasting of the "constrained" vision to the "unconstrained." The concept of the lesser of two evils is characteristic of the constrained vision. (This is the second feature of true tolerance we have identified with the constrained vision; the first was the affirming of an enduring human nature or essence proposed by Aristotle.) The constrained vision, largely corresponding to the conservatism of today, is wary of the dangers of overweening governmental authority and human and social frailty. The unconstrained vision, which underlies contemporary liberalism, is markedly optimistic about human nature and the ability of social institutions to withstand imposed changes and renovations. Sowell says of the difference in the practical approach of these two visions, "The unconstrained vision promotes pursuit of the highest ideals and the best solutions. By contrast, the constrained vision sees the best as the enemy of the good—a vain attempt to reach the unattainable being seen as not only futile but often counterproductive, while the same efforts could have produced a viable and beneficial trade-off."[13]

The practical import of this axiom of the lesser evil for a practical doctrine of toleration can perhaps best be seen by way of a legal and political controversy sparked by radical Islamists' September 11, 2001, attacks on the World Trade Center and the Pentagon.

A feature of the Bush administration's response was to propose a policy that would limit immigration into the United States from terrorist-sponsoring nations like Saudi Arabia, where sixteen of the nineteen hijackers were from. Plenty of civil rights groups cried "discrimination!" and "intolerance!" Such a policy was racist and an obvious violation of the Fourteenth Amendment, the "equal protection" clause of the U.S. Constitution, they said. The administration countered that national security interests required a different reading of the Fourteenth Amendment in this case. Most Americans agreed with the administration's desire to curtail such immigration. In Sowell's terms they saw such limitation of immigration as a commonsense tradeoff: the downside of inconveniencing innocent would-be émigrés from terror-supporting nations (e.g., they would have to postpone their travel plans) was trumped by the upside: increased national security. It was a matter of the lesser of two evils. The world is an imperfect place, human discernment is fallible, sin can be insidious and inconveniences (or worse) are simply part of the human condition. In short, we live in a world thoroughly affected by original sin, and trying to impose a regime of absolute fairness (in this case, allowing all émigrés in, perhaps even dismantling borders) is foolish. So a sober realism about the world and the inevitability of imperfection—both fundamentally Christian propositions—can assist the prudent application of tolerance in the real world rampant with exigencies an abstract utopia knows nothing of.

Individual Christian Conscience and Toleration

Summoned to defend his viewpoint before the Diet of Worms, Martin Luther (1483-1546)—whose ninety-five theses had initiated the Protestant Reformation, a spiritual revolution in Europe—said bluntly, "Unless I am convinced that the testimony of scripture, or by an evident reason . . . I am held fast by the scriptures adduced by me, and my conscience is taken captive by God's Word . . . I neither can nor will revoke anything, seeing it is not safe or right to act against my conscience."[14]

In these remarks we have, according to R. E. O. White, the appeal to biblically informed individual conscience characteristic of the Reformation.[15] This accent on inner experience, this keen straining to hear the voice of conscience, would make a notable Christian contribution to the formation of a true toleration, integral to which is freedom of conscience. Among the thirty-nine axioms comprising the useful "Counsels of Tolerance" proposed by J. Budziszewski in *True Tolerance* is one highlighting conscience and discourse: "Each person is entitled to defend his understanding of the good by rational arguments . . . and to attempt to persuade others that it is, in fact, true."[16]

Luther's insistence that the Christian be free to believe according to conscience is reinforced by fellow Reformer John Calvin (1509-1564), who rooted this tenet in the sovereignty of God. He wrote: "In the obedience we have shown to be due to the authority of governors, it is always necessary to make one exception, and that is entitled to our first attention—that it do not seduce us from obedience to [God]."[17]

If this is reminiscent of the battle cry of the American Revolution, it is no accident: the Protestants of the colonies were heavily Calvinistic, and the colonists saw their revolt against the English king as rebellion against immoral imperial policies and hence obedience to God. Fotion and Elfstrom sum up the impact of Protestant individualism on the overall development of toleration in this way: "The rise of Protestantism in Europe, with its emphasis on the centrality of the individual conscience in religious belief, contributed eventually to the culmination of the struggle concerning religious toleration and a shift to political toleration as the new arena of discussion."[18]

The Patristic Insights into Political Tolerance

Professor J. Budziszewski observes that the Christian church was much slower to realize the political implications of tolerance than the importance of tolerance as an idea in itself.[19] In an appendix to *True Tolerance* he adduces an impressive array of passages from Christian thinkers in the early centuries of the faith who nonetheless did show a nascent but still significant understanding of the implications of the gospel for tolerance in a political sense.

For example, he cites John Chrysostom (c. 347-407), the archbishop of Constantinople: "[It is] not right for Christians to eradicate error by constraint and force, but to save humanity by persuasion and reasonableness and gentleness."[20] Chrysostom was concerned that too close an association between church and state would bode ill for the church: "When a Christian ascends the imperial throne, far from being shored up by human honors, Christianity deteriorates."[21]

A similar cautionary note can be found in the work of the fourth-century bishop of Alexandria Athanasius. He is most famous for his penetrating, persistent and decisive defense of the full divinity of Christ against the widely proclaimed error of his contemporary Arius, who held that Jesus Christ was not God. Athanasius was no fawning apologist for imperial authority and its undue influence on the Christian faith. On the contrary, he sharply cautioned against interference by the emperor in church affairs. Further, he held that even true doctrine was not to be promulgated by imperial force, a force that would overrun reason and destroy the liberty of faith. Athanasius wrote, "For the truth is not preached with swords or darts, nor by means of soldiers, but by persuasion and counsel."[22]

Christian patriarchs such as Chrysostom and Athanasius were ahead of their time in making the distinction between church and state, between civil and religious authority. A great span of time would yet pass before this distinction would develop into the purposeful, planned separation of church and state, with its implications for full political toleration.

The Wars of Religion

The wars of religion that followed the sixteenth-century Reformation—with Catholics and Protestants bloodying each other for three decades across Europe—are often adduced by antireligious ideologues as proof that religion is the antithesis of toleration. They argue that the internecine carnage of the Thirty Years' War, *fought four centuries ago,* irrefutably demonstrates the inverse relationship between toleration and religion: the less religion, the more toleration. Not content to reason as they will against the use of religious ideas in public discourse, they would eradicate from the public square even the slightest whiff of religious commitment or sentiment. Their wide-eyed, scrupulous "seasonal hunts for Nativity scenes and Santa Claus," writes satirist R. Emmett Tyrrell Jr., have become in the last decades boringly predictable—and ominously effective.[23]

Yet the multifaceted concept of Western toleration and the virtues integral to its practice are exemplified by the Judeo-Christian heritage and secondarily by Hellenistic thought from Socrates through the Stoics. Moreover, the American Revolution—certainly the most important political boon to civil toleration—was intrinsically rooted in the Judeo-Christian tradition of faith and practice.

In this light the Thirty Years' War (1618-1648) is easily understood as uncharacteristic of the Judeo-Christian heritage. This conflict was only partly a Roman Catholic-Protestant struggle, it was also a political and territorial struggle by different European powers.

Still, this period does show the dark side of religion misconstrued. But it is important to remember that the decisive critiques of the confusion, fear and hypocrisy that fomented the Thirty Years' War *came from within Christianity,* from such Christian thinkers as John Locke (1632-1704).

Though the carnage was horrifying—the conflicts cost hundreds of thousands of lives—they were not in vain, as Carroll and Shiflett point out: "[A] marvelous thing happened as a result of these convulsions. Western society reconsidered holy war as a political option—and rejected it."[24]

Providentially, Western Christianity, even when plundering itself, serves as an example that theological and intellectual differences cannot be homogenized and that simply abiding them is a much more desirable circumstance than seeking to eradicate them.

England's Religious Turmoil

The religious and political turmoil of post-Reformation Europe shook England during the reign of Henry VIII (1509-1547), whose divorce from Catherine of Aragon led to his self-appointment as head of the Church of England, which had separated from the Roman Catholic Church. Theologically, Henry understood himself as continuing as a Catholic, which theology and sacramental system he favored over the Reformers'. So the Church of England continued in this style until Henry's death. His son and successor, Edward VI, was heavily influenced by Calvinism, and he revamped the Church of England to reflect the Reformers' biblical understanding. Mary I, a Roman Catholic queen, succeeded Edward VI and thrust out Protestant reforms and reformers with such violence that she earned the nickname "Bloody Mary."

This to-and-fro theological gyration—Catholic to Protestant, Protestant to Catholic—would characterize the throne for many decades and with such lurching that it would be humorous if it had not been so painful. Mary was succeeded by Elizabeth I, a Protestant queen, who wished to retain in the Church of England a Catholic ambiance while making its theology decidedly Protestant. King James, next in line, amplified the Reformers' stress on Bible study by commissioning an English translation of Scripture, famously named after him. When he was succeeded by the Catholic king Charles I, Protestant Puritans led by Oliver Cromwell revolted in the name of Parliament, beheaded Charles and declared a kingless commonwealth. But after a season Charles's son, a Roman Catholic, returned from exile and was crowned king. He was followed by the Catholic King James II, who was deposed by the Protestants William and Mary, who passed the landmark Act of Toleration of 1689. The Act, while retaining the Church of England as the nation's established church, allowed many dissident congregations to openly practice their faiths.

In addition to the prompting of the Act of Toleration, England's stormy religious history after Henry VIII produced two other signal developments in the evolution of toleration. The first was stimulating Enlightenment philosopher John Locke to write his influential *Letter Concerning Toleration;* the other was causing the emigration of religious dissidents from England to the American colonies and thus unintentionally causing a most extraordinary experiment in self-government and toleration.

We will now turn to a consideration of some Enlightenment figures' role in furthering tolerance as well as contributions from the early American experience.

THE ENLIGHTENMENT
AND BEYOND

I disapprove of what you say,

but I will defend to the death your right to say it.

VOLTAIRE

The Enlightenment of the seventeenth and eighteenth centuries stressed a confidence in human reason and the abilities of human beings—apart from divine revelation—to morally guide themselves. "Sapere Aude," or "Dare to Know," Enlightenment philosopher Immanuel Kant urged his colleagues.[1] This sentiment, though in fallen human hands became the seed of secularism that would centuries later balefully bloom, served as a powerfully motivating force for human reflection, including meditation on the necessity of toleration.

John Locke

It was during the reign of Charles II that John Locke was provoked to write and promulgate his *Letter Concerning Toleration,* published in 1689. The effects of this letter were so striking and influential that Locke has been called "the leading champion of toleration in the history of British philosophy."[2]

At age thirty-five John Locke was a private physician and counselor in philosophy in the employ of the first Earl of Shaftesbury, a Whig leader. He had taken this employment in 1667, having left his position as an Oxford don. Shaftesbury was in Parliament during the reign of Charles II, who admired Shaftesbury's support of religious toleration— and counted on him to promote toleration for Catholicism in England.

Though the king and Shaftesbury shared similar convictions on toleration, they differed in its practical application. The Catholic king was most concerned to extend toleration to Roman Catholics, who rejected the spiritual authority of the Church of England. In contrast Shaftesbury was most concerned about the cause of the Protestant Dissenters, such as the Quakers.

Shaftesbury had invited Locke, his philosopher-in-residence, to build a case for toleration, especially for dissenting Protestant groups. This is the general origin of Locke's *Letter Concerning Toleration*. Locke's essay is a grand achievement in religious toleration, one that would have great effect throughout the American colonies.

Locke's *Letter* did not recommend disestablishment of the Church of England—and in this respect, it would fall short of the American founders' insistence, soon after the *Letter*, that no church be the established American church. Yet Locke's essay cogently rebukes the Church of England's usurping of the consciences of its dissenters. Notably, Locke does not make his case as a secularist but as a Christian, and he reverently quotes the New Testament to counterpose the use of civil force to compel belief to Christ's nonviolent invitation to faith. Such militant force was not, said Locke, the mark of the true Christian. He writes: "The business of true religion is not . . . instituted in order of erecting an external pomp, nor to the obtaining of ecclesiastical dominion, nor to the exercising of compulsive force."[3]

Against the background of the Thirty Years' War of religion and politics, Locke reminds us that Christ is the "Prince of Peace" whose followers should not be "armed with the sword, or other instruments of force, but prepared with the Gospel of peace, and with the exemplary holiness of their conversation. This was his method."[4]

Despite Locke's concern that the churches must be duly restrained from imposing sacred doctrine on citizens, he (with the American founders, later) views the church as the principle protector of morality. This put Locke's position in opposition to that of a later theorist of toleration and freedom, philosopher John Stuart Mill, who revolted against what he saw as exterior influences on individual conscience, including that of the Christian church. Maurice Cranston contrasts Locke's position to Mill's: "From Locke's point of view, to take away the authority [on the individual] of first the church, then of the society itself, would leave the state as the only source of authority, and that really would be a formula for [individual] enslavement."[5]

Yet Locke's chief theme is the fundamental distinction he makes between the church and the state. He finds two functions of the church: (1) the organization of liturgy, public worship and ethical superintendence, and (2) the regulation of lives in terms of virtue and piety. He applies this principle to both the Church of England and the various dissidents, writing, "These religious societies I call churches; and these I say the magistrate ought to tolerate: for the business of these assemblies of the people is nothing but what is lawful for every man in particular to take care of; I mean the salvation of their souls: nor, in this case, is there any difference between the national church and other separated congregations."[6]

Civil government has different functions altogether from religious societies. It is charged principally with the promulgation and enforcement of civil law—by *force* if necessary. Given their decisively different purposes and aims, Locke says, secular and religious institutions ought, indeed must, peacefully coexist

John Stuart Mill

With Locke, John Stuart Mill (1806-1873) made an important, though lamentable, contribution to the idea of toleration, mainly through his book *On Liberty* (1859). Unlike Locke's work, which sought to debunk political and religious intolerance, Mill's work extended the meaning of intolerance to include nonlegal practices such as social pressure, ostracism and stigma. Mill argued for wide "experimentation" in lifestyles and opinions, and the discounting of behavioral traditions as traditions. For Mill, established morality was suspect simply because it was established, and what he called the "despotism of custom" was always to be resisted.[7]

But Mill's diatribe against what he viewed as social intolerance, his relentless uplifting of eccentricity and denigration of tradition, had its critics. One of the more trenchant ones was Mill's contemporary, James Fitzjames Stephen. Stephen answered Mill in his scathing book *Liberty, Equality, Fraternity*. That Stephen's name is not well-known today says something about who won the argument, at least in influential intellectual circles. Yet Stephen's critique of Mill has caused new interest in our times as the dubious effects of Mill's policy, which in time was more or less adopted in the West, have stimulated a rethinking of his vision of liberty sans tradition: Was Mill wrong?

The Mill-Stephen controversy is not merely a nineteenth-century curiosity but a dispute with far-reaching implications for tolerance today. In terms of Sowell's "conflict of visions," Mill directly fits the "unconstrained vision": the revolt against tradition, the eccentric as the true hero of civilization, the malleability of human beings.* Understood in this way Mill's *On Liberty* is the father of 1960s American cultural turmoil and all it has lamentably bequeathed us. In his bestselling critique of modern liberalism, *Slouching Towards Gomorrah,* Robert H. Bork notes the significance of what transpired in the sixties: "It is important to understand what the Sixties turmoil was about, for the youth culture that became manifest then is the modern liberal culture of today."[8] Therefore, reflection on the Mill-Stephen controversy supplies insight into the culture wars of today.

Stephen, in his writing, concedes that tradition is hardly beyond critique and that intelligent iconoclasm actually advances culture. Yet the conservation of tradition holds a central place in Stephen's style of "constrained vision," and he is clearly less optimistic about the casual proliferation of eccentricity and unorthodoxy than is Mill.

John Stuart Mill's father, James, was an ardent admirer of the first prophet of utilitarianism, Jeremy Bentham, and sought to groom young John for a career as a political reformer. John would fulfill that ambition, eventually developing in the body of his overall philosophical work a version of utilitarianism considered more nuanced than Bentham's.[9]

Mill was by nature and training a controversialist, both in political philosophy and his personal life. In 1830, when he was twenty-four, Mill began an affair with Harriet Taylor, the wife of the London merchant John Taylor. After John Taylor's death they married and Harriet Taylor,

---

*Interestingly, Mill's emphasis on emotion and iconoclasm in his thought can easily be seen as reaction against his strict and even sterile upbringing as the highly (and privately) educated son of the eminent philosopher James Mill. Having had a socially stunted childhood, in his intellectual life Mill indulged the romanticism and rebellion he never experienced as a child. For description of Mill's early years, see Timothy Luther, *The Political Philosophy of Democracy* (Boston: Houghton Mifflin, 1998), pp. 321-22.

whose special intellectual interest was women's rights, collaborated with her husband on a number of works.

Mill's masterwork *On Liberty* was an application of utilitarian principles in the defense of social toleration. It broadly enlarged the principle of toleration, exalting the renegade and the reformer but trivializing the traditionalist. Mill did not establish toleration on a theory of natural rights but on the principle of utility: the toleration of unconventional views inclines to produce the greatest good for the greatest number. Mill gives four reasons for tolerating unconventional opinions, which have been celebrated by a large swath of Western intelligentsia ever since their pronouncement. Startling to many in their time, today they are conditioned into contemporary consciousness.

First, since opinions contrary to society-sanctioned opinion may be true, to suppress them would deny the vital effects of this truth to society, thereby leaving it in dangerous error. Second, opinions that are suppressed may contain a degree of truth, and the promulgation of a whole truth is better than a partial one. Third, even when a publicly held opinion is indeed true, its mechanical reception and uncritical embrace is incompatible with its deep comprehension by those who know it by rote. Fourth, the meaning and significance of a doctrine that has ceased to be debated is in danger of being lost or weakened, for an unexamined truth is undercut in its power to form character and shape conduct.[10] Mill's vision of liberty turns on what would later be called his "harm principle": that everyone may do as he or she pleases as long as harm is not done to his or her neighbor. It is a testament to Mill's baleful influence that this very rationale is routinely trumpeted in contemporary America, from the editorials of the *New York Times* to the lurid displays of human dysfunction televised on the *Jerry Springer* and *Rikki Lake* shows. Indeed, as one critic of Mill notes, Mill has been so influential to the modern mind that to employ "liberal language has been taken to be *intelligent:* to reject it evidence of *stupidity.*"[11]

Acknowledging that *On Liberty* is a masterpiece of liberal polemic, contemporary conservative social critic Roger Kimball wants to distinguish its rhetorical prowess from the cogency of its arguments, which Kimball sees as devastated by Stephen's *Liberty, Equality, Fraternity* (1873), a book that was a deliberate response to Mill's work.

Stephen's title, *Liberty, Equality, Fraternity*, alludes not only to the banner of the French Revolution but to a motto crystallizing the new secular faith, of which Mill was an adherent: the Religion of Humanity, most famously exposited by French philosopher, atheist and self-styled vicar of all humanity, Auguste Comte (1798-1857).

Mill did not accept wholesale Comte's philosophy, but he did agree with the ambitious humanist that human potential was basically limitless and tradition need not be regarded as any serious caution against rolling the dice of social, political and religious change.

Stephen insists that Mill defines liberty, equality and fraternity in ways corrosive of traditional social arrangements. Mill's view of liberty, for instance, epitomized by the negative "harm principle," is primarily opposed to moral systems that by nature critique human character. But the expressions of human character are the very stuff of life, the single most direct producer of quality of life, both individual and social.

Mill insists, though, that society has no business deciding anything to be morally wrong that solely concerns the individual—including, he says, gambling and fornication. Yet, notes Kimball, even these two examples are problematic in a social context. Kimball asks, recognizing the social ramifications and consequences of individual choices of action, "should a person be free to be a pimp? Or to keep a gambling house? Mill thinks these are exceptionally difficult questions."[12]

These are not difficult questions, says Stephen; the state has the right to regulate them and many other things people might want to do with their liberty.[13] This is simply the basis of civilization, and it is a quite impoverished understanding of human liberty that places it in an intellectual vacuum, separated from any admitted knowledge of human nature, human ends, the good in general and God himself.

Stephen anticipates two strands of the "unconstrained vision" in Mill: Mill's anthropology, which sees the human person au natural as ego-transcending and inclined to the good, and Mill's view that morally evolved persons do not act with special kindness toward their intimates but display equal and disinterested benevolence to all. Both propositions, says Stephen, are contrary to human nature, and to base a personal ethic and social policies on them is to invite disaster, all in the name of freedom and goodness.

The American Experience

The Calvinist Christianity that first established itself in the North American colonies contained a knowledge, sometimes imperfectly expressed, of the imperative of social and religious toleration. This burning insistence on freedom of conscience and belief would eventually kindle the American Revolution and help establish the first truly tolerant democracy on earth.

In the Puritan distrust of secular and hierarchical ecclesial power and its form of government slept the seeds of American democracy, and of a new fullness of toleration that transcended the toleration accorded to religious groups by England's established church. Various religious forces were at work in the colonies too—including the Quakers, Anabaptists, deists, the Roman Catholics of Maryland and others. The ferment of all these forces would fuel revolution and lead not just to representative democracy but also to formal disestablishment: the renunciation of one national, superintending church.[14]

The first amendment's insistence that "Congress shall make no law respecting the establishment of religion" must be understood in light of our earlier remarks concerning the turmoil that an established church had caused in England. The purpose of separating church and state is not to protect the state from religious influences. Rather, it is to preserve the freedom of religious belief. Commentator George Will plainly explains the first amendment's purpose: "The intention of the framers of the Establishment Clause . . . was to ensure government neutrality between religious factions, not between religion and irreligion."[15]

Yet the desire for governmental religious neutrality was not the only force behind disestablishment and religious toleration in postrevolutionary America. Dinesh D'Souza argues that the principle of checks and balances contributed mightily too. Pointing out that a variety of Protestant sects predominated in the United States from the beginning, it was simply in the practical interest of each group to "live and let live." He writes: "The ingenuity of the American solution is evident in Voltaire's remark that where there is one religion, you have tyranny, where there is two, you have religious war; but where there are many, you have freedom."[16]

And there were other practical ways to steer Americans clear of interdenominational animus, says D'Souza. One of these was the promotion of a vigorous capitalism, which encouraged an appreciation of this-worldly prosperity.[17] The founders knew if they could encourage an economy that invited each person to improve his or her station through hard work and prudent living, there would be a diminution of vicious energy for the likes of interdenominational religious conflict. Paradoxically, then, opportunities for worldly success would mitigate religious conflict. D'Souza summarizes his idea as follows:

> The American founders solved two great problems—the problem of scarcity and the problem of diversity—that were a source of perennial misery in ancient societies, and that remain unsolved in the regimes of contemporary Islam. The founders invented a new regime in which citizens would enjoy a wide berth of freedom—economic freedom, political freedom, and freedom of speech and religion—in order to shape their own lives and happiness. By separating religion from government, and by directing the energies of the citizens toward trade and commerce, the American founders created such a rich, dynamic, and tolerant society that it is now the hope of countless immigrants and a magnet for the world.[18]

D'Souza's point is well-taken: the origin of religious toleration in American life was not only idealistic or philosophical, but it was also founded on a practical, realistic understanding of human nature and human needs.

The Role of Christian Clergy

Indispensable to the beginnings of the new nation is the explosive impetus that the American clergy gave to the American Revolution. Peter Oliver, a Tory writing in 1781, rebuked the "black regiment, the dissenting clergy" for fomenting the revolution.[19] Most influential among early colonial Protestants were the Puritans and their well-educated, plainspoken clergy—a people whom Edmund Burke described as "the most adverse to all subjection of mind and opinion" in their radical adherence to Reformed or Calvinist Christianity.[20] It was the Puritans' fierce commitment to the absolute sovereignty of God over all of life that sealed their resistance to any compulsion viewed as undivine. Winthrop S. Hudson and John Corrigan write: "It has been said of the early Calvinists that they feared God so much that they could not fear any man, be he king or emperor."[21]

While conventional textbook approaches to the revolution typically suggest that colonial solidarity against British rule was mostly a function of a series of political outrages such as the Stamp Act, the revolution's true prologue is spiritual: a solidarity produced by a colonialwide spiritual revival in the decades preceding the celebrated rallying points such as the Stamp Act—a revival aptly called the Great Awakening.

If the initials G. W. come to mind relative to the American Revolution, they rarely remind of clergyman George Whitfield—but they ought to, despite the inimitable role of George Washington. For it was Whitfield who piqued the Great Awakening, which historians credit as indispensable to the revolution's success. Had the awakening not inspired interdenominational Christian solidarity among Baptist, Puritan, Catholic, Lutheran and Episcopal colonists prior to 1776, the pitch of revolutionary fervor required for success may not have been achieved. Typical is John Mark Terry's assessment of the Great Awakening in his book *Evangelism:* "The Great Awakening served to unify the colonies and increase their awareness of each other. . . . In this the revival prepared the way for the American Revolution."[22]

The Christian dynamism that stoked the revolution has been excised from secular textbooks. In the custody of our secular princes—law professors, judges, history professors and journalists—the Christian fervor that inspired our national beginnings has been basically ignored. As Michael Novak points out, if the words of warning in George Washington's "Farewell Address" that we must not forget our religious origins are to be taken seriously, then this historical amnesia is troubling for the American future.[23]

Why do public school textbooks tend to leave out elaboration of the decidedly unsecular roots of American democracy? At least three other reasons may be added to the point made by Novak about the secularity of American elites.

Most of them turn on a convoluted contemporary understanding of toleration. The first is an absurd application of the separation of church and state doctrine—too much positive mention of Christianity in a textbook is seen as a state endorsement of Christianity and as "intolerance" toward other faiths or nonbelief altogether. The second is a twisted psychology of self-esteem: non-Christians students may feel "marginalized" or "offended" by the truth that the revolution was largely a Christian revolt. The third reason is the anti-Western bias of many educators and textbook authors who—rightly so—associate Christianity with Western culture but, according to their bias, wish to credit Christianity with as little good as possible.[24]

Yet truth be told, it was a solidarity based on interdenominational Christian cooperation produced by the Great Awakening that unified colonial will before the revolution. It was Christian preaching that heartened American patriots and steeled the continental army during the revolution, and a Judeo-Christian ethic that not only prevailed in the Constitution of 1789 after the birth of the nation, but thereafter gave Americans the will and insight to make the United States—the "New Order of the Ages," in the founders' words—practically flourish through two centuries, with toleration as one of its finest fruits.

A historic moment that pictures with special poignancy both the vitality of tolerance in America and the central role of faith in its founding was that of the First Continental Congress at prayer on September 7, 1774. Early in September members of this Congress rode from all points in the colonies to Philadelphia to make clear to King George III the rights they expected to be honored by the British crown. Rumors were rife of a British attack on Charleston.

Some delegates proposed that the meeting begin with a prayer; a few opposed the motion, arguing that the wide variety of religious sentiments held by delegates—Presbyterian, Quaker, Episcopalian, Congregationalist, Anabaptist—precluded a common prayer. Samuel Adams stood up and announced that he was no bigot and would hear a prayer from any true patriot and man of piety. He suggested the Reverend Duché, an Episcopalian minister, and the motion carried. So it was that the first act of the First Continental Congress was the commissioning of a prayer.

The next day, Reverend Duché read aloud before the Continental Congress Psalm 35 from the *Book of Common Prayer*. It began:

> Plead my cause, O Lord, with them that strive with me: fight against them that fight against me. Take hold of shield and buckler, and stand up for mine help. Draw out also the spear, and stop the way against them that persecute me: say unto my soul, I am thy salvation.

John Adams, who would be the second president of the United States, was deeply moved by the prayer, and he wrote to his wife Abigail that he had never heard a better prayer or one so well pronounced. "I never saw a greater effect upon an audience. It seemed as if heaven had ordained that Psalm to be read on that morning. . . . It was enough to melt a heart of stone. I saw tears gush into the eyes of the old, grave pacific Quakers of Philadelphia. . . . I must beg you to read that Psalm."[25]

All this should give pause to those who, counter-historically, insist that religion has no place in public life—that since religion is intrinsically divisive, its rhetoric should be muffled in the public square.

Certainly, the founders thought differently. We have already alluded to George Washington's panegyric in his "Farewell Address" to religion as an indispensable buttress of those virtues required for self-government.[26] We could reiterate this point through multiple citations from a host of founders, but we will let suffice this statement from John Adams in 1798: "We have no government armed with [the] power of contending with human passions unbridled by morality and religion. Avarice, ambition, revenge, or gallantry, would break the strongest cords of our Constitution as a whale does a net. *Our Constitution is made only for a moral and religious people. It is wholly inadequate to the government of any other.*"[27]

PART TWO

TRUTH AND
THE CULTURE WARS

With some understanding of the history of tolerance, and a clear picture of the Judeo-Christian identity of the American nation as it was originally conceived, we can now turn to the contemporary struggle over tolerance in American society.

The proper apprehension and practice of tolerance depends on a clear understanding of truth. Yet in the United States and Western culture generally today, truth is a foggy idea, regarded at best as a specter of the premodern past. This imperils the rich legacy of Western tolerance we have traced. In an effort to more fully bring to bear on our contemporary cultural divisions this heritage of tolerance, we will consider the condition and conception of truth today.

In this section we will examine the idea of truth and the necessarily interrelated character of truth and tolerance, then take the measure of the two primary combatants in the American culture war—American secular liberalism and evangelical Christianity—and consider how they respectively understand and apply the concept of truth in the context of contemporary American pluralism.

THE TRUTH
ABOUT TRUTH

[Truth] allows us to cooperate with reality, whether spiritual or physical, and tap into its power. As we learn to think correctly about God, specific scriptural teachings, the soul, or other important aspects of a Christian worldview, we are placed in touch with God and those realities. And we thereby gain access to the power available to us to live in the kingdom of God

J. P. MORELAND

In ancient times they asked, "Who is your God?" A generation ago, they asked your religion. Today your creed is a preference. Preference? "I take my coffee black, my wine red, my sex straight, and my shirts lightly starched. Oh yes, and put me down for Islam."

CHARLES KRAUTHAMMER

As the typical American today would be quick to point out, there are many ways to understand truth. And, such a person would probably hasten to add, the more individual and subjective the understanding, the more respectable it is. Both academically and popularly truth seems to be regarded as a suspicious idea today, and if it has any pretensions beyond the purely private, it may likely be regarded as downright arrogant. Indeed, it is a profound irony and social tragedy that truth—and any claim to know the actual truth about a given matter or proposition—is more likely to be associated with intolerance than tolerance, with narrow-mindedness and bigotry rather than intellectual good faith and genuine concern for human well-being. This is a phenomenon that no commonwealth can long endure.

The depth and significance of our cultural confusion over the nature, meaning and application of truth as a concept is difficult to overestimate. It seems as though we are schizophrenic about truth: we use it in our daily lives concerning the likelihood of rain, our bank's accurate accounting of our money on deposit, and whether the president was quoted correctly in the newspaper, but we seem allergic to recognizing the possibility that our opinions about politics, ethics or religious belief might be seriously mistaken or outright false.

The mind-independent quality of some types of truth is hard for the contemporary American to accept, yet in a very real sense it is this kind of transpersonal truth for which we most deeply hunger. God has placed "eternity in the hearts of men" (Eccles 3:11), a natural yearning to know him and his ways, and unless we are open to the reality of objective, transpersonal, mind-independent truth we risk never finding the fulfillment that is in him alone.

This personal need for transpersonal truth is paralleled by our culture's need for an awareness, acceptance and acknowledgment of public truths, basic moral propositions that can order our society.[1] All societies need such principles if they are to endure. Both individuals and communities are doomed to the fog of confusion and the myopia of self-centeredness if we are unwilling to always hold open the possibility that not only objective truth exists but that it may be what we don't want it to be or think it should be.

This surpassing existential and intellectual commitment to truth—wherever it leads—is at the center of Christian consciousness. Paul, in 1 Corinthians 15:13-19, explicitly declares that Christian faith itself is wholly futile and even a lie against God if Jesus has not been resurrected from the dead as he, the other apostles and the early church had been proclaiming. Paul's personal investment in Christianity was to be discarded if at any time, through any means, the physical resurrection of Jesus was shown to be objectively untrue.

This is a sobering fact for believers and one that should always be kept in mind for three reasons. First, all human beings seem to have a remarkable ability not to let the facts get in the way of what they want to believe, and remembering the contingent nature of Paul's faith will help us remain intellectually honest, not only with respect to religious matters but also as a general habit of mind.[2]

Second, the overriding devotion to truth, whatever the consequences, will in time teach us that God is not afraid of any of our questions or confusions, and that in the end, he alone is the author of truth.[3] Just as there is nothing that can happen to us in our lives that the absolutely sovereign God has not either directly willed or allowed to come to pass, so too there is no true event or circumstance that he does not fully know and understand, and is able to ultimately use (in ways we may recognize and understand or not) to affirm his own utterly pure, unassailable justice and love, whether in history, society or individual lives.[4]

Third, insisting on the controlling nature of truth and subordinating our own noetic (that is, mental) preferences to what is indeed the case about matters cannot help but lead us to humility of mind. If we acknowledge as Paul did that our own convictions are always in some way evidential and therefore falsifiable by counterevidences, we preserve a winsome philosophical submissiveness as well as an implicit commitment against complacency of reflection and the intellectual arrogance so common to the settled mind.[5]

Truth and Humility in the Christian

Indeed, this kind of humility of mind is mandated for the Christian, and the failure of some contemporary Christians to evince this virtue has helped close cultural and personal doors that might otherwise be more amenable to the Christian worldview. As Richard John Neuhaus notes:

> As St. Paul reminds the Corinthians, our apprehension of [truth] is always partial, something seen through a glass darkly in anticipation of the time when we will know even as we are known [1 Cor 13:12].
>
> Few things have contributed so powerfully to the unbelief of the modern and postmodern world as the pretension of Christians to know more than we do. . . . If Christians exhibited more intellectual patience, modesty, curiosity, and a sense of adventure, there would be fewer atheists in the world.[6]

Still further troubling is the indulgence by some Christians in what has become an American culture of anger. A powerful case can be made that anger is at the heart of the contemporary American experience, and the effects of this fury, from murder to road rage to divorce to nasty politics, are all around us.[7] The entry of Christians, including some Christian intellectuals and leaders, into this derby of personal destruction is obviously counterproductive to Christian critique and witness, and it is unbiblical. Occasionally, this unholy rage manifests publicly, as when one prominent pastor, after delivering a stirring Sunday sermon, seized a young church staffer who had inadvertently done something during this "man of God's" sermon that upset him and delivered a blistering attack on the frightened underling—with his lapel microphone still on! The tirade was broadcast to the entire church campus, from the nursery to the prayer room.[8]

The church too has been infected with the culture of anger, and this, along with the intensity of the American culture wars, has produced a perverse anger among Christians toward unbelievers. This hostility and its theological and cultural consequences also hinder Christian witness, and certainly lead Christians to sometimes manifest an attitude and demeanor, both personally and intellectually, that is regrettable.[9]

Peter's adjuration in 1 Peter 3:15 to explain Christian belief—as well as its ethical requirements and implications—to non-Christians with "gentleness and respect" must be taken not as an unattainable ideal but rather as a moral requirement. Recognizing the partialness of our own knowledge and understanding will help us fulfill this mandate.

Of course, we should always remember the paradoxical nature of God and the Christian gospel. The God of the Christian tradition deliberately frustrates human pretensions to intellectual and spiritual self-sufficiency (1 Cor 1:19). He urges us to become small in order to become great, to become servants in order to become rulers, to become dependent on him in order to become truly independent, to lose ourselves in order to find ourselves, to aspire to self-negation not self-aggrandizement and so forth.[10] Indeed, God's habit of confounding human understanding extends to those who we think belong in his kingdom and those who we are sure do not. Knowing this should generate a healthy, ethically essential respect and tolerance for the faiths and worldviews of those we disagree with. As one Christian philosopher put it:

> Every religious culture and experience should be deeply respected—even
> if not adopted and even if regarded as mistaken in important respects.

Christians above all *should* know of God's habit of turning up in the wrong company, where according to the official view He absolutely *could not* be. . . . The partisan of one religion must extend the same generous openness and hopefulness to the practitioners of other religions as he would want them and the atheist to extend to himself.[11]

Our human habit of shutting off the kingdom of God to others is our enemy when seeking to cultivate an authentically humble sense and style in our communication of Christian truth. The old quip is all too true: "When you get to heaven, you'll have two surprises: you'll be surprised whom you see there—and they'll all be surprised to see you."

Theories of Truth

Effectively contending for the truth in contemporary culture—whether the truth claims of Christianity, the facts of society and politics, moral truth or the psychological and emotional truths of the human experience—requires we have a comprehensive understanding of truth itself, and the various manners and contexts in which it can be experienced, demonstrated and understood. Toward that end it will be helpful for us to briefly survey the outlines of seven common theories of truth, their respective theoretical and practical virtues and applications, and their significance for our study.[12]

Truth is whatever you want it to be. This relativist view of truth is of course a rejection of truth itself in any public or objective sense, and an inadequate and unrealistic way of understanding life. No one actually lives as a relativist, and as a conceptual disposition relativism is really nothing more than an exercise in self-justification and rationalization, substituting one's own preferences or wishes for any realities that do not coincide with those personal desires. Relativism is fundamentally childish.[13]

That said, Christians should not reject altogether the subjective realities relativism conveys, particularly in a time such as ours, which is substantially emotive and narcissistic in its ethos. Relativism can function as an adequate theory of truth as long as the ideas being asserted are simply expressions of personal preference and make no pretensions to anything beyond that. For example, "I tend to prefer hamburgers to hotdogs," "I like mystery novels," and "I want to hold a grudge against Bill" would all be true statements about a person who inhabited each of those mental and emotional states. A relativism intending to communicate purely transient private realities is nothing more than a description of one person's inclinations and therefore has a certain usefulness. But as we ascend to public, political, ethical and metaphysical contexts, relativism loses all legitimacy and explanatory competence.

Truth is what works. This pragmatic understanding of truth is still essentially relativistic; it reduces truth to what *I think* works or what currently *works for me* or what, in light of current social arrangements or realities, is useful for me to do or think. Pragmatism is a reduction of truth to utility and sets truth on a foundation of shifting sand—it is *me,* and not external reality, that determines what *I think* is pragmatically right at the present time. My definition of "usefulness" may change later, as may my aims, hence what is pragmatically true for me now may not be pragmatically true for me in the future.

Further, what is true is not always practical (facing death and paying taxes), and what is practical sometimes violates our moral intuitions (stealing when I know I cannot be caught). As G. K. Chesterton famously noted, the devotion to pragmatism does not answer to the needs of the human heart, to our fully human character, since, as he noted, "Man's most pragmatic need is to be something more than a pragmatist."[14]

Despite its philosophical limitations, pragmatism is deeply rooted in the American mind and history, and continues to order the lives of many. From William James to John Dewey to Richard Rorty to Jeffrey Stout, the pragmatic approach to the theoretical and practical problems of life and society has always influenced the American mind.[15] And certainly, to say that a certain attitude or practice (e.g., getting paid in cash to aid in avoiding reporting your income to the government) "works" is true, but only as a procedural verdict about its efficacy to achieve a given end, however much the amorality of pragmatism violates our moral sense. Of course, sometimes the utility of a practice does coincide with its morality, as, sometimes at least, with tolerance. It is practically and financially useful for us to cooperate interpersonally and economically, though we may not see eye to eye on a great many values questions. But as the final word on truth and understanding the human experience, pragmatism amounts to little more than relativism with a nod toward the fact that I must interact with others.

Truth is what we can sense and sensually perceive. The attraction of this empiricist theory of truth is notorious in American popular and intellectual life today but none the more coherent for it. The empiricist criterion for knowledge—all that I can know is mediated through my five senses (taste, touch, smell, sight, and sound)—is self-refuting because it cannot itself be verified by the human senses. Neither of course, can our senses always be trusted, as when we experience a mirage or a hypnotically induced state.

Further, if bare sensation is accepted as the authoritative touchstone of knowledge and what is really there, then important aspects of knowledge and reality—*as commonly presupposed by our daily lives*—are lost to us or at the very least called into serious question. These would include, for example, moral and other values, minds, past and future events, theoretical entities (e.g., atoms, unconscious drives or thoughts), and intellectual appreciation of film, to name a few. Reducing knowledge and truth to the claustrophobic arena of the five senses is finally an arbitrary move and one executed usually in the service of the worldview of scientism, the confusion that only "science" and the scientific method provides a reliable way of understanding human experience and the world.[16] Certainly though, while an empiricist theory of truth is ultimately too confining, it is still important to give due attention to the empirical data of our body, values and actual experience.

Truth is what reason declares. Rationalism, the exaltation of reason and thought processes to the royal throne of knowledge, suffers the same self-refuting defect of pragmatism, empiricism and relativism: it cannot be proved by its own standard. Reason alone needs recourse to other dimensions of reality and human experience—formal logical truths like the law of noncontradiction (x cannot equal non-x), deep sentiment (like a father's inclination to protect his children) and romantic attraction—to properly recognize and understand the human condition. Some dimensions of life and the world are simply ineffable in their wonder and truth, and the finite human mental apparatus is not competent to completely process it.* Reason is important, but it is not all that is important.

Truth is the coherence of a group of ideas. The "coherence theory of truth" is widely influential today and holds that truth is the coherence or harmony among a set of ideas. Again, though, a problem of intelligibility intrudes. The partisan of this theory of truth seeks to vindicate this perspective not by showing that it *coheres* with other related ideas about truth and knowledge but rather that it matches up with what we mean when we say "true," that it corresponds with what we believe ourselves to understand when we affirm that a given idea is true. By appealing to correspondence to vindicate coherence, it disproves itself.

Further, this approach to truth is too insular and self-contained to be of great use to us in our daily lives. When we assert or affirm a given state of affairs, an idea or an event is true, we are claiming more for it than a certain quality about its relation to other similar or relevant states, ideas or events. We are not making simply a statement about relationships among similar ideas but rather a statement about the relationship between a certain idea and the world outside or beyond that idea. We naturally want our concept of truth to be able to address realities "out there" and independent of the ideas in our minds.[17]

Though inadequate as the final word on truth, certainly the concept of coherence is one we expect our true ideas to fulfill. We quite rightly intend that values we practice and advocate cohere with other truths we hold about the nature of the world and society. Though coherence is not itself the final criterion for truthfulness, it is an indicator and property of it. Coherence is a necessary condition for truthfulness, but not a sufficient condition.

Truth is what corresponds to reality. The correspondence theory of truth is certainly to be preferred to other candidates, and it best captures

---

*The film *Grand Canyon* (directed by Lawrence Kasdan, Twentieth Century Fox, 1992) is a provocative illustration—using the metaphor of Arizona's profound Grand Canyon—of this transcendent dimension to the world and human experience. Deep grief has also been advanced as a "signal of transcendence," in sociologist Peter Berger's phrase. For powerful reflection on these lines, see the truly stunning work of Gerald Sittser, *A Grace Disguised: How the Soul Grows Through Loss* (Grand Rapids: Zondervan, 1995). For discussion of the concept of "signals of transcendence," which Berger defines as "phenomena that are to be found within our 'natural' reality but that appear to point beyond that reality," see his book, *A Rumor of Angels: Modern Society and the Rediscovery of the Supernatural* (New York: Doubleday, 1969), pp. 52-75.

what we most fundamentally mean as we use and interact with the concept of truth. When we say or believe that X is true, we are understanding ourselves to be describing an actual state of affairs, a quality of genuine reality. If we are assured an event is true, we believe it in fact happened; if we are convinced a situation is true, we think that situation prevails and may actually affect us or someone else, and so we act or recommend action accordingly; if it is proven to us that a proposition is true, we have concluded that the proposition portrays a distinct mind-independent reality as that reality essentially is. There is a matching-up or a decisive connection between the statement and the reality it refers to. The actual nature—or some aspect of it—about the world external to us is properly conveyed to us by true statements. Further, that actual nature of the world is not changed or affected by our correctly or incorrectly describing it. The final truth of ideas or events is discovered by people, not created by them.[18]

Truth is whatever I feel. Last, and by way of introducing our next discussion, we should note the emotive outlook on truth. Truth is what I feel; truth is found wherever my emotions lead me. As with so many habits of the contemporary mind, its childishness and indefensibility does not prevent it from achieving widespread currency and practice.

Still, there is no reason to believe our feelings are an infallible or even reliable guide to reality, and emotivism embraces a deeply uncritical stance toward ourselves and our emotions. Could it be my feelings of dislike toward someone and my conviction he is a person of bad character are based on jealousy, resentment or unresolved anger in my own life projected toward him? Any equation of emotional impulse and truth falls far short of considering all the evidence—which unless I am entirely self-absorbed I must admit may lie outside of my own mind and experience—that would be relevant to determining the truth of any given matter.[19]

This is not to say that feelings cannot be a part of the truth of a matter (e.g., I feel revulsion at the photos of the grisly crime scene, emphasizing to me the injustice and brutality of what was done), but they alone should not be allowed to steer our lives. We must not *identify* truth with feeling. Whether as individuals or as a society, such a move would give rise to impulsiveness, violence, irresponsibility and eventually anarchy.

Truth Today

If there were a headline to describe the state of truth in American life today, it might be "Truth in Trouble" or "Tough Times for Truth." Our essentially postmodern times have created and sustained this confusion over truth, so it is entirely appropriate that postmodernism—this nihilistic Hydra that is part literary criticism, part artistic and architectural style, part philosophical orientation and general sociocultural mood—has come under heavy critical attack.

We will not comprehensively cover the range of postmodernism's incoherences as an intellectual framework.[20] Suffice it to say, it is essentially only subjectivity and relativism wearing many different linguistic costumes. What is little more than "do your own thing" becomes talk of the centrality of "historical embeddedness," the necessity of recognizing our "socio-linguistic constructedness" and the unavoidability of "discourse communities." What passes for deep thought in postmodern academia is often little more than an uncritical and rampant skepticism and subjectivity toward anything traditional or not politically correct by the standards of contemporary liberalism.

Postmodernism's attachment to the absolute subjectivity of values and worldviews inflates a careful and intellectually responsible awareness of subjectivity to absolute proportions, creating a false dichotomy between either wisely incorporating the reality of human subjectivity into our thinking and believing or intellectually operating solely on (putative) subjective grounds at the expense of even the possibility of objective conclusions or bases to our thinking and believing.[21]

This apotheosis or exaltation of subjectivity to a godlike position is a mistake that inheres in postmodernist analyses by its nature. Complete and total subjectivity prevents any interpersonally authoritative conclusions whatsoever, and it insulates us from criticisms external to ourselves since there will always be recourse to the trump: "That's just your perspective." But this extreme subjectivism is obviously self-refuting, foreclosing on the possibility of employing public argumentative criteria and the very transpersonal distinctions it needs to sustain its own critique of objectivity. While postmodernists may revel at what they take as the demolition of tradition, they are not so easily able to fill the holes they think they create in the foundation for living that the traditional Judeo-

Christian worldview has provided American society. As Professor J. Budziszewski remarks,

> A postmodernist thinks *life* is fragmented. He doesn't believe his life is going anywhere, that it has a theme, that it's *about* anything, and he doesn't think yours is either. At most, he thinks, life is just a series of "projects" and relationships. . . . The biggest problem postmodernists face is meaninglessness.[22]

The unrealistic postmodernist orientation toward life proves terribly unsatisfying for the human soul. It ultimately has an isolating effect, disconnecting the person from the relationships and institutions that provide meaning and significance to life, leaving the individual as a lonely bundle of desires and preferences, adrift in a sea of choices with no way to order life's options into a morally sensible hierarchy of goods, and no way to realize any point or goal to life, because there *is* no real, overarching purpose to human existence or anyone's individual human experience as a whole.[23]

This isolating effect also prevails when it comes to truth. Under the regime of postmodernism there can be only "truth for me" or truth that I choose within my social setting, there cannot be any public or objective truths. Social practice is the final authority to all critique for the postmodernist, so such norms themselves cannot be the subject of critique. To the postmodernist, truth—as a "construction" of either my own desires or my community at either a micro or macro level—is created, not discovered; it is chosen, not revealed. So truths remain private and only binding on me, with my consent.[24] I need not assent to the truth of any moral or philosophical idea that, for whatever reason, I do not want to be true. I create my own reality, and anyone who does not cede to me the reasonableness of doing so is foisting on me a constricting, suffocating alternative.

In fact, since I as a postmodernist believe all truth is exclusively self-created, those who don't and seek to dispel my view, are, in my eyes, *imposing* on me their own private perspective. Since there can be no public truths to which they can legitimately be seeking to gain my assent, they can only be engaged in a kind of conquest of me, an attempt to move me away from my own autonomously chosen preferences and into what they, for their own reasons, want for me. In this way the solipsism or unrelenting self-focus of postmodernist ideologies forecloses on debate itself, ceasing to tolerate dissent and dialogue that, if it claims more for itself other than the purely subjective expressions of the speaker, is sinister. Inevitably this devotion to subjectivity becomes tyrannical and obscurantist. Postmodernists refuse to lift their eyes above the horizon of their own wants and preferences, including what they individually want to be true. The belief in truth as subjectivity short-circuits discussion, construing challenge as imposition. It is a dehumanizing perspective.

It is easy to see how postmodernism—and the larger secular liberalism of which it is really just an academic expression—leads to a suffocating orthodoxy and intolerance to challenge. Postmodernism is not usually the subject of such charges, and that is one of the cardinal ironies of our times. That which is thought to be broad-minded is narrowminded, that which is thought to be intellectually adventurous is uncritical and unreflective, that which is thought to be liberating is constricting, and that which is thought to permanently safeguard truth by locking it away in the heart of personal preference or social convention has confined it in the solitary and dark prison of self-obsession.

Postmodernism's derelict handling of the idea of truth has only exacerbated our culture wars by leaving us without common philosophical ground on which to dialogue about social controversies. The cultural chasms created by the denial of the possibility of objective truth are proving too expansive for adherents of different worldviews to communicate across. Furthermore, the contemporary reduction of truth to personal preference is stagnating our ethic of toleration, which, like a river, must remain active if it is to support the vitality and diversity of life it is intended to support. We will now turn our attention to how truth, rightly conceived, both requires and supports authentic tolerance.

TRUTH
AND TOLERANCE

*If there is no real truth, there is no reason for me to be tolerant. With-
out some kind of beliefs which cause me to value you as a person,
even though I disagree with you, why should I be tolerant towards
you? If you are getting in my way, why shouldn't I walk over you, if I
have the power to do so? . . . Contemporary tolerance is like a cartoon
character who has run over the edge of the cliff, and is still running
for all he's worth, without yet realising that there is nothing under-
neath him holding him up. . . . If there is no real truth, we cannot
place any limits on tolerance. If society is to be able to function, we
need some shared beliefs that will move us to value other people as
people, even when they disagree with us, but which will also enable
us to put limits on our individual freedom of choice, for the good of
society as a whole.*

DAVID COUCHMAN

Tolerance needs truth in order to be a coherent, functioning concept
in public life. But it is also the case that truth as a reflective goal for individuals and communities in contemporary life needs an operative ethic
of toleration, that is, a clear and compelling understanding of why the
pursuit and practice of truth in human relationships and public policy
needs a context of right-minded toleration to flourish in.

Before pursuing those ideas, though, we must make the preliminary
point that the reason for so much of our social dysfunction with respect
to the notion of truth and its relationship to tolerance is that the contemporary ethos—at times relativistic, always antitraditional (at least at the

level of elite or opinion-making culture)—has restricted to us the range of credible explanations for our social ordering. In other words, the trajectory of contemporary American society since at least the middle of the twentieth century has been to rule "out of bounds" the assumption that objective truth about matters moral, political and religious exists, is knowable to a substantial degree and is a legitimate pursuit. Reducing matters of ethics, politics and faith to strictly personal taste and preference disconnects in the public mind these subjects from questions of truth. It becomes inappropriate, oppressive, closed-minded and otherwise rude to speculate about the actual truth of these matters because they really are just matters of choice, after all.*

Cobbling together a personally pleasing collection of ideas from the various outlets of religious traditions, self-help gurus and other sources of popular inspiration becomes the usual and culturally "reasonable" way of navigating life.[1] What Peter Berger calls the "plausibility structures" of contemporary society, those social forces and assumptions that work to either legitimize or stigmatize beliefs and practices, incline us away from taking seriously the possibility that objective truth and reality are relevant considerations to enterprises like religious belief, moral judgments and public policy programs.[2]

Without the wide acceptance of joining our ultimate concerns with the conviction that there is a mind-independent nature to those concerns, we are left with a culturally pervasive yet intellectually degraded concept of truth and the related confusion that authentic tolerance lies in *recognizing* and *acknowledging* this misunderstanding about truth and belief. So we are left with a widespread misapprehension of both truth and tolerance. Let's then seek to remind ourselves about some foundational truths about truth, which is to say its fundamental nature, and then reflect on why toleration must be joined with this proper outlook in order for truth to operate in our lives in the manner we really know it should.

---

*This social shift is partly the result of the sociological factors associated with the rise of modernity and then postmodernity in addition to the ideological ones under consideration here. For discussion of the sociological dimension that has induced this pervasive condition of subjectivity, see Peter L. Berger, *The Heretical Imperative* (New York: Doubleday, 1979). See also Peter L. Berger, Brigitte Berger and Hansfried Kellner, *The Homeless Mind: Modernization and Consciousness* (New York: Vintage, 1974).

The Nature of Truth

We intuitively know a great deal about the logic of truth if we simply think about it. So we will now take a sort of quick inventory of some of its features.

In our daily lives we operate according to a correspondence view of truth; it is unavoidable. Furthermore, what is valid in all other theories of truth depends on correspondence. That is, to the extent that those theories of truth work or are true, it is because they describe a reality or state that exists as it is described. So, truth is the matching up or linking up of an idea to reality.

But having said that we must note that this does not mean that truth will necessarily be verifiable. An event or idea may be true apart from our knowing it to be so. Similarly, it may be false even though we claim it to be true. Further, what we believe or say about objective reality is not made true by our act of believing or saying. The "hardness" of truth is not softened by my preferences, however intense they may be. I may not want my roof to be leaking during the rainstorm, but if it is, it is, and I cannot wish or will away that fact. What I want to be the case about a given matter and what is the case bear no *necessary* relationship to each other. What I think about something or how I perceive it or how I talk about it are all independent of how it really is, the properties it actually has, whether it is God, the resurrection of Jesus of Nazareth, the moral rightness of keeping my promises under normal circumstances or the humanity of pre-born human beings. I don't change the nature and essence of reality or the properties of an entity itself by thinking about it or talking about it or believing it to be the case.[3]

Truth and belief, then, are separate, and this principle applies to ethical and religious spheres as well. Moral laws (e.g., don't murder or torture people; under normal circumstances you ought to treat other people the way you want to be treated) and religious reality (e.g., the existence of God, the divinity of Jesus of Nazareth, the actuality of postmortem consciousness) are no less real than physical laws and realities like gravity and fatigue. Physical realities cannot be denied away and neither can nonphysical realities. Any denial of the authenticity of nonphysical reality is arbitrary and completely presuppositional, with no reason to compel its acceptance other than its consonance with the spirit of our age. But what is socially or academically normative is not therefore right and true. A belief, like physicalism, may be widely held and still be wrong. The failure then to see the distinction between truth and belief is at the heart of our disordered view of truth in American culture today, and it is what allows us to treat truth as taste and genuine tolerance as subscription to this mistake.

Tolerance Too

In contemporary life, though, it is not enough to simply affirm that truth is not malleable, and that the way things really are in the world apart from me (and sometimes within me as well) are not a product of my feelings, will or consciousness. We must also reflect on how and why it is that even a realist understanding of truth must embrace—both as a matter of philosophic fact and of practical necessity—toleration. We would like to advance three reasons, one practical and two philosophical, along these lines.

First to the practical. The condition of contemporary life is what we might call a deep pluralism. We live with a multifaceted diversity and heterogeneity of cultures, beliefs, practices and commitments, and this variegation is still developing. We must note that this condition and its various manifestations are not necessarily inherently good, as the uncritical mantra of so many of our governmental and educational institutions would have us believe.[4] But as a social reality, deep pluralism is a phenomenon we must be cognizant of.

Indeed, it obligates us who assert truth claims to be aware of the many influences shaping and conditioning the perspectives of those who hold different views, and to realize that in all likelihood their views are held with an intensity of commitment equivalent to our own. Thus belief and presentation of what we assert is the truth about matters of moment must proceed with human sensitivity and common sense. Such winsomeness, apart from being prudent and politic, is also a moral duty in the contemporary context. It generates and preserves toleration toward others' views and a humanizing ethic of dialogue that takes stock of both the social and cultural factors that have shaped those views and the personality of their holders, as well as of the potential for those people to develop and change personally and ideologically. To seek to communicate important truth to someone is not an intellectual exercise or a debating game, it can change lives and human relationships, and an enterprise with such serious consequences must be practiced with a spirit of patient respect for other people and their social context.

Philosophically, too, we can point to a pair of reasons underlining the unity of the pursuit of truth with toleration. First, the contingent nature of the world around us means that our conclusions about the most important questions of life, (e.g., what is its purpose) may never rise to a level of apodictic or 100 percent certainty. That is, even my most strongly held commitments never rise past strong probability in terms of their *philosophical* warrant or justification. This is not to affirm an arid rationalism or to say that beyond the gateway of faith the believer cannot experience what is understood to be a profound existential confirmation or ineffable personal validation of his or her convictions. Rather, it recognizes that the cognitive pathway to faith traversed by finite people in a complicated world may seem imperfect and difficult to them.[5]

This is by no means a problem for religious dedication, because probability is really the basis of most of our actions and commitments.[6] I go at a green light believing it is probably safe; I fly in a plane believing it is probably safe; I am a theist because it is more probable than not that God exists; I begin to believe in the bodily resurrection of Jesus of Nazareth because that seems more probably true than not.[7] Because rational probability is the general character of our decisions and beliefs (even our most important ones), the reality of potential error as well as the imperfect manner that people process and evaluate Christian truth claims—hindered perhaps by their cultural setting, family heritage, intellectual ability, personal knowledge of hypocrisy in the lives of professing Christians they know, past personal tragedy or trauma, and so forth—call on us to manifest a patient forbearance toward those who for reasons of whatever type resist the gospel message.

Indeed the intellectually honest and authentic pursuit and advocacy of truth in the world today would seem to suggest a willingness on our own part to subject our own convictions to counteradvocacy and critical examination. To wish others to dialogue with you so that you can share your faith in Christ with them obliges you to be the recipient of "non-Christian evangelism," so to speak. This belief that truth can be transmitted through dialogue, discussion and debate directly implies and goes a long way toward creating a context of tolerance for worldview discussions.

A second philosophical reason why the affirmation of truth must be married to a carefully tolerant disposition must be considered.

There can be no question that the communication of the gospel as permanent truth, irrespective of cultural norms or conditions, is at the heart of the Christian faith. Jesus affirms this emphatically in Matthew 28:18-20, saying:

> All authority in heaven and on earth has been given to me. Therefore go and make disciples of all nations, baptizing them in the name of the Father and of the Son and of the Holy Spirit, and teaching them to obey everything I have commanded you. And surely I am with you always, to the very end of the age.[8]

Indeed, the fact that the great commission to evangelism is the final statement Jesus made to his disciples on earth speaks to its essentiality and the importance Jesus attaches to this duty and privilege.

But this charge of Jesus presupposes the intellectual autonomy of the hearers. Jesus declares that "all authority in heaven and earth" belongs to him, but then he immediately sends his disciples out to preach his message. He does not assure them that he will compel the belief of their hearers, nor does he suggest they will even gain a favorable response from their audiences. It is understood that the response to the disciples' message is outside of their control and that Jesus himself will not in any overt, public or impersonal way force or compel people to embrace the gospel. Of course, elsewhere we learn that God is active in history and that the Holy Spirit is active in the minds and hearts of unbelievers as they encounter Christian truth, but always the mind and personality of the human individual encountering the Christian message is uncoerced.

This tells us something very important about human nature, which Jesus obviously knew: *people are existentially touched only by a received truth they do not have to affirm.* That is, truth genuinely holds us only when we come to it ourselves in an unforced, personally desirous manner.

Keeping that in mind we must remind ourselves that the logic of the Great Commission and Christian soteriology itself asserts that the truth of the gospel is personally transformative, subsequent to "whosoever will" receive it.[9] While this transformative power is unique to the truth of Jesus Christ himself, there is also an existentially jolting character to truth about any significant matter. In other words important and humanly significant truths—for example, about the objectivity of morality or human dignity as opposed to whether today is one of the two Fridays a month on which the street-sweeper truck passes in front of my house—should affect us. Truth has a compelling character to it, and it ought to existentially impinge on us. We have a human duty to ensure, to the best of our ability, that it does. If I know a proposition of gravity and moment is true and yet willfully ignore it, I am guilty of a human and moral failure, an inauthenticity and failure of my humanity. Truth should change us and decisively order our interaction with the world around us.

This fact, joined with the insight about human nature just noted above—that people are moved and touched by truth the way truth is intended to move and touch them only when they individually assent uncoerced to that truth—shows us that truth needs a context of tolerance to do its work, to be itself, to function in people's lives the way truth by its own character is intended to function. This applies to Christian proclamation and also to the articulation of personal, social and moral truths of all kinds. Truth needs tolerance just as a fish needs water.

Thus the declaration of truth entails or brings with it an ethic of tolerance. Every Christian should remember this and bear in mind that obviously God, as the author of human nature and the character of truth, wills us to preach Christ only in the context of tolerance. A truth claim must be situated within the intellectual setting of tolerance just as a diamond ring features its precious stone within a beautiful surrounding, such as a gold setting. Their interrelationship is natural and complementary.

Emerging then is this paradox, frightening to the secular mind: Christianity, with its commitment to timeless and objective truths, provides a solid foundation for tolerance, not the secular liberalism that has in our time so arrogantly laid claim to the mantle of broad-mindedness, all the while elbowing the Judeo-Christian tradition out of the American public square like a pathetic, aging beauty queen intent on hogging the stage for one more preening swagger down the runway.

Englishman Ian Markham, in his important book *Plurality and Christian Ethics*, argues similarly.[10] He says it is Christian theism, providing, as it does, for the intelligibility of the universe and meaningfulness to human experience (and thereby the sensibility of truth claims), which supports the enterprise of toleration amidst our deep pluralism.

Having jettisoned the legitimacy of any traditional, transcultural assertions of public truth—and therefore the enterprise of morally grounded debate that alone can provide a general, transcultural and transpersonal canopy of meaning, stability, and applicability to public arguments—secular reason is no longer able to render any convincing and fair public rationale for its conclusions, including the tolerance imperative. All of its prescriptions, including the call to tolerance, according to its own logic, never rise above personal preference, socially constructed community or culture-specific norms. So it has no consistent and persuasive bases to protect against those very violations of moral common sense that it rightly denounces, such as fascism, racism, and human rights abuses all over the globe.

Without a bedrock commitment to the concept of foundational truth in general and a commitment to overarching truth about some specific matter (e.g., the moral imperative of equal treatment under the law irrespective of skin color), the secular liberal cannot appeal consistently to any grounds to persuade others of the wrong of transgressions like racism or intolerance, or the right to resist such wrongs.*

But rather than explicitly admit the nonrelativity of truth and the noncontingent nature of some moral principles, the secular liberal wants to have cake and eat it too. These liberals want to continue to denounce the moral traditionalism of the Judeo-Christian heritage on putative relativist grounds (because they dislike its moral traditionalism, particularly on sexual matters), but they still assert the wrongness of racism, the state establishment of religious belief or other violations of individual autonomy. Secular liberalism wants to be skeptical and relativist toward traditional morality but still affirm the unconditional truth of its preferred moral judgments—for example, the moral legitimacy of same-sex marriage or abortion on demand—and thus advance its *particular* ideological agenda and worldview. This is inconsistent and hypocritical.

This incoherence of secular liberalism is especially exposed on the is-

---

*See the discussion "What Is American Secular Liberalism?" in chapter seven for a general definition of secular liberalism as a political ideology.

sue of tolerance because secularists must abandon their relativist pretext—so useful when confronting traditional moral claims—and at least tacitly assert to listeners their *obligation* to exercise the objective value of tolerance when the secularists wish to vigorously defend unconventional moral truth claims they find attractive. But the official relativism of secular liberalism can offer no firm reason why people *ought* to be tolerant and give new ideas a hearing when they may not want to. Tolerance, loosed from the mooring of objective truth and duty, can only float away into the vast sea of individual preference. I may want you to be tolerant of me, but I cannot give you any binding reasons why you should be if all moral duties are optional and mind-independent truth—anchored in the unchanging, unalterable being of God, the ultimate foundation of human life and relationships, and the grounding of their significance—does not exist.

It is the Judeo-Christian moral tradition of Western culture—with its moral realism and commitment to transcultural and transpersonal truth—that decisively has the conceptual resources to mandate tolerance and consistently denounce immoral practices.

The Christian and Truth

Having reflected on the joined character of truth and tolerance, we want to reaffirm the centrality of truth to the Christian. Repeatedly, Jesus and his disciples declare that truth is at the core of the Christian message. God wants everyone to come to the knowledge of the truth (1 Tim 2:4); Jesus is the truth (Jn 14:6); Jesus was born for the purpose of bearing witness to the truth (Jn 18:37); the word of God is truth (Jn 17:17); truth came through Jesus Christ (Jn 1:17); authentic disciples who know the truth are liberated (Jn 8:32). And statements about the truth continue on and on, showing unequivocally the imperative that Christians understand the objective, illuminating and life-giving nature of truth.[11] It is undeniably impossible for a Christian to be a relativist with respect to the truth, either philosophically or existentially. The truth is there, uncreated by human consciousness, and disciples of the One who came to proclaim the truth in all its dimensions are to be transformed by it.

This absolute character to truth must be continually in the forefront of the believer's mind because it is so contrary to the spirit of our age. The

Christian conception of truth swims upstream in the contemporary world, which is enthralled by an array of movements and ideas that have distorted understandings of truth. The Christian's consciousness is one of opposition and resistance, of an alien voyaging through a foreign land. Of course, this does not mean Christians should be hostile, pugnacious or petulant but rather they should never expect a warm welcome in the salons of secularism when bringing the message of human lostness apart from the person and work of Christ.

Of course, Christians have by no means handled the truth well in recent decades. Assorted trends in Christian theology have enthusiastically rushed over the precipice of relativism in pursuit of their own single issue.* Further, it must be noted that Christians have not always understood one of the most important consequences of the centrality of truth in Christian consciousness: the imperative of self-criticism. When we enter into the full realism of truth, we also enter into the crucible of self-criticism, where the call to self-examination and introspection regarding our motives and purposes for thinking and doing is always heard. David said:

> Search me, O God, and know my heart;
>   test me and know my anxious thoughts.
> See if there is any offensive way in me,
>   and lead me in the way everlasting. (Ps 139:23-24)

We always are to subject our own worldview and its components, including the psychological and emotional ones, to reflective analysis and contemplative scrutiny, informed first by Scripture and also by the Holy Spirit and the historical deposit of Christian wisdom.

This continuing existential self-analysis underlines for us the reality

---

*Such issues range from the nineteenth-century criticism of the Scripture to the old liberalism of the early twentieth century, to the situation ethics and death of God movements of the 1960s, to the liberation, black and feminist theologies of the same period, to the dying mainline churches of the religious left today, which some scholars bluntly portray as essentially faithful adjuncts of the Democrat party in terms of their social values and political affections. See Stanley Hauerwas and William Willimon, *Resident Aliens: Life in the Christian Colony* (Nashville: Abingdon, 1989), p. 38, cited in Thomas Reeves, *The Empty Church: The Suicide of Liberal Christianity* (New York: Free Press, 1996). See Reeves's valuable work for a survey of the decline of Protestant mainline churches in the United States. See also the older study by John Warwick Montgomery, *The Suicide of Christian Theology* (Minneapolis: Bethany House, 1970).

that truth is only meaningful when it is freely embraced. Love is not authentic if given in response to a demand; personal moral virtue is not real if imposed externally on an individual; and faith is not genuine if coerced by threat or force. In the same way, truth is not truly known apart from free assent to it. The Christian as an ambassador of the truth must handle truth of all sorts, ever aware that it is intended to touch and transform, and that it can only do so in the presence of cognitive freedom and the commitment to preserve that freedom—no matter how intense the sound and fury of the surrounding cultural war may be.

7

AMERICAN
SECULARISM

*Every year the church in the United States draws closer and closer to
the situation faced by the New Testament church: an embattled minority living in a pluralistic, pagan society.*

PHILIP YANCEY

*Liberal Tolerance is a sham. Although portrayed by its advocates as an
open, tolerant, and neutral perspective, it is a dogma whose proponents tolerate no rivals. Those of us who are concerned with presenting
and defending our faith in a post-Christian culture must be aware of
this sort of challenge, one that masquerades as open, tolerant, and liberating, but in reality is dogmatic, partisan, and coercive.*

FRANCIS J. BECKWITH

Likening American cultural conflict to a war has become common
today, and it is an accurate if lamentable description, given the vitriol
of much public debate. Indeed, James Davison Hunter argued in his
landmark book, *Culture Wars* (1991), that America during the last part
of the twentieth century had moved into a new and uniquely deep cultural division.[1]

In this arena of civic conflict there are a number of different constituencies identified by various labels, but it seems every scheme of
classification is imperfect and partial. Whether it be left-right, liberal-
libertarian-conservative, populist-elitist or some other systematization,
inevitably some ideological party will feel inadequately described.[2]
For the purposes of our discussion, though recognizing this complexity,

we will straightforwardly reckon the two poles of the culture war to be secular liberalism on the one end, and evangelical Christianity on the other end. Though using other explanatory categories has some validity, our consideration of the present cultural contention over the meaning of tolerance is best served by these two general categories, as they in fact starkly portray the primary themes of our social struggle to understand tolerance, an idea so integral to a viable cultural pluralism. Let us now then examine one of these outlooks, secular liberalism.

What Is American Secular Liberalism?

In his comprehensive critique of contemporary American secular liberalism, *Slouching Towards Gomorrah,* Robert H. Bork presents its two philosophical foundations: radical egalitarianism and radical individualism.[3] The former is a commitment to equality of outcomes rather than simple equality of opportunity; the latter insists on eliminating virtually all social and legal curbs on personal gratification. Egalitarianism, enforced by the state and its bureaucratic apparatus, and hyperindividualism, enforced by both antibourgeois activist courts and the culturally ambient hedonism that characterizes American life today, combine to propel American culture down the paradoxical path of intellectual conformity and personal debauchery.[4]

Contemporary liberalism, spawned from the intercourse of American leftism with classical liberalism, which took place in the context of the new affluence, moral adventurism and cultural restlessness of the 1960s, has come to carry little resemblance to the rational tradition whose name it bears.

Bork sees contemporary liberalism as the creation of a complex confluence of factors. He holds that classical liberalism, with its heavy accent on liberty and equality as values, has always carried within itself the seeds of its own devolution into its modern perversion. But for most of this country's history there were bulwarks against this degeneration, specifically a vigorous, traditional Christian religious practice; the dominance of the Judeo-Christian moral tradition; a body of law closely hewn to the constitutional principles of the founders and the simple reality of hard work as a prerequisite for economic survival.[5] Throughout the convulsions of the twentieth century (WWI, the Great Depression, WWII), these realities prevailed. But with the onset of remarkable affluence and the concomitant boredom of the 1950s, along with the technologizing of life and the overweening valuing of personal convenience it brings, Americans grew impatient with the religious, moral and legal traditions that circumscribed their lives and their now energized pursuit of self-gratification.[6] This tide, joined with the swelling influence of intellectuals and literati, collided with the socialistic student radicals and national up-heavals of the 1960s (John F. Kennedy's assassination, the Vietnam War, Martin Luther King Jr.'s and Robert Kennedy's assassinations), settling in the antibourgeois, nihilistic, hedonistic and collectivist configuration recognized today as contemporary liberalism.

The liberalism of today is a decisive rejection of the true liberal tradition and the American mores that tradition has been so central in forging. A profile of the new liberalism, secular liberalism, as practiced in this country at the end of the twentieth century is not flattering. It would include the assertions that this viewpoint is (1) addicted to the politics of victimization; (2) averse to the nuclear family; (3) reluctant to genuinely condemn out-of-wedlock births; (4) supportive of racial quotas and race-based policies in government and public education; (5) supportive of group identification and doctrinaire multiculturalism; (6) disinclined to advocate personal moral accountability, instead blaming criminal behavior on economic conditions like poverty; (6) obsessed with the categories of race, class and gender; (7) supportive of misandrist gender feminism and quotas for women; (8) profoundly disrespectful of prenatal human life; (9) indifferent at best toward traditional religion and opposed to open, public expressions of religious conviction, especially by those of the conservative Christian and Jewish faiths; (10) supportive of judicial activism and using the courts as agents of cultural change; and (11) intolerant toward those who oppose its positions, routinely replacing debate with ad hominem attacks such as "racist," "sexist," "misogynist," "homophobe," "mean-spirited" and so forth.[7]

This lamentable political condition is at the heart of American secularism. The conformity of political correctness, along with a hostility to conservative Christian faith (recall the famous incident a few years ago when a *Washington Post* reporter in print described evangelical Christians as "largely poor, uneducated and easy to command"), is de rigueur for those who desire the patina of cultural sophisticate that only the elites of secular liberalism can confer.

Relativist? Yes and No

In discussing the dysfunctions of contemporary American society fueled by secular liberalism, it is customary to characterize it as relativistic and driven by the wild, chaotic winds of moral subjectivism. But the fact of the matter is that this diagnosis only tells half of the story. In order to rightly understand American secularism and our contemporary confusion over tolerance, it is important to turn over the rotten apple of modern liberalism's moral relativism to see what is on the other side. This will give us a full and more accurate understanding of our cultural conflict today.

Relativism is bankrupt as a moral philosophy, and no one is actually a real relativist, including the contemporary secular liberal. Secularists today make a whole host of moral judgments, and they do so unhesitatingly. Racism is wrong; failing to observe the separation of church and state (as they misconstrue this idea) is wrong; forbidding by law gay marriage is wrong; outlawing or seriously restricting abortion practice is wrong; affirmative action is morally right; people should be tolerant; and on and on.

The relativism of the secular liberalism that is so prominent today and that has drawn so many well-deserved criticisms is only relativist when it is resisting traditional Judeo-Christian morality. This is an extremely important point that must not be missed. The values and convictions that compose the substance of secular liberalism are defended fiercely by their supporters, but when presented with the moral judgments of traditional morality, they resort to an inconsistent "Who's to say?" relativism and "That's just your view" moral subjectivism.

For example, secularists who oppose restricting marriage to two people of the opposite sex assert that this traditional insistence is merely a matter of arbitrary taste and convention. Secularists who disagree with regarding homosexual practices as unhealthy and morally wrong reduce the view to a matter of personal preference. Opposing abortion on demand is seen by them as an unreasonable foisting of personal dispositions and desires on all of society. Thus traditional morality is dismissed by secularists on grounds of moral relativism (either through appeal to cultural diversity or individual preference), yet those values and moral judgments favored by secular liberals (e.g., same-sex marriage, abortion on demand, the banning of Christmas crèches in front of city hall) are defended as objectively right, just and constitutionally appropriate in themselves. Secularists do not argue simply on the basis of personal preference or even social convention but insist they are right for everyone, on principle.

This intellectual inconsistency and hypocrisy is at the core of what Francis Canavan calls the "pluralist game."[8] It is a kind of "bait and switch" cultural scam in which relativism and ethical "neutrality" in our pluralistic setting are held out as the grounds on which to disapprove and reject moral traditionalism, but suddenly the new morality of secular liberalism is embraced and advocated on nonrelativist grounds. The covert moral particularity of secular liberalism—dressed in the cloak of the neutrality and misunderstood tolerance that are thought to be required by our pluralism—is smuggled in to our law and social consciousness. But the result is anything but tolerant—a tyranny of the minority effectively stigmatizes as "homophobic" or "antichoice" those communities of belief with strong, transcendent moral traditions. The true "pluralist game"—our political attempt to reconcile the social disagreements arising out of pluralism—has thus become a shell game in which respect for pluralism and diversity becomes an unrelenting engine for secular transformation.[9]

In this way secular liberalism, unwilling to subject itself to its own critique, has created a group of "new absolutes" regarding the norms of family life, sexuality, the place of religion in society, male-female relations and tolerance.[10]

This strategy has been profoundly successful for secular liberalism, and it both affirms and draws its massive popular appeal from the relativist spirit of our time. The zeitgeist, or spirit of our age, is deeply inflected with a relativist tone. In a society so saturated with an unending smorgasbord of images, ideas, cultures and options nested within a powerful capitalism and drive toward materialism, "I'm OK, you're OK" and "Do your own thing" become alluring themes around which to organize our lives.[11] There is great pressure in contemporary American life—a kind of mass peer pressure—to be relativistic toward the values of moral traditionalism not affirmed by the mass culture, and this greatly abets the bait-and-switch approach of secular liberalism.

This selective use of relativism in the culture wars today is enabled by essentially two unfortunate habits of the American mind. First, we have failed to make a consistent and clear distinction between relativism and pluralism. Relativism philosophically commits us to epistemological and moral subjectivity. What is true and right is what each individual regards as true and right for him- or herself at the moment, since such things cannot be known objectively. Relativism is prescriptive and states how things must or ought to be. Pluralism, by contrast, simply describes a phenomenon, a social condition brought on by the growing heterogeneity of the population, continued mass immigration, the media and information revolutions, and a whole host of other features of contemporary American experience. Pluralism, strictly speaking, is only a sociological fact; it implies nothing about the respective merits of the different values and habits and cultural practices that comprise pluralism. Relativism, on the other hand, exalts pluralism to a moral ideal by asserting that "we ought to have a pluralistic society." It opportunistically attaches a normative, value-laden boost to pluralism that is a confused use of the term *pluralism,* but this move proves a useful strategy of subverting moral tradition. Relativism has become the unwarranted standard inference drawn from the phenomenon of pluralism today. Just because there is a diversity of views, it does not follow that none of them are uniquely right. Simply because there is a dispute about what is true, it does not follow that there is no truth or that it cannot be known.

A second feature of American intellectual life that has empowered the concept of relativism is what we might call "value formalism." This is an extremely subtle yet powerful and corrupting practice of American public life. It is essentially the reduction of political debate to sloganeering.

Consider words like *diversity, change, choice* and *tolerance.* They all are very popular, even ubiquitous, today. And who would dare say they are against these concepts? Certainly no one, for they have attained the cultural status of an unquestionable good. But what do these words actually mean? Their connotative definition, that is, what they mean in the public square, is generally abstract and vague. Few people you might meet on the street would be able to render a specific, coherent definition of each of these terms.

Their complexity has proved very useful to the social engineers of secular liberalism though. These terms are themselves value neutral, which is to say neither good nor bad. The morality of each depends on the social and personal context it is applied to. Is *diversity* inherently a good thing? Not if all the options or alternatives being added to a choice or practice are bad and harmful. Adding a half dozen children of bad character to a classroom full of children of good character would certainly bring diversity to the class, but not in a good way. What about *change?* It depends on the moral direction of the change. Introducing vague, impractical and unnecessary changes to a good and efficient law would not be good. Changing from a gentle person into an angry person would not be good either. The goodness and desirability of a change depends on the nature and direction of the change. Change is not good in and of itself. So too with *choice*. Choice itself is not a moral value; it is only a mental act, like adding two and two. Making a decision, a choice, is not automatically good in itself. It depends on whether what has been chosen is good. To choose to become a Nazi or a compassionate, competent dentist are both choices, but they are not equally good choices. *Tolerance* also is not intrinsically good. It is only good if I am tolerating what ought to be tolerated and in the right manner. If I am at the beach and I witness a large truck dump a thousand gallons of motor oil into the surf, and I tolerate it by not informing the police, a lifeguard or any government official, I have not acted morally well, and no one would say otherwise.

Values like diversity, change, choice and tolerance (and others such as "self-expression" and "self-esteem") can never be morally good apart from their context and the ends they are applied to. *In conceptual or ethical isolation* they are only shells or empty forms, like baking molds, that can be good if used for good ends or bad if used for harmful ends. If I use a gingerbread-man-shaped cookie mold to make delicious gingerbread cookies, I've used the device well; if I use it to beat my dog, I have not.

The formal nature of these values has made them ideal tools of social transformation for secularists because they can be filled with the particular ideological substance of secular liberalism, yet they retain their social status as ideologically neutral and obviously desirable social goods. They have become sociocultural Trojan horses, welcomed and embraced by individuals and institutions who feel great pressure not to resist them (and invite charges of bigotry, parochialism, misogyny or intolerance), only to find, sometimes approvingly sometimes disapprovingly, that they have been filled with the ideological components of secular liberalism. Secular liberals enlist the considerable social capital of these pleasant-sounding words and phrases (e.g., "change is good," "pro-choice") to institutionalize their politics.

The sneaking-in of particular norms under the culturally indisputable auspices of pseudovalues such as "choice" and "change" is particularly insidious when it comes to tolerance. For once values of secular liberalism, such as abortion on demand, are culturally ensconced (i.e., they have become the status quo), it is easy through language to present them as "neutral" and "value free," and thus any attempt to change them becomes a cynical case of the dissenter being "intolerant," trying to "legislate morality" or to "impose her values" on what is taken to be the blissfully neutral, politically open public square. This is a political strategy of the secular left, and it is very effective even though it completely sidesteps the moral issues at stake (e.g., is it morally good to choose to kill a pre-born human being) by hiding them behind socially impeccable but abstract and vague concepts (like "choice").

Secular liberalism has perverted tolerance for the sake of advancing its own agenda. Seeing the political utility of playing the tolerance card (i.e., charging those who expose the politically and morally partisan content of culturally dominant pseudovalues like "choice" with intolerance and closed-mindedness), it has created a socially dominant but confused understanding of tolerance as agreement with the prevailing liberal social ethos, and in the process it short-circuits real debate and political dialogue. Secular liberals have changed the cultural definition of tolerance into "acceptance" and "respect," as though dissenting from their ideology is rude and mean-spirited. Tolerance has evolved from *abiding the objectionable* to *affirming the rightness* of the diverse and nontraditional.

This is how liberalism has become intolerant. It intimidates its critics into silence and casts the weight of cultural suspicion at them by first ignoring its own moral particularity, then infusing culturally approved values with that particularity, and then posturing these values as neutral and their critics as moral imperialists seeking to impose and foist *their own* partisan ideology on society. It is a pretty clever trick, but it stifles real debate. The obvious fact that every group and ideology—left to right—is seeking to advocate and codify the values it believes best for society is ignored, and politics devolves into little more than a power play. The search for the good and vital public argument are buried under clever slogans and deceptive rhetoric. It seems that secular liberals, who misuse tolerance in this way and thereby become truly intolerant themselves, do not genuinely value diversity, nor do they truly believe that their own ideas would win out in a culturally open and informed debate. Thus they do not argue fairly against moral traditionalism and the classical Judeo-Christian worldview, but they suppress that perspective from gaining a serious cultural hearing in the first place, ruling it beyond the pale of reasonable consideration through labeling it "intolerant" or "narrow minded."[12]

The Elites

This mechanism of secular liberalism—in conjunction with its army of foundation-funded, public-interest-group litigators ever in search of test cases to unravel any vestige of traditional American life—which has transformed our society is not widely supported by the general American public, even those who vote for the politicians who skillfully play the pluralist game. Secular liberalism's cultural battles are planned and executed by secular liberal elites. These are the opinion-makers and knowledge-class employees at universities and major print and electronic news organizations, and those with high profile positions in entertainment and government. These intellectuals, writers, commentators and public figures function as the arbiters of what ideas, images and social assumptions are "respectable," "sophisticated" and "serious."[13] This is not the mirror image of a "vast right-wing conspiracy," but it is the sociological reality that explains how the pathological public policies of political correctness we have documented could proceed to fully colonize American educational, journalistic and other public institutions.

In sociologist Peter Berger's famous phrase, America is a nation of Indians governed by Swedes. That is, if India is the most religious country in the world, and Sweden the most secular, we find in the United States that the forces of secularization work to propel its supporters to the social and political top. These elites wield and protect control of social institutions, creating an insular world that sees secularism and contemporary liberalism as the only credible worldview. As the late cultural critic Christopher Lasch remarked:

> Our public life is thoroughly secularized. The separation of church and state, nowadays interpreted as prohibiting any public recognition of religion at all, is more deeply entrenched in America than anywhere else. Among elites [religious belief] is held in low esteem. . . . A skeptic, iconoclastic state of mind is one of the distinguishing characteristics of the knowledge classes. Their commitment to the culture of criticism is understood to rule out religious commitments. The elites' attitude to religion ranges from indifference to active hostility.[14]

Thus, as Richard John Neuhaus argued in *The Naked Public Square,* Christian concern is steadily marginalized and degraded as a respectable worldview.

Worldview Themes of Secular Liberalism

The controlling worldview of secular liberalism is first and foremost hostile to expressions of traditional morality and piety. Despite the direct challenge such expressions represent to the secular creed, the ultimate source of this aversion to traditional Christianity is found in the commitment of the secular mind to its own self-styled trinity of meaning: *individualism, autonomy* and *rights.* These ideas, though misapplied in liberalism today, are arguably the foundation of its worldview.

Individualism, in the secular-liberal intellectual milieu, is detached from its traditional emphasis on self-responsibility and a sober pursuit of the *telos,* or end, of human nature. Instead it features the human being as little more than a bundle of desires and preferences shorn of natural, unchosen ties to family and community. Here a truncated and unfulfilling understanding of freedom as "doing my own thing" prevails, and the person is unconstrained by tradition, convention or any defect of human nature.[15]

Autonomy, similarly, is understood in a starkly isolated way. To be self-ruling is to be unhindered by tradition or custom, especially religious in character, and to be free to strike out into the world unburdened by a person's familial, cultural or religious past. Far from regarding tradition as the embodiment of the wisdom of human experience, or believing that an individual might learn from well-lived lives of the past, the peculiar version of autonomy informing the secularist's worldview is of necessity limited to one's own wits and self-derived insights.

This approach, which the secularist regards as courageous, may just as well be seen as arrogant or naive. The exercise of true autonomy calls for the recognition that my own good is inseparable from the good of others and the community, that there is a continuity to human action, and that no one person can conduct his or her life in isolation from the lives of others. The denial of these conditions for realizing true autonomy gives us a glimpse of the misanthropy inherent in the secularist's conception of human freedom and behavior. Such "courage" turns out to embody a disregard for the well-being of self and others.[16]

The conception of rights within the worldview of secular liberalism has done much to distort American society, primarily by unhinging rights from their natural complement: responsibility. As Professor Mary Ann Glendon writes:

> An intemperate rhetoric of personal liberty . . . corrodes the social foundations on which individual freedom and security ultimately rest. . . . Our rights talk, in its absoluteness, promotes unrealistic expectations, heightens social conflict, and inhibits dialogue that might lead toward consensus, accommodation, or at least the discovery of common ground. In its silence concerning responsibilities, it seems to condone acceptance of the benefits of living in a democratic social welfare state, without accepting the corresponding personal and civic obligations.[17]

For the liberal secularist though, the obsession with rights and their exercise serve the important purpose of not only liberating the individual from responsibility as a personal ethos but also obviating any consideration of the genesis of responsibilities to others and the source of their human rights that oblige the individual to them. As we remain busy with our "rights," we are all the more able to suppress from our minds the Source of those rights and what that might imply about our lives and how we interact with others, including those with whom we disagree. A one-sided emphasis on individual rights obscures the obvious question: Who has the responsibility, the duty, to observe and respect others' rights?

Secularism is a worldview every bit as much as Christianity or Buddhism, though it is comparatively unsystematic, unreflective and untested by time. Those who are committed to it see all of life through its lens, and, as with any devotee to a creed, are personally invested in its vindication. Thus, puncturing the self-enclosed seal of this worldview is difficult.

Christianity as a worldview is certainly unique in explicitly stating the circumstances under which its adherents should renounce it.*Expect no such articulations from the secularist, whose faith amounts to nothing more than self-devotion and the pursuit of whatever one wants to pursue at the moment. This wholesale self-devotion ensures the continued appeal of secularism as a worldview, and in fact those Americans identifying themselves as secular has doubled since 1990, up to nearly 16 percent.[18] Not surprisingly, then, since 1991 the number of adults in the United States who do not attend church has also nearly doubled, up to 75 million people, according to a Barna Group survey.[19] Though secularism is proliferating, it will retain its inevitably unfulfilling character—as Augustine observed centuries ago in a heartfelt prayer in his *Confessions,* "Without Thee, what am I but a guide to my own destruction?"[20]

---

*See Paul's discussion in 1 Cor 15:14-17: "If Christ has not been raised, our preaching is useless and so is your [Christian] faith" (v. 14).

8

EVANGELICAL
CHRISTIANITY

*It is the only serious sin left. Even murder has its mitigating factors,
but not this one. It is the pariah sin, the charge that makes you un-
touchable without need for further explanation. The sin is intolerance
and the greatest sinners in twenty-first century America are evangelical and fundamentalist Christians. America is sick of intolerant people and it's not going to tolerate them anymore.*

DANIEL TAYLOR

How then should we understand the rival worldview to American
secular liberalism, the other major perspective in the contemporary cultural conflict? Though using the label "evangelical Christianity" to desig-
nate moral and social Christian conservatives broadly, we realize it is imperfect. It will of course not convey the fact that a few moral and social
conservatives are indeed secular, and a minority of evangelicals are politically on the left. And as a term evangelical Christianity does not include other Christians and Jewish or other religiously minded people
who participate in the attempt to preserve the moral heritage of the
Judeo-Christian tradition.

We want to consider evangelical Christianity because there is in fact
an especially sharp and intense conflict between evangelicalism on
the one hand and secular liberalism on the other, not least because of
the evangelical mandate of a biblically grounded faith and ethic. Indeed, perhaps the most important intellectual nexus of the American
culture wars is between conservative Christianity and the practical
meaning of tolerance upheld by the secular liberal elites. Evangelical

Christianity offers a robust, articulate and systematically coherent worldview, and so it can represent well the objections to secular liberalism.

We will discuss that shortly, but suffice to say at this point that the appellation evangelical Christianity is offered not in a triumphalist sense but rather in the "mere Christian" sense of C. S. Lewis's humble apologetic of that title.[1] Although we will be describing the worldview of evangelical Christianity and showing its consonance with true tolerance, much of what we say will also be applicable to those Christians standing in the tradition of historic Christian orthodoxy, believing the substance of the three primary historic creeds of Christianity, the Apostles', Nicene and Athanasian creeds and affirming the actual truthfulness of the Christian metaphysic: the triune, personal, infinite Creator has offered redemption to humanity through the atoning sacrifice of Jesus of Nazareth, God the Son incarnate; and the Holy Spirit is at work in individuals, communities and history to bring people to that saving knowledge; and postmortem all persons will be judged by God.

What Is Evangelicalism?

Defining evangelical Christianity in precise sociological or theological terms is a difficult task.[2] But certainly some essential themes that yield a reliable gestaltic or general-sense definition are identifiable. We suggest five primary poles of evangelical consciousness that provide a framework for the perspective.[3]

1. a deliberate focus on the person of Jesus Christ and his death on the cross

2. the holding of Scripture as the primary authority for spirituality, doctrine and morality

3. an emphasis on deliberate, purposeful conversion (the "new birth") as a life-changing, spiritually and ultimately morally transformational experience

4. the imperative of witnessing or sharing the faith, especially through explicit evangelism

5. a serious concern about the culture's steady movement toward secu-

larism and relativism, and a conviction that we are living in times of social crisis.*

Sociologist and researcher George Barna has offered his own somewhat more restrictive definition of *evangelical*. Besides having confessed their sins to God and made a commitment to Jesus Christ as Savior and believing on that basis that they will go to heaven when they die, he describes evangelicals as those who believe the Bible is

> totally accurate in all that it teaches; that their faith is very important in their life today; believing they have a personal responsibility to share their religious beliefs about Christ with non-Christians; believing that Satan exists; believing that eternal salvation is possible only through grace, not works; believing that Jesus Christ lived a sinless life on earth; and describing God as the all-knowing, all-powerful, perfect deity who created the universe and still rules it today.[4]

Those who meet these criteria in their religious lives, Barna says, are about 5 percent of the U.S. population, or approximately 15 to 20 million Americans. Barna pegs the share of the population that are "born again" Christians, which includes a wider range of Christians from among all denominations and traditions, as approximately 40 percent of the U.S. population. This larger figure is more consonant with a recent Gallup poll, which found that 46 percent of Americans described themselves as evangelical or born-again Christians, as well as a PBS/*U.S. News and World Report* poll, which asserted 32 percent of Americans are evangelical Christians.[5]

Whatever then the precise numbers of evangelicals, evangelicalism is a worldview shared by a very substantial portion of the nation. The general evangelical mindset manifests marked differences from the three ideas foundational to the worldview of American secularism, individualism, autonomy and rights. Individualism within this religious worldview

---

*This well-founded concern is what has spurred evangelical involvement in American politics over the last forty years or so. But conservative Christians have been hampered in their efforts to powerfully shape public policy and cultural assumptions by their inability to offer "public arguments," that is, arguments for positions consistent with biblical faith that draw on extrabiblical sources, like history, human experience and natural law principles. For discussion of the imperative of transcending the "biblical politics" that has characterized evangelical thought and action in the public square, see David L. Weeks, "The Uneasy Politics of Modern Evangelicalism," *Christian Scholar's Review* 30, no. 4 (summer 2001): 403-18.

is a call to self-reliance and to antistatism, that is, an antipathy to activist government. It invigorates an effort to embody as an individual human person a Christlike character of self-giving to God, family and community.[6] Autonomy in this moral spiritual frame does not align with secularism's flight from the authority of tradition (and revelation) but rather establishes a self-governance within the framework of Christian teaching, commitment and community. The Christian ethic is formed by the surrender of the individual's life to God alone in order to find it, a purposeful submission of every aspect of the self under God. Thus autonomy is not an end in itself but rather a means toward glorifying God. Similarly, rights are not conceived as weapons against the norms of tradition or history. Neither are they simply a means toward self-actualization. Rather, rights, both civil and natural, are laden with the responsibility for their sound stewardship exhibited in their morally informed careful exercise. Their use shapes a person's character and inexorably carries him or her—and quite possibly family and friends—closer toward or away from God. In the Christian frame rights and responsibilities are essentially inseparable, two sides of the same coin, and must receive similar emphasis for the individual and community to be formed by right reason and virtue.

The evangelical Christian worldview, and really the more broadly conceived classical Christian worldview, in contradistinction to the ethos of secularism, will always stress a God-centered consciousness over a human-centered one, objective moral authority over relativism, ethical principle over pragmatism, reason over feeling, and a recognition for the need of opinions objectively grounded and authority promulgated by convictions, not merely personal preference.[7]

Through such a Christ-centered lens the Christian sees a much different social and religious reality than does the secularist. The interpretation of events and concepts is decisively shaped by this prism. Acknowledgment of having a particular perspective does not constitute a vindication of relativism, by any means. We all view things from a certain perspective, but this does not entail that all are equally true or good. Acknowledgment of such competing comprehensive perspectives points up the depth of division in American culture. Evangelical, traditional Christianity and American secularism are not just differing sets of metaphysical beliefs and personal commitments. In essence they are nothing less than different ways of being human, utterly incompatible world-views that distinctively affect the psychology and interpreted life experience of their adherents. This is not to say conversation between them is impossible or common ground nonexistent, but it does remind us of the patience that is required to foster and participate in truly civil public argument in contemporary American life.

Strengths and Weaknesses

Evangelicals, particularly those connected with academia, journalism and the arts, seem somewhat embarrassed by their religious pedigree. Having been culturally derided as the intellectual equivalent of the nerd with high pant cuffs, white socks and black shoes, they seem especially willing to flagellate themselves for being a part of this segment of the American population.

Immediately after the quintessential religiously intolerant atrocities of September 11, 2001, one author (Brad) attended a Christian film festival devoted to studying cinematic portrayals of evil. Evangelical participants impaneled after the film were unable to bring themselves to say that Americans had been unjustly victimized by the attacks and that the perpetrators had been in the service of great evil.[8] For so long have evangelical intellectuals and artists been cultural outsiders, never accorded the respect that their secular peers receive, that a great many are timid and tepid when it comes to articulating their true sentiments. This is unfortunate since evangelical Christianity is contributing much to the preservation of American society today. Its moral critique, opposition to the brutal culture of abortion (which harms children as well as mothers and fathers), affirmation of the socially essential need of limiting marriage to one woman and one man, the development of faith-based treatment and recovery programs as well as a host of other charitable and socially minded endeavors are a great force for good in this country.

On the other hand, what the evangelical intelligentsia lacks in nerve is often more than made up for by the often brash expressions of evangelical pulpit prowlers and activists. Sometimes, it seems, evangelicals' zeal to imitate Paul's affirmation of shamelessness at being identified with the gospel of Christ (Rom 1:16) leads them to practice boorish behavior, as when a missionary in Japan made it a habit to park his car across the street from a Buddhist temple and blare in a bull horn during funerals and other ceremonies, "Repent you heathen, or burn in Hell!"[9]

As rude as that is, a deeper weakness in contemporary evangelical Christianity is its acculturation and obscurantism. Both theologically and philosophically, anti-intellectualism has plagued evangelicalism over the last century.[10] Happily, this trend is reversing, and many evangelicals, even at popular levels, are pursuing serious biblical, philosophical and cultural studies.[11]

Is It Tolerant?

But certainly the most urgent question facing evangelical Christianity in America today is not its social or intellectual dysfunctions but rather the presumption against its very legitimacy as a religious orientation in a pluralistic culture. The fact is that the very heart of the evangelical Christian consciousness articulated by Jesus himself—"No one can see the kingdom of God unless he is born again" (Jn 3:3)—is widely regarded as a bigoted attitude. For example, a commentator on National Public Radio, responding to a statement from a gathering of Southern Baptists that affirmed the existence of hell and the need to evangelize non-Christians, said, "The evaporation of four million [people] who believe in this crap would leave the world a better place."[12] To assert—as the New Testament does repeatedly—that salvation is to be found in Jesus Christ alone is to be regarded as intolerant by a great many Americans today, especially those with access to the centers of influence, like the universities, media, television and film. Are they right?

Without a sliver of doubt we think secularists are completely mistaken to respond to the proclamation of the good news of God's sacrifice of his Son for *all* humankind with the reflexive charge of intolerance. Such a charge is an example of twisting tolerance into an unrecognizable counterfeit of the true ideal.

Why so? The attempt to persuade another person is not being intolerant of that person. In fact, it shows respect for his or her intellectual agency and dignity of mind. To urge that someone adopt a new point of view about a matter is in no way to mistreat him or her. We encounter

ideas we disagree with every day of our lives. It seems a strangely petulant and hypersensitive move to respond to those who present them to
us by calling them intolerant. There exists no right not to be offended,
not to have our views unendorsed, not to hear ideas we do not like or
that trouble us in some way. It is not intolerant to fail to affirm another
person's opinions about religion, politics or ethics. It is not intolerant to
warn people of a danger you believe they face or to tell them that you
believe they are flawed and in need of spiritual help. None of those activities can reasonably be described as intolerant in an authentic sense.

Presenting and discussing the gospel in a respectful, decent and civil
manner—as Christians are directed to do (1 Pet 3:15-16)—is not a true
moral offense. Admittedly, it can be done in a rude or contemptuous
way, just as nearly any activity can, but there is nothing inherently oppressive about Christian proclamation. After all, if someone hears the
preaching of the cross and does not like the story or for some other reason disapproves of it, he or she can simply reject it. Conversation or
proclamation only becomes intolerant when it is accompanied by coercion in some form.

The intolerance charge against Christian evangelism also mistakenly
posits a necessary connection between believing Christianity true and
other religions largely untrue on the one hand, and on the other hand,
therefore mistreating and disrespecting non-Christians. It is simply not
true that disagreeing with someone (even if we regard this world as religiously ambiguous) about religious truth amounts to being mean, malicious or somehow intolerant toward that person. In fact the particular,
widely known injunction from Jesus to love your enemies and do good
to them shows what is truly entailed by the Christian faith. Despite all
charges to the contrary, Christianity is built on the reality that not only
humans but also God can love persons while rejecting their false beliefs
and immoral behaviors. Love aims for the gracious transformation of the
person, not the external coercion of mind or body.

Secularists and others who render the charge of intolerance also make
the logical mistake of assuming that the phenomenon of religious diversity in and of itself means that no one religious orientation is veridically
superior, that is, completely true or substantially true in a way the alternatives are not. The fact of religious pluralism does not itself render the

Christian gospel untrue or inaccurate. It merely shows that persons disagree about such things.

Similarly, Christian claims about truth are not false or unreliable strictly because they are believed by some to militate against human harmony and peace. The putative referent(s) of any set of truth claims exists or does not exist irrespective of the effects or consequences of advancing those particular truth claims. (Nevertheless, Christians are taught to hope that indeed the truth they know in Jesus Christ will eventually come to fruition in a true, just and lasting peace for all those who receive it.)

Further, charging Christians with intolerance for declaring their faith is itself intolerant and a convenient lapse in respect for diversity. After all, even the most cursory survey of the New Testament will find passage after passage declaring the message of salvation in Jesus Christ alone (e.g., Jn 3:3; 3:16-17; 5:24; 6:63; 8:31-32; 11:25; 14:6; Acts 4:12; 10:43; 16:31; Rom 3:26; 6:23; 10:9-13; 1 Tim 2:5). This theological principle and its pronouncement are integral to Christian identity. It is inseparable from this worldview, just as supporting female suffrage is inseparable from feminism, monotheism inseparable from orthodox Judaism or the redistribution of wealth from active socialism.[13] To acknowledge and respect diverse viewpoints on all matters is to let Christians be Christians and convey the logic of human salvation that is inherent in their worldview. We cannot say we appreciate human diversity without allowing the various worldviews to articulate their own philosophy. An open society that affirms the right to free expression will inevitably lead us to encounter ideas we do not embrace.

Some say the reason the Christian gospel is intolerant is because it asserts some people will go to hell. This is mean-spirited, they believe, and possibly psychologically unnerving to non-Christians, so it ought not be spoken. In response we might repeat all the above points and add that extending the contemporary demand for tolerance to metaphysical propositions like hell is perverse. Should our life here and now in the context of our mixed pluralistic society control and define what is acceptable to suppose about the hereafter? This is tyrannical indeed. Ascertaining the social good of certain religious propositions can only reasonably be confined to an evaluation of their influence on our lives now, in human society. For example, those who affirm on the basis of a metaphysical mandate that "infidels" must be killed the world over, as does Wahhabist, bin-Laden style Islam, must be judged as genuinely intolerant. It is a religious idea that directly impinges terribly on social and political life here and now, and so it should be subject to an evaluation of its (in)humanity. But to assert, as Christians do, that a person may in some way suffer postmortem is a claim about life after death, that does not in itself negatively effect the way Christians treat non-Christians.*

In fact, other well-known and acknowledged Christian teaching calls Christians to patient forbearance and forgiveness toward non-Christians (Rom 12:14-21; 1 Pet 3:9; 4:13-14, 19; 2 Pet 3:9). It is a mistake to assume that unjust treatment of those with whom Christians, or even adherents of other religions, disagree follows automatically or directly from claims about the ultimate truths of their beliefs, including that of hell.[14] The whole of their teaching would have to be apprehended, including any explicit directives about proper treatment of those with whom an adherent disagrees, before judging whether or not a particular religion promoted unjust and inhumane treatment.

In addition, telling Christians not to talk about hell assumes they are doing it with malicious intent. But Christians believe they are warning others, just as a fireman might warn someone in a burning house, about a danger they face. They understand themselves to be motivated by compassion and concern, not mean-spirited sadism. Simply because a topic is unpleasant does not mean it must not be spoken. Simply because an individual experiences unpleasant thoughts or feelings on hearing about an unpleasant prospect, it does not follow that no one should mention that unpleasant prospect to such an individual.

Last, we should point out that the Bible itself touches on the concept of tolerance quite substantially. Paul urges believers to let their gentle-

---

*Damnation, of course, is unfair or unjust only if no one deserves it. It is far from clear that such is the case. Peter Berger once noted that "There are deeds that demand not only condemnation, but *damnation* in the full religious meaning of the word—that is, the doer not only puts himself outside the community of men; he also separates himself in a final way from a moral order that transcends the human community, and thus invokes a retribution that is more than human. . . . The massacre of the innocent . . . suggests the necessity of hell—not so much as a confirmation of God's justice, but rather as a vindication of our own" (Peter Berger, *A Rumor of Angels* [New York: Doubleday, 1969, pp. 67-69]). For important reflection on hell, see Jerry Walls, *Hell: The Logic of Damnation* (Notre Dame, Ind.: University of Notre Dame Press, 1992); William Crockett, ed., *Four Views on Hell* (Grand Rapids: Zondervan, 1997).

ness be evident to all (Phil 4:5); he tells them to live humbly and not be busybodies (1 Thess 4:11; 2 Thess 3:11-12; 1 Tim 5:13); he instructs them not to be easily angered and not to keep a record of wrongs done to them (1 Cor 13:5); he models a tolerant and sensitive declaration of the gospel amidst religious diversity (Acts 17:16-34); and Peter tells Christians to always answer questions and challenges to their faith with respect toward the questioner (1 Pet 3:15). Indeed, the entire Christian ethic of loving one's neighbor and returning blessing for cursing is itself a call to toleration. So clearly any biblical faith must vigorously affirm the practice of tolerance, rightly understood.

Pluralism

Despite the fact that the phenomenon of pluralism has been perverted into a normative proposition in both religion and politics—in religious belief the various faiths are all assumed to be "true" or "salvifically effective,"[15] and in politics "diversity" and "multiculturalism" require us to affirm a counterintuitive egalitarianism of cultural values across different ethnic communities and nations[16]—the fact is that pluralism as a social reality is not at all undesirable, and for Christians it can be an ideal social arrangement. After making a few clarifications about the meaning and implications of the reality of pluralism as it relates to ethics and Christian life and witness, we will discuss why it should be regarded as a wonderful opportunity by Christian believers.[17]

Pluralism does not mean that all people are right in the views they advocate; neither does it mean that the various values affirmed by them are good or ought to be affirmed by the culture as a whole. Reality and truth are absolutely not in themselves pluralistic in character. Simply because a given view inhabits the panoply of diversity of worldviews, that does not mean it is true or accurate in any important way. It might be, but it might not be. Faiths and worldviews are not true or faithful records of reality simply because we want them to be. Such matters have to be examined closely. The resulting raucous conversation of worldview voices—and the practice of true tolerance that ensures that each is culturally audible—should be welcomed by Christians, who should believe that their tradition speaks in a uniquely wise and powerful way to the human condition. Pluralism is not to be loathed or feared but rather embraced as a forum for the free and vigorous examination of ideas and understandings, about matters great and small.

Thus even though since the Enlightenment and with a quickening pace over the twentieth century and even more so in recent decades, Christianity has lost its cultural prerogative of presumed moral and religious authority, Christians should not understand God's work as disadvantaged or impaired by this context. The omnipotent, omniscient, personal, infinite, creative God of the Judeo-Christian tradition will not be thwarted by human societies set against him. The message of the cross of Christ does not require cultural privilege or social affirmation in order to flourish. To the contrary its message of the inevitable frustration of a life devoted to worldly ideals and satisfactions resonates especially well in the human heart when it is relegated to a reviled status, though people may not acknowledge its piercing truths.*

Even though the structure and character of contemporary moral thinking is defined by its victim consciousness, and even though Christianity is widely regarded as the historical victimizer—and thus "rightly" the recipient of all manner of slights, insults and mocking**— Christians must still insist in a Christlike manner on not only their legal protections and civil rights but the civility accorded by true tolerance and pluralism rightly observed. Strategies from litigation to electioneering to lobbying to op-ed writing to popular protest should all be sensibly pursued. Though we are obviously living in a politically correct atmosphere where non-Christian outlooks are permitted to be culturally and ideologically aggressive and polemical in ways that Christians would be pilloried as bigoted and shamefully insensitive if they followed suit, we nonetheless should wisely and winsomely insist on oc-

---

*Individual believers too should take heart in a culture that exhibits hostility and, in many places in the world, virulent persecution toward them, for the One who inhabits them is greater than the one who is in the world (1 Jn 4:4). It is sobering to note that more Christians have been murdered because of their faith in the twentieth century than in all the previous centuries of Christianity combined. For important survey of the persecution of Christians in totalitarian, Islamist and communist regimes the world over, see James Hefley and Marti Hefley, *By Their Blood,* 2nd ed. (Grand Rapids: Baker, 1996), and Nina Shea, *In the Lion's Den: Persecuted Christians and What the Western Church Can Do About It* (Nashville: Broadman & Holman, 1997).

**Recall the infamous *Piss Christ* image of artist Andres Serrano, a picture of a crucifix submerged in a jar of urine, financed, courtesy of the American taxpayer, by a $15,000 National Endowment for the Arts grant.

cupying our seat at the diverse table of pluralistic society.

Last, Christians will take to the chilly waters of American pluralism when they realize that it, as with all else, is providential. God is not asleep at the wheel; history has not snuck up on him. The times we live in, in all their challenge and complexity, are a brushstroke rendered by the master Artist's hand, devoted to purposes and designs we may not fully perceive and understand. But our lack of comprehension is not indicative of a lack of divine intention. Equipped with this understanding we can welcome our lives in this pluralistic context and stand among our neighbors humbly advocating Christian theological and moral truth, bearing witness to the enduring kindness of God's loving heart, confident that he as at work within us accomplishing his good purposes in *his* world.

PART THREE

THE TRUTH ABOUT TOLERANCE

F̲ew maladies are as insidious as auto-immune diseases like rheumatoid arthritis or the human immuno-deficiency virus (HIV), which cause the body to turn against itself and undermine its own ability to function well and resist further attacks against it. The lamentable misunderstanding and misapplication of tolerance in our time could be seen as socially analogous to such afflictions; it causes culture and essential social institutions to work against the commonweal by stifling dialogue and chillingly stigmatizing as "intolerant" points of view that diverge from today's dominant ideology: secular liberalism.

In this final section we will focus on tolerance itself. First, we will view its distortion in American media, in debates over homosexuality and in education, particularly higher education. Then we will turn specifically to the animus against traditional Christianity being cultivated today in the name of tolerance. Finally, we will articulate a positive understanding of true tolerance through the delineation of ten propositions that will clarify the meaning and function of this idea so central to the quality of American public life today—and tomorrow.

9

TWISTED TOLERANCE
AND DOUBLE STANDARDS

Obviously the modern idea of toleration has turned upon itself,

producing in many cases greater bigotry

than anything it sought to eradicate.

A. J. CONYERS

There are two kinds of people in the world,

the conscious dogmatists and the unconscious dogmatists.

I have always found myself that the unconscious dogmatists

were by far the most dogmatic.

G. K. CHESTERTON

Sometimes with secret pride I sigh

to think how tolerant am I;

Then wonder which is really mine:

Tolerance or a rubber spine?

OGDEN NASH

When considering the perverse misapprehension of tolerance that has settled over contemporary American culture, we must first note that it is not a stand-alone phenomenon but rather a component of the larger drift of our society into selective secular relativism. As this ideology and way of understanding the world has permeated our social consciousness, it has activated all types of confusions, of which the "new tolerance" is one. So to study the twisting of tolerance, it is necessary to view it within some of the institutional contexts where it occurs. Thus we will briefly glimpse the new tolerance through the bizarre looking glass of political correctness and secular liberalism as we find it in three representative aspects of contemporary society: The media, the cultural controversy over homosexuality, and education. After these cultural snapshots, we will investigate the treatment of Christian conviction under the regime of secular liberalism, with its redefinition of tolerance, and show how the misunderstanding of tolerance today is a growing threat to free and open public debate for all as well as to the unhindered exercise of biblical Christianity.

The Influence of the Media

To say that the American news media has a leftward political slant is now a truism. As Bernard Goldberg showed in his bestseller exposing the ideological commitments of the news industry, *Bias,* the information industry in this country has its own distinct culture that inclines it strongly toward secular liberalism. This orientation is decisively at odds with most Americans. Study after study confirms journalists and media workers are much more likely to identify themselves as politically liberal than the general population; they are less likely to get married and have children than the general population, less likely to own homes, less likely to do volunteer work and community service, and less likely to attend church or synagogue.[1] The influence of media workers is profound, and their particular worldview influences our culture in a disproportionate way. The moral and behavioral attitudes they approve of are cued to the American public as the correct and reasonable attitudes to have. The attitudes they disapprove of are viewed as unsophisticated or simplistic. Much of the moral mindset of elite American media is nearly the polar opposite of the traditional Judeo-Christian ethic and worldview, as the following examples indicate:

- A recent Pew Research Center survey showed that although 20 percent of the American public identifies itself as liberal and 33 percent identifies itself as conservative, 34 percent of journalists identify themselves as liberal and just 7 percent as conservative.[2] The disconnect between reporters' values and the general public's became so obvious at the *Los Angeles Times* that John Carroll, the paper's editor, wrote a memo to his section editors admitting that their newsroom was a "political atmosphere that is suffused with liberal values *(and is unreflective of the nation as a whole).*"[3]

- Nina Burleigh was a writer for *Time* magazine, a national news magazine that serves as a primary source of political opinion and analysis for a great many Americans, when she declared her devotion to abortion rights, "I would be happy to give him [former president Bill Clinton] [oral sex] just to thank him for keeping abortion legal. I think American women should be lining up [to do that] to show their gratitude for keeping the theocracy off our backs."[4]

- A 1999 *New York Times Magazine* story about an anti-abortion protestor noted in an aside, "It is a shared if unspoken premise of the world that most of us inhabit that absolutes do not exist and that people who claim to have found them are crazy." Thus opponents of moral relativism who disagree with the urbane inhabitants of the *New York Times's* "reasonable" world are not just wrong, they are mentally ill.[5]

- National news media extensively covered the vicious murder of Matthew Shephard, a young gay man in Wyoming killed by two thugs. But they ignored the rape-torture-murder of thirteen-year-old Jesse Dirkhising by two adult homosexual neighbors. Neither the *New York Times* nor the *Los Angeles Times,* CNN, ABC, CBS or NBC reported on the shocking story in even *cursory* ways.[6]

Secular liberalism is the default position of American media. It is a part of the mental atmosphere of the news industry.[7] Certainly it is true that there are an increasing number of conservative media alternatives that hold the Judeo-Christian worldview in higher esteem, but the cultural influence wielded by the liberal guardians of information—CBS, NBC, ABC, CNN, the *New York Times*, the *Washington Post, USA Today* and the *Los Angeles Times*—is still unrivaled.

The Issue of Homosexuality

The cultural drift in our country toward the mainstreaming of homosexuality is profound, and the pressure to approve of it is comprehensive and persistent. Emblematic of this mainstreaming and the generally accepted character of homosexuality today, the New York City public school district recently announced it was opening a new public high school exclusively for gay, lesbian, bisexual and transgender students. "This school will be a model for the country and possibly the world," said the new school's proud principal, William Salzman.[8] It is now widely regarded as nearly unthinkable that anyone seeking public office would directly assert homosexual conduct to be morally wrong and harmful to society if widely practiced and affirmed.[9]

The determined march toward the embrace of homosexuality is sometimes strident, sometimes soft, but always insistent on an emphatic moral judgment: There is nothing morally wrong or socially or personally damaging about homosexuality. The following four examples, or events similar to them, transpire in the United States and Canada regularly:

- Dr. Christine Brody refused on religious grounds to artificially inseminate Lupita Benitez, a lesbian who wished to become pregnant, give birth and raise the child with her partner. Benitez is suing Dr. Brody for violating her civil rights and discriminating against her.[10]

- In 2000 the Democrat-controlled California State Legislature passed two laws, AB 1785 and AB 1931, which require public school students be taught "appreciation of the diversity of California's population and discouraging the development of discriminatory *attitudes* and practices" toward, among other groups, homosexuals. This teaching of "tolerance" effectively establishes that any student who refuses to acknowledge the moral legitimacy of homosexuality will be guilty of intolerance and a discriminatory attitude, and subject to reeducation and possible disciplinary action.[11]

- A proposed California law, AB 196, authorizes fines of up to $150,000 for businesses—for example Christian bookstores and Boy Scout councils—that refuse to hire transsexuals or "drag queens" (i.e., men who dress as women). The bill prohibits discrimination based on "gender," the definition of which includes "identity, appearance and behavior" not necessarily associated with a person's sex at birth.[12]

- Nickelodeon, a child-oriented cable television channel, aired a thirty-minute report titled "My Family's Different," hosted by journalist Linda Ellerbee. The show features Ellerbee amiably chatting with teenagers who have heterosexual parents and homosexual parents living in same-sex relationships. It also features comments from a gay school principal and a homosexual firefighter who is a father of three. Ellerbee provides a classic example of doublespeak and the twisting of tolerance by saying in the show's introduction, "The following program is about tolerance. . . . It is not about sex. It does not tell you what to think." But its clear purpose is to communicate the moral and familial legitimacy of same-sex relationships, and suppress criticism of it as mean or ignorant. Commenting on the program, Ellerbee explains, "It is never wrong to talk about hate. . . . That's all our show is about. It is not in any way about the homosexual lifestyle. It's not even introducing the subject to most kids. They know. But quite frankly, many of them know it from a hate standpoint without even knowing what they're talking about."[13]

- North America's first legal gay marriage took place in June 2003 when a Canadian appeals court ruled that the heterosexual definition of matrimony was unconstitutional. Canadian Deputy Prime Minister John Manley said approvingly, "I think it's time for us to recognize that same-sex marriages are part of our societal norm."[14]

As the assumption of moral equivalence between homosexuality and heterosexuality settles in our culture, the traditional Christian sexual ethic and understanding of marriage is increasingly being viewed not as a legitimate criticism of such conduct but as a bigoted and *inherently* flawed perspective.

The Role of Education

Since the publication of Alan Bloom's *The Closing of the American Mind* (1987) and Dinesh D'Souza's *Illiberal Education* (1991), the rigid and imperious secular liberalism of both American higher education as well as elementary and secondary education has been under a well-deserved and steady attack. Education at all levels increasingly has taken on the character of the indoctrination of certain values and viewpoints and the discrimination against others, all of which shuts down moral deliberation. But this should not be surprising since secular liberalism, having unhitched knowledge from wisdom and education from any conviction about the ultimate ends or purposes of human persons as such, has transformed the enterprise of education from its classical sense of formation in goodness into a relativist's paradise, little more than a trade school for politically correct thinking. For example:

- A poll by the National Association of Scholars found that 73 percent of graduating college seniors in the United States chose the statement "what is right and wrong depends on differences in individual values and cultural diversity" as the message their professors most frequently conveyed to them.[15] Only 25 percent of American college students think the values of their country—freedom, legal equality, civil rights, capitalism, religious freedom—are superior to the values of other countries.[16]

- In 1997 the conservative *Cornell Review* student newspaper at Cornell University editorialized against the accuracy and philosophy of courses offered by the Black studies department there. In response members of the Black Student Union stole and burned two entire editions of the newspaper. The dean of students at Cornell not only failed to condemn the black students' actions as censorious or intolerant but praised them for "claiming their First Amendment Right."[17] No action was taken against the Black Student Union.

- At Wabash College in spring 1995 a conservative student newspaper, the *Wabash Commentary,* criticized an African American history course on the basis of enrolled students' comments about it for its "feel-good pedagogy" and for stressing personal rather than historical exploration. The college president, Andrew Ford, responded by telling incoming students the next fall that "What happens in a classroom stays within the classroom. . . . [T]he honesty we need to confront issues requires us to be insiders. We must never break trust with one another." The conservative paper was discontinued by the university, and its funds were reallocated to a student publication of the College Democrats club.[18]

- Francis Cardinal Arinze, a Vatican official, recently delivered a graduation speech at Georgetown University, a Catholic school, extolling the value of family and traditional religious beliefs and ethics, saying,

"Happiness is found not in the pursuit of material wealth or pleasures of the flesh, but by fervently adhering to religious beliefs." After the speech over seventy faculty members signed a letter to the dean of the university decrying what they called Arinze's "wildly inappropriate" remarks. One professor, Teresa Sanders, *a professor of theology,* was so outraged by Arinze's remarks that she simply stood up and walked out of the commencement while the cardinal was speaking.[19]

- *Teaching Tolerance* magazine, a publication of the Southern Poverty Law Center, which is respected and consulted by teachers' unions across the country, assures on its website "Tolerance can be taught, not just talked about. . . . Tolerance is an idea that is universally relevant, and it belongs everywhere in the curriculum." That sounds nice. But then come the implicit value judgments and ideology that define *tolerance* for this publication—and secular liberalism generally. We have italicized the words in the next quote that are freighted with particular ideological meaning, which is conveniently never explicitly described. "Here [on the website] you will read about teachers and students working together to *improve* race relations, *respect* religious *diversity* and ability differences, dispel gender *bias* and *homophobia*, confront *hate* and build classroom *community.*"[20] Decoded, with its partisan political and religious assumptions exposed, that sentence would read: "Here you will read about teachers and students working together to emphasize white guilt, affirm the truthfulness of non-Christian religions and individual intellectual homogeneity, assert that there are no intrinsic psycho-emotional differences between men and women and that homosexual practices are not immoral, denounce those who criticize socially pathological behavior and urge conservative students to remain silent about their ideology."

- During the Iraq war a community college instructor explicitly forbade his student from using the *Weekly Standard,* a conservative magazine of opinion, or *any other* conservative sources in a paper examining the rationale for the war.[21]

- Nicholas DeGenova, as assistant professor of anthropology at Columbia University, speaking at a campus "teach-in" protesting the Iraq war, said that he would like to see "a million Mogadishus," referring to an ambush a few years earlier in Mogadishu, Somalia, that killed eighteen American soldiers. The scholar continued, "The only true heroes are those who find ways that help defeat the U.S. military."[22]

- David Horowitz, once a leading young leftist, now a conservative social critic, sought to place a paid advertisement in fifty-one college newspapers across the country, arguing against the morality of the American government paying reparations to black citizens who are the descendants of slaves. Only nine papers agreed to run the ad, two of which immediately apologized to "outraged" students for doing so. At the University of Wisconsin, protestors stormed the newspaper's offices; police had to warn paper staffers to lock their office doors.[23] At Brown University a coalition of students who found the ad "offensive" demanded free advertising space in the newspaper and a "donation" by the paper to a student group of their choosing. When the paper refused, all four thousand copies of it were removed from campus by the aggrieved students. Later, more newspapers were printed and delivered to campus locations under police escort.[24]

- An alternative student newspaper at the University of California, Berkeley, the conservative *California Patriot,* printed an article written by a group of conservative students criticizing the Hispanic student group MEChA (Movimiento Estudiantil Chicano de Aztlan) for calling white people "Gringos" and calling for a national "revolt" against Caucasians. Shortly after the article the newspaper's offices were burglarized and ransacked, and members of the group that authored the article received death threats. MEChA denied any responsibility for either episode.[25]

- Conservative former Israeli prime minister Benjamin Netanyahu was forbidden from delivering a scheduled speech at the University of California Berkeley when hundreds of chanting students, in protest to his presence, blocked the entrance to the theater were he was to speak.[26]

- A professor of physics at the University of Massachusetts, Amherst, declared "[The American flag is] a symbol of terrorism and death and fear and destruction and oppression."[27]

- State departments of education and textbook publishers carefully supervise images and language to ensure that an antitraditional ethos of political correctness is observed. As a matter of routine practice, according to historian of education Diane Ravitch, major publishers require that their books are void of pictures showing women cooking, men acting assertive or old people walking with a the aid of a cane. Men and boys must not appear larger in photographs than do women and girls, and Asians must not appear shorter than non-Asians. Forbidden words include *co-ed, actress, brotherhood, anchorman* and of course *policeman.*[28]

- Undeniably, there is a notorious liberal slant to the professorate generally. A poll commissioned by the Center for the Study of Popular Culture to study the political views of Ivy League humanities professors found that in the 2000 election, 84 percent voted for Al Gore, 6 percent for Ralph Nader and 9 percent for George Bush. Fifty-seven percent of the professors said they were Democrats by party affiliation, but just 3 percent said they were Republican (compared to 37 percent of the general public identifying themselves as Republican and 34 percent Democrat). Six percent of the professors said they were conservative or somewhat conservative; 23 percent claimed "moderate" as their orientation, and 64 percent were liberal or somewhat liberal.[29] The self-perpetuating nature of this ideological homogeneity in academia is seen in Edward Rozek's claim that in *forty-three years* as a professor in the political science department at the University of Colorado, Boulder, he was the *only* Republican in the department; all of his colleagues were Democrats.[30]

Tolerance: A One-Way Street

The picture emerging here is one that has been developing since the 1960s. Many college campuses and educational curricula at lower levels as well as the tides of American life generally are avowedly antitraditional and committed to the creed of secular liberalism. The backdrop to this social shift is the view that the American nation and the Judeo-Christian creed that has nursed it are irredeemably corrupt. Without question, public culture generally and elite and influential venues like media, the law, and academia in particular are repressive to the cognitive minority within them (i.e., traditional Americans).

A fundamental sentiment driving this secular-liberal juggernaut is the conviction deep in the psychology of contemporary liberalism that lib-

erals are good people, and that conservatives are not just wrong on issues as a matter of policy but that they are *bad* people. Conservatives
think liberals are wrong; liberals think conservatives are mean-spirited
and bad.

This basic assumption received absurd academic expression in an article recently published in the American Psychological Association's *Psychological Bulletin.* The article, which was based on research of professors from Berkeley and Stanford, divined the psychological habits
common to all conservatives. It turns out that the conservative soul is
characterized by "fear and aggression," "dogmatism," and "uncertainty
avoidance." According to the authors, typical figures of conservatism
who embody the sort of psychology that leads to political conservatism
include Hitler, Mussolini and Ronald Reagan. Presumably Satan himself
is a conservative too. This article, which was not intended as satire, is an
apt parody of the combination of self-righteousness and hysteria that
characterize liberal polemic in American politics today.[31]

Indeed, contemporary liberals' sense of personal moral superiority,
plainly on display in this "study," drives much of today's wholesale re-
vamping of traditional education and mores. Thus sensitivity training, victim studies, values clarification and the lexicon of secular liberal euphe-
misms governing public life follows in train, energized by zealous belief.

Speech codes, now ubiquitous on campuses, are a key component of
education into the secular worldview. They are an especially effective if
insidious way of sneaking partisan political and moral judgments into
the intellectual life of a university and by implication, eventually, the
larger society of which it is a key part. As Alan Charles Kors, a professor
of history at the University of Pennsylvania notes:

> At the theoretical level, speech codes deny things that should be self-
> evident: the indispensability of freedom to learning; the dignity and
> strength of meeting speech that one abhors with further speech, with rea-
> son, with evidence, with cold contempt, or with moral outrage and moral
> witness. Prejudice and ignorance do not disappear when their expression
> is suppressed; rather, they simply go deeper into people's souls. . . . At
> the practical level, speech codes have created an arena of double stan-
> dards, of arbitrary, partisan enforcement, and of the raw use of power to
> enforce a political agenda. . . . In a nation whose essential soul—and, in-

deed, whose minority rights—depend upon equal justice under law, the double standard of speech codes at our universities is teaching the worst possible lesson: that one's freedom should depend upon one's local power. . . . The feelings of moderate, religious, or assimilationist students are given no standing whatsoever in the alleged sensitivity to pain and underlying protection from free speech and free expression. You may call an evangelical a "Jesus Freak" or "Born-Again Bigot," any veteran a "baby killer," any black with white friends an "Uncle Tom," any antifeminist a "Barbie Doll." It is an unconscionable hypocrisy. Education, to be edifying in a free society, must occur in conditions of liberty of expression and of equality before the law. Neither exists on most campuses today.[32]

Tolerance easily becomes a one-way street in such environs. Those who hold traditional views and values must be unceasingly tolerant of their opponents, but their opponents may be unceasingly critical. Criticism of the traditional from the antitraditional is open-minded and free-thinking; criticism going the other direction is insensitive and intolerant or simply identified as hate speech. The campus is an arena for worldview transformation, and any traditionally minded student who resists this is retrograde and narrow-minded, not simply well-intended but wrong.

Marcuse on Campus

Professor Kors places the intellectual impetus for this widespread misuse of tolerance with twentieth-century Marxist philosopher Herbert Marcuse (1898-1979). Marcuse's ideas were highly influential in the 1960s, featuring a melding of Freudian and Marxian themes into an allegedly emancipatory understanding of human beings as polymorphously sexual creatures who must transcend the suffocating morals of bourgeois or middle-class life and experience complete freedom from tradition in every area of life. In a 1965 essay titled "Repressive Tolerance," Marcuse railed against the freedom of assembly and the freedom of speech integral to true tolerance, and instead advocated, mainly through the institutions of academia, what he called "liberating tolerance."

"Liberating tolerance," he explained, "would mean intolerance against movements from the Right, and toleration of movements from the Left."[33] Marcuse simply wanted "not 'equal' but *more* representation of the Left" in American institutions of all sorts, particularly universities.[34] In other words, he wanted to hear less from those who disagreed with him and more from those who agreed with him. Believing traditional tolerance and the doctrine of legal equality as themselves repressive in the thoroughly corrupt and exploitative American capitalist society, he thought rights and liberties should be reassigned unequally in order to redress historical wrongs. If this had to be done by "extralegal means," Marcuse thought that was permissible. America was so infected with "false consciousness" that free and open debate in the context of civility and toleration was pointless because the general consciousness itself, the whole of society, was rotten.[35] So it is that *tolerance* becomes a synonym for totalitarianism, and *discrimination* based on ideology becomes a positive good.

It is striking to hear in the childish despotism of Marcuse the rationalizations of the guardians of today's political correctness. Their voices are alarmingly similar, and speech codes along with the Orwellian vocabulary of *sensitivity, diversity, tolerance* and so many other cardinal doctrines of today's restrictive secular liberalism owe their philosophical parentage to this anarchic misanthrope. As Hilton Kramer and Roger Kimball note:

> The casual brutality of Marcuse's program of "liberating tolerance" is breathtaking. But it would be a mistake to think that such fantasies of control are confined to academic radicals. . . . The [contemporary] liberal betrayal of [classical] liberalism is also evident throughout the policies and attitudes that constitute political correctness, "diversity training," and the like. . . . [I]ts dictates are increasingly felt in schools and colleges, in the workplace, and in governmental offices. Wherever one discovers a publicly bruited "commitment to diversity," one can be sure that policies designed to assure lockstep conformity are not far behind.[36]

Indeed, the damage done to classical liberalism by the likes of Marcuse is profound. John O'Sullivan summarizes perhaps their most important conquest, the pirating of the meaning and practice of tolerance. He writes:

> The basic [classical] liberal notion of tolerance has now been transformed in two directions. Not only is it no longer extended to protect ideas that run counter to the doctrines of modern liberalism, but in addition it elevates liberal ideas *above* criticism. Where once it meant a willingness to

tolerate ideas and behavior of which one disapproved, it now means an obligation not to criticize them openly. Criticism and vigorous debate, far from being the testing ground of truth and error, are now themselves seen as intolerant. . . . Tolerance thus becomes a device to elevate certain liberal ideas and constituencies above public criticism rather than trusting that they will eventually emerge victorious on their merits in open public debate.[37]

This is a civilly destructive trend, especially in so pluralistic a society as ours. The secular liberal should be as concerned about this misuse of tolerance as anyone, not only because of its intrinsic wrongness but also because today's in-group may be tomorrow's out-group. The social capital of secular liberalism could, in the future, be dissipated by means hard to anticipate today, and the lash of twisted tolerance could be directed against it.

But without question, in the zeitgeist of American life today the whipping boy is traditional Christianity.

·10·

CHRISTIANITY
IN THE
CROSSHAIRS

We are always in the forge, or on the anvil; by trials God is shaping us for higher things.

HENRY WARD BEECHER

How did orthodox Christianity, whose spread throughout the world was predicated in great part on its inclusiveness ("Come to me, all you who are weary and heavy laden"), come to be a symbol of exclusivity and intolerance? One possible answer echoes the sentiment seen on the church signboard: "If you feel distant from God, guess who moved?" It seems so simple. Christians have stayed true to a 4,000 year-old revelation of moral truth, ultimately rooted in God's eternal nature. Naturally this offends the "do your own thing" sensibilities of talk-show hosts, Hollywood filmmakers, White House spin doctors, and those who follow after.

DANIEL TAYLOR

While contemporary secular liberalism certainly has many foes and ideological opponents, its bête noir is traditional Christianity, and in particular the evangelical variety, which by its nature—intellectually and spiritually—explicitly seeks to challenge and transform. Thus when so potent a weapon as the new tolerance is in the political, cultural and institutional hands of secular liberalism, it should not be surprising at whom it is pointed.

An Acceptable Target

Secular liberalism's self-serving redefinition of tolerance has placed conservative Christianity under a dark cloud of suspicion, culturally. The social and cultural prerogative of authority and moral credibility that orthodox Christianity enjoyed until the Scopes debacle of the 1920s has now been substantially eroded.

Fundamentalist is now a common epithet in American life, signaling a contempt and anger as intense as any contemporary slur. Ditto for the *religious right,* now an invective so potent it is equally applicable to Islamist clerics who advocate terrorism and to Bible-believing Christians, as when the *New York Times* explained that following the atrocities of September 11, 2001, the Saudi Arabian government was reluctant to rein in the Islamist clerics in its country who incite terrorist violence, fearing doing so "would have inflamed the religious right."[1] Again, just after the 9/11 attacks, a *New York Times* correspondent explained that terrorists opposed "values cherished in the West as freedom, tolerance, prosperity, religious pluralism and universal suffrage, but abhorred by religious fundamentalists (and not only Muslim fundamentalists) as licentiousness, corruption, greed and apostasy." The reporter's implication is obvious: conservative Christians, like Muslim fundamentalists, hate freedom and tolerance.[2] Similarly, *Times* columnist Bill Keller complained that (now former) Republican senators Phil Gramm, Jesse Helms and Strom Thurmond have "harnessed their collective century of seniority to the Taliban wing of the American right," equating Christian conservatives with the sadistic and misogynistic reign of the former Afghan government.[3]

The term *evangelical* hardly fares any better, evoking in the social consciousness images of flamboyant, sweaty televangelists incessantly appealing for "love gifts" and pleading theatrically for the blessings of "Gawd." Roman Catholics, too, with their explicit hierarchy and high valuation of tradition, are regular—and socially acceptable—targets of ridicule. This fact was recently evidenced at a Princeton University "art" exhibit in which Roman Catholic images—a torn Sacred Heart of Jesus, pictures of naked female torsos arranged in the shape of a cross, and various devotional items all strung together under the heading "Shackles of the AIDS Virus"—were displayed. When Catholic students at the uni-

versity rightfully complained that the exhibit (which was titled "Rican-
structions") represents Roman Catholics as murderers, a dean of the university said she was sorry the exhibit had "caused pain" to the students,
but it would remain because she said it has "educational value" to the
community.[4] It is impossible to imagine that elements of Muslim or Jewish faith and practice, or symbols of African American culture would be
allowed to be laid out for public ridicule, let alone have that desecration
deemed educational.

This cultural sneering and the confidence that it will resonate across
much of the American population are further exemplified in four recent
public statements by opinion leaders:

- Bill Moyers, icon of public television, voiced all the appropriate sentiments of elite secularism when he declared that Republican Christians
  in offices of national leadership, beginning with George W. Bush,
  would "force pregnant women to give up control over their own lives
  . . . transfer wealth from working people to the rich . . . [give] corpo-
  rations a free hand to eviscerate the environment . . . and [practice] se-
  crecy on a scale you cannot imagine. . . . [I]f you like God in government, get ready for the Rapture."[5] Moyers is regarded by his media
  colleagues as a seasoned, temperate and reflective professional. One
  wonders what the fringe of liberal opinion might sound like.

- Anthony Lewis, an opinion columnist of the *New York Times* for thirty-
  two years, said at his retirement that he has learned that "Certainty is
  the enemy of decency and humanity in people who are sure they are
  right, like Usama bin Laden and John Ashcroft."[6] The typical contempt
  of elite media for conservative Christians like John Ashcroft is seen in
  this absurd equivalence between an aspirant to genocide and a mass
  murderer and the Attorney General of the United States who is a known
  Bible-believing Christian. But if certainty is the enemy of humanity in
  people who are sure they are right, Mr. Lewis must be quite unsure
  about his own judgment, or perhaps his epistemological principle, self-
  refuting though it is, does not apply to *secular* fundamentalists.

- In 1999 a CBS news producer said Gary Bauer, a high-profile Christian
  activist, was a "little nut" in a program meeting. Nobody participating
  in the meeting objected or registered any concern, according to a par-
  ticipant in the meeting. Media mogul Ted Turner publicly called Chris-

tianity a religion "for losers," and one Ash Wednesday, while striding through a newsroom, Turner saw employees with ash on their foreheads and derided them as "Jesus Freaks."[7]

In early 2002 a Democratic party strategist recommended that to counter President Bush's rising popularity, Democrat spokespersons should equate conservative Christians with the Taliban, the repressive and theocratic former government of Afghanistan. As a reporter explained, "The theory goes like this. Our enemy in Afghanistan is religious extremism and intolerance. It's therefore more important than ever to honor the ideals of tolerance—religious, sexual, racial, reproductive—at home. The GOP is out of the mainstream, some Democrats will argue [this year], because it's too dependent upon an intolerant 'religious right' "[8] Recall that the Taliban, in their unspeakable brutality, eliminated religious liberty and rights to free expression, covered women from head to toe, forbade them suffrage and other basic rights, and practiced public mutilation and capital punishment for acts of property theft. But this Democratic strategist was so confident in the hypnotizing power of the tolerance mantra—and in people's fear of being thought "intolerant"—that however hyperbolic comparing Republicans to the Taliban was, it would not matter. People would hear the word *tolerance,* and robotically nod their assent to the value judgments of secular liberalism. Note, of course, that in the strategist's remark, the specific position to be taken on the range of issues presented (religious, sexual, racial, reproductive) does not even need to be explicitly stated. The value judgments, the positions of secular liberalism, are encoded into the phrase "honor the ideals of tolerance." Observing the ideals of tolerance in secular liberal newspeak means, with reference to the categories the strategist mentioned (religious, sexual, racial, reproductive): Do not believe any one religion is uniquely true; accept the moral equivalence of homosexuality and heterosexuality along with the legitimacy of same-sex marriage and gay adoption; support racial preferences and the idea that America is still deeply racist; be absolutely pro-choice on abortion. Anyone dissenting from these ideas may be branded as intolerant, under the social and political rules of engagement that prevail in America today, a protocol spawned by the ideology of secular liberalism and its too frequent acolytes in the Democrat party.[9]

This attitude of cultural contempt has direct and practical consequences for conservative Christians' faith and practice. Public attitudes
change and social consciousnesses develop, and given the powerful
tides of secularization that oversee life today (e.g., the information media, entertainment media, democratized higher education, global travel,
widely diffused religious and ethnic diversity), it would be unsurprising
if in many places, including the United States, evangelical and otherwise
conservative Christians found themselves increasingly crosswise of the
emotive and cognitive assumptions of their cultures. Consider the following recitation of culturally sanctioned encroachments on the Christian worldview:

- In 1997 Grinnell College defunded an evangelical Christian student
  group that refused to allow homosexual students who had been attending the group's meetings to become group leaders. Whitman College in Washington state, Middlebury College in Vermont and other
  schools across the country have similarly denounced or penalized
  Christian student fellowships who do not allow gay students to lead
  their organizations, saying the evangelical groups, in so doing, violate
  campus rules that stipulate student groups are not permitted to consider one sexual orientation morally preferable to another. *U.S. News
  & World Report* columnist John Leo remarks on the cause and implications of this type of institutional bias—so prevalent on American
  campuses—against traditional ethical views: "The politically correct
  left now relies far more on coercion than on persuasion or moral appeal. The long-term trend is to depict dissent from the gay agenda as
  a form of illegitimate and punishable expression."[10]

- The same coercive policy was at work in the spring of 2000 when a
  Tufts University student board called the Tufts Community Union Ju-
  diciary voted to "defund" the evangelical Tufts Christian Fellowship.
  The reason? The Christian group was violating Tufts' antidiscrimination policy by forbidding an openly bisexual student from assuming
  a leadership role in the Fellowship. The board's decision meant Tufts
  Christian Fellowship could not use the university's name, could not
  reserve rooms on campus to meet in, and would no longer be eligible
  for the approximately $5,000 allotted to student organizations. Re-
  marked the Tufts dean of students, "[University] funding is not the

right thing to provide to a group that doesn't make its membership totally open to everyone."[11] We wonder if the university would reason in this way if an evangelical Christian joined and sought to lead the Gay-Lesbian-Bisexual Student Association? Or if an orthodox Christian sought the chairmanship of the campus Hillel Jewish group? Certainly teach-ins and solemn candlelight vigils urging respect for diversity would soon appear.

- The same surreptitious usurping of evangelical Christian creed and conscience—cloaked in the benign names of diversity, fairness and nondiscrimination—was on display recently at Rutgers University. In fall 2002 the Rutgers chapter of InterVarsity Christian Fellowship was informed by the university that it was being suspended for violating the university's mandate that campus groups be open to all students and that any active member be allowed to run for a leadership position in the organization. InterVarsity Christian Fellowship quite reasonably responded that while membership was open to all, only students "committed to the basis of faith and the purpose of this organization are eligible for leadership positions."[12] After several months of negotiation, the university relented, and allowed IVCF to select leaders who shared its values and beliefs. The absurdity of this conflict—should a Buddhist student group have to accept a leader who believes in Christianity, or the Pagan Student Association a Mormon?—points directly to the ugly reality that the real purpose of such "antidiscrimination" policies is *to discriminate,* to cripple or annihilate religious groups that assert a biblical opposition to homosexuality. John Leo, who followed the Rutgers affair closely, summed up the matter well:

> Though written in the bland language of brotherhood, anti-discrimination laws give critics of private groups "a public hammer with which to beat groups they oppose," said Richard Epstein, professor of law at the University of Chicago. Such laws provide a way for outsiders to reach into a dissenting group to determine its membership, policies and officers. Using a verbal screen of "diversity," "fairness" and "non-discrimination," university officials delegitimize religion by substituting campus orthodoxy for religious principles.[13]

The larger cultural trend in this same direction extends beyond campuses and into government employment, the commercial workplace, public life and the general social ethos where comments dissenting from the zeitgeist can be construed as everything from creating "a hostile environment" to "offensive and personally hurtful" to simply "discriminatory." Christian conviction and practice are colliding with the now widely diffused (mis)construal of toleration as acceptance and affirmation. For example:

- A recent headline in *USA Today* declared: "Americans Less Tolerant on Gay Issues." The first sentence of the story reads, "Americans have become significantly less *accepting* of homosexuality." Later, the article explains, "After several years of growing tolerance, [Americans show] a return to a level of more traditional attitudes."* So, the definitions in the lexicon of the new tolerance are clear: *tolerance* means "acceptance," which is to say, approval; *traditional attitudes* (read, Judeo-Christian disapproval of homosexuality) equal "intolerance," which is to say, a morally wrong, unreasonable and in certain contexts (e.g., employment at a church summer camp or Christian college) a discriminatory outlook.

- Democratic New York state assemblyman Sheldon Silver recently advocated, in two women's health bills, that all hospitals, irrespective of religious belief or affiliation, be required to offer pharmacological abortifacients—the so-called morning-after pill—arguing that failing to do so is a violation of antidiscrimination law.[14]

- Brenda Nichol was suspended from her job at a Pennsylvania public school for wearing a one-and-a-half-inch cross around her neck. The cross violated the Pennsylvania Public School Code that prohibits religious messages. A federal judge later ruled that Ms. Nichol's Constitutional rights were violated by the code.[15]

- The British Columbia College of Teachers, in Canada, refuses to cer-

---

*"Americans Less Tolerant on Gay Issues," *USA Today,* July 29, 2003, p. 1A (italics added). The public poll this story concerned still showed substantial support for regarding homosexuality as morally and socially equivalent to heterosexuality. This fact, plus the very well-funded and aggressive gay lobbies like GLAAD (Gay and Lesbian Alliance Against Defamation) and the continuing integration of gay themes into popular culture, particularly television, all underscore the truth of what we mentioned earlier, that homosexuality is being mainstreamed in American life.

tify as professionally competent teachers graduating from Trinity Western University, a Christian university, because it says their belief in the morally objectionable character of homosexuality may harm students in the classroom. Perfectly displaying the softheaded equation of tolerance with license and commitment to the antitraditional, a Canadian Supreme Court Justice, reviewing the case said, "It's all very well to say, 'love the sinner but hate the sin,' but is that not a contradiction in terms? While the religious may preach tolerance, religion is often an engine of intolerance."[16]

Svend Robinson, a gay member of Canada's liberal New Democratic Party, advanced an ultimately unsuccessful effort to broaden Canada's hate-crimes laws to include as criminal any action or statement that would "incite or promote hatred of homosexuals." Opponents of Robinson's proposal expressed concern that the law, if passed, would effectively criminalize the Bible. They cited as precedent for their apprehension a recent ruling by a Canadian judge that a newspaper ad that quoted a passage from Leviticus in support of its argument against the morality of homosexuality had "exposed homosexuals to hatred." Robinson's efforts were not helped by one member of parliament's recollection that Robinson had recently confronted a Roman Catholic priest protesting homosexuality on Parliament Hill, and, after arguing with the cleric about the issue, grabbed the sign the priest was holding and heaved it over the embankment the men were standing on.[17] In a similar turn, in 2002 the Swedish Parliament passed a bill criminalizing "hate speech" against homosexuals and other minority groups. The bill explicitly includes "church sermons" as the avenues of expression that could fall under the bill's purview. Prominent Swedish homosexuals were quick to publicly declare that they will report to Swedish authorities Christian preachers who "speak disparagingly" about homosexuality from the pulpit.[18]

It can only be the most naive exercise in denial to believe that such legal innovations could not transpire in the United States. After all, American progressives are renowned for looking to Canada and Europe as America's exemplars of sophistication and good sense. As we have seen, there is already precedent on America's campuses for such anti-Christian censorship and constraint in the name of tolerance.

The New Obscenity: The "G" Word

A part of the reason the new tolerance is successful in inculcating its twisted definition of tolerance into the American mind is because of the increasingly virulent public and legal hostility in American life to any public expressions of theistic, let alone Christian, sentiment. The G-word, *God,* is the new obscenity. More conservative Jewish people and some Christians have always refused to say or print the name or title of God out of reverence and awe. But today cultural references to God are abbreviated or deleted altogether because, according to the contemporary consciousness and secular extremism, any public voicing of God is *verboten.*

- ABC entertainment executives bleeped-out the word *Jesus* when a daytime talk show hostess said "Thank you, Jesus" for her success in losing weight.[19]

- A Chicago family participating in a fundraiser and beautification project for a local park purchased a single brick to be placed in a new brick walkway in the park. The Christian family wanted their inscription on the brick to read "Dear Missy, E. B. and Baby, Jesus is the cornerstone. Love, Mom and Dad." The Park District in Chicago told the family they were not allowed to print the name "Jesus" on their brick, as it might offend others.[20]

- An honor guard at a New Jersey cemetery was fired for saying, during the presentation of the American flag to grieving relatives at a funeral service, "God bless you and this family, and God bless the United States of America."[21]

- The United States Supreme Court declined, without comment, to hear the appeal of Mr. Brian Rohrbough, whose son Danny was murdered in the Columbine High School massacre. Mr. Rohrbough was seeking permission to mention God on a four-inch tile to be placed among four thousand other tiles along a school corridor.[22]

- A public-interest law firm sued the New York City public schools, asserting the district "expressly permit[ted] and encourage[d]" the display of a Jewish menorah and the Islamic star and crescent during a holiday program at a public school, but directly forbade a Christian parent's request to provide the school with a nativity scene to display.[23]

- In the wake of the 9/11 attacks, a public school in Rocklin, California, displayed a sign on its front lawn: "God Bless America." The local ACLU chapter threatened to sue the district if it did not immediately remove the sign, calling the phrase a "hurtful, divisive message."[24]

- Two students at a high school in Virginia were banned from singing at their graduation ceremony a Celine Dion song that mentions God. Besides mentioning the G-word once, the song contains the phrase, "Lead us to a place, guide us with your grace. / Give us faith so we'll be safe." Mentioning God and the offending phrase breaches the separation of church and state, according to an attorney for the school district.[25]

- After a local chapter of the American Civil Liberties Union threatened a lawsuit, U.S. park officials removed three bronze plaques that overlooked the Grand Canyon. The plaques, which were placed over thirty years ago, were inscribed with Bible verses from the book of Psalms, including Psalm 104:24, "O LORD, how manifold are thy works!" (KJV).[26]

- The United States Ninth Circuit Court of Appeals ruled that the words "under God" in the Pledge of Allegiance must no longer be said, as they constitute a violation of the separation of church and state.*

- Los Angeles County, under threat of lawsuit from the ACLU, decided to remove from its official seal a small cross, which signified the historical role Roman Catholic missions played in the settling of the region. Many other images related to the history of the area appear on the seal—oil derricks, a cow, the Hollywood Bowl, a tuna fish—all larger than the cross. Among these other symbols is another religious one, Pomona, the Roman goddess of gardens and fruit trees. But the enforcers of secularism at the ACLU said the cross may make some non-Christians "feel unwelcome," and so history must be rewritten.[27]

- In a textbook case of secular hysteria, what might be termed a "secu-

---

*"Pledge Ban Set for March 10 in Nine States," March 3, 2003 <www.cnn.com/2003/LAW/03/03/pledge.of.allegiance.reut/>. The decision was later stayed, and the U. S. Supreme Court ultimately refused to rule on the case, saying the petitioner lacked legal standing, thus preserving the reference to God in the Pledge, for the time being. For discussion of the centrality of theism to the American nation, see M. Stanton Evans, *The Theme is Freedom: Religion, Politics and the American Tradition* (Washington, D.C.: Regnery, 1994).

lar witch hunt" is on in the state of Utah. The ACLU chapter there has issued an "action alert" on its website in pursuit of a Ten Commandments monument. Some fifty years ago a charitable group in Utah donated nine Ten Commandments marble monuments to the state for display. Through the years the ACLU has systematically searched for and found these monuments and, through litigation or the threat thereof, compelled the removal of them from any public grounds. But the ninth and final copy of the Ten Commandments is missing, and, the guardians of civil liberties explain, it must be found—and banned. The description from their website—which describes the appearance and probable location of the monument is classic:

> There is one monument left in Utah on government property. We need your help to find the last monument. Please go visit your local public parks and city buildings to see if the monument is there. We are particularly interested in looking for the monument in Logan, Brigham City, Hurricane, Midvale, Midway and Tremonton. The monuments are made of a reddish gray marble, are rounded on the top and are in the form of two tablets side by side. If you find it, contact our office at . . .[28]

Society Without Religion

In what is another strategically clever but philosophically and civically corrupting move, the guardians of secular tolerance have transmuted the separation of church and state into the separation of religion and society. The former does not require or even imply the latter, as so many customs of American civil religion—from Congressional prayers to using the Bible in swearing-in ceremonies to "In God We Trust" on our coins—attest. But it is an effective way to sanitize the public square of religious ideas some may find distasteful.[29] The utter exaggeration of the separation of church and state into the banishment of any Christian symbol or value from public consciousness is a prominent characteristic of American life today, and it is the fruit of secular liberalism's thriving.

What we see then is a combination of factors at work continually inculpating the traditional Christian worldview and the ethics bound up with it. Christianity rightly understood is not simply a collection of arid propositions, it is an existential faith as well as a propositional one that conditions and pervades all of the believer's consciousness. Whether the subject is the source of norms for social policy, the morally proper expression of human sexuality or the nature of the afterlife, the Christian speaks out of a moral tradition of ultimate convictions that regards itself as omnicompetent (i.e., able to address all of life, if not directly, then by moral or practical inference from clear biblical principles and time-tested Christian tradition). To assail conservative Christians, then, for asserting the immorality of same-sex marriage or the postmortem misery of those who have rejected Christ is to criticize their religious beliefs. This is certainly permissible, and as we have argued, Christians above all should insist on the permissibility of religious criticism. But the idea afoot today that Christian believers are somehow speaking out of bounds when they render social or moral criticisms predicated on their faith is first a misapprehension of the meaning of Christian religious faith and also an ad hoc and intellectually arbitrary drawing of the line of permissibility in debate.

Domineering secular liberalism and its relocation of the chief concepts of contemporary politics—change, choice, diversity, discrimination, tolerance—into that movement's ideological lexicon, stealthily freighting those terms with the particular values of secular liberalism while trading on those words' social capital and presumption of moral impeccability, is culturally crowding out conservative Christianity. The first step in restraining this push is to expose the rhetorical sleight of hand and emphatic moral judgments of the American secularist worldview.

The transformation of tolerance by secular liberalism into a vessel to carry its ideological agenda has been particularly successful and civically damaging. Secular liberalism is generally the dominant ideology on American campuses, in newsrooms, in the entertainment industry, among the Democrat party and portions of the Republican party, in mainline Protestant denominations as well as a substantial swath of Roman Catholicism. This intellectual hegemony has enabled it to rapidly proceed in replacing of traditional tolerance with a new concept loaded with politically partisan meaning. But this counterfeit inhibits *real* social dialogue and hobbles the ability of the body politic to traverse the minefield of the contemporary culture war.

An apt cinematic analogy to the tragedy of tolerance today is found in the 1956 film *Invasion of the Body Snatchers,* directed by Don Siegel. The movie tells the story of Dr. Miles Bennel (played by Kevin McCar-

thy), a small-town physician who returns home from a medical confer-
ence to find his office inundated with patients claiming their friends and
family have been replaced by imposters. As the story unfolds, the at-first-
skeptical Dr. Bennel comes to believe that indeed people all over town
are being physically replicated and replaced by aliens. The aliens look,
sound and speak like the people they have replaced, but inwardly they
are different. The mind, emotions and personality—the genuine substance of the victims, their identity—is missing. They are only the shell
of their old selves. Sinister alien duplicates have taken over their bodies,
removed the internal substance of the person and are now using this
outward resemblance to further their own agenda of world conquest.

In the same way the concept of true tolerance has been replaced by
an imposter that uses the same name. The false tolerance of today bears
the verbal image of its authentic twin, and it trades on the social capital
and general cultural respect that true tolerance so rightly is accorded.
But the new tolerance is an imposter; it manifests a robotic affirmation
of virtually any idea that is nontraditional and unthinkingly condemns
criticism of its own judgments as bigoted or intolerant. The alien tolerance of today is incoherent when challenged, and it is dehumanizing in
practice as it works to shut down debate and squelch criticism, both of
which are quintessentially human endeavors which help us to come to
know the truth, and thereby truly know ourselves and our destiny.

TEN TRUTHS OF
TOLERANCE 1

We have a long tradition of political and religious tolerance in our country. It's true that perhaps it has not always been lived up to, but we have that tradition. But that idea of tolerance was based upon the idea that tolerance is good. It was based upon the idea that there is moral truth, that there is a right and wrong way to treat other people; and in the absence of that tolerance itself is without foundation. The only basis of tolerance is truth. Tolerance has suffered a great deal recently in our religious and political and educational areas. And tolerance, because truth has been pulled away from it, has slipped over into the idea that everything is equally right. No longer is tolerance a matter of saying, "I disagree with you and I believe you're wrong, but I accept you and I extend to you the right to be wrong." That's not enough. We're now in a situation where everyone must be equally right, where you cannot say that people are wrong and still claim to love them. We used to say humorously, "Love me, love my dog." Now we in effect say, and entirely without humor, "Love me, love my opinions—love my views." And this is humanly disastrous.

DALLAS WILLARD

Let us now turn to the right and responsible apprehension and application of tolerance. We have seen that true tolerance is not the province of the secular liberalism that so strongly flavors American life, and that unfettered debate about traditional moral convictions—especially religiously grounded ones—is ironically imperiled by what passes for tolerance today.

We have also observed that genuine tolerance truly belongs to those who embrace the Judeo-Christian religious tradition (including its evangelical expression). The Judeo-Christian conviction regarding the operation of true tolerance in a largely secular and pluralistic society can be summarized in ten basic principles, concepts which are equally applicable and practicable to those outside of that religious tradition. While some of these principles—and therefore our discussion of them—naturally overlap with themselves and with some of what we have said earlier in our study, this analysis will allow us to gain a clear and comprehensive understanding of the essential idea of toleration.

Principle 1

Tolerance, rightly understood, is a patience toward a practice or opinion one disapproves of. This understanding may come as a surprise to many people today who imagine that tolerance is simply a synonym for the words *acceptance* or *agreement*. Why include the harsh word *disapprove* in the definition of tolerance, some may wonder?

The classical idea of tolerance has been marked by a clear understanding that toleration entails disagreement yet respect, that is, a difference of opinion accompanied by a firm moral commitment to the decent treatment of the person with whom one disagrees. The famous formulation of tolerance is attributed to the eighteenth-century philosopher Voltaire, "I disapprove of what you say, but I will defend to the death your right to say it." So by technical definition, tolerance is "A policy of patient forbearance in the presence of something which is disliked or disapproved of."[1] The English word *tolerance* is derived from the Latin *tolerare,* meaning "to bear," so the concept of forbearance or putting up with something not agreeable is inherent in the concept of tolerance. Thus logically built in to the very idea of tolerance is the *presence of disagreement*. It would make no sense to be tolerant of a public policy or practice we agree with. The concept of tolerance is not relevant when there is no dispute or discontent about the way things should go or the way they should be done. Toleration need only be brought to bear when there is tension, when there is a disagreement about what is fitting and proper, whether the context be public or private.

For example, I may disapprove of my community's decision to support a raise in my property taxes, but I tolerate this decision of local government and abide by it rather than fail to pay my taxes or attack my neighbors. Similarly, in a private context, I disapprove of my spouse's smoking habit and wish she would quit it, but I do not physically seek to restrain her from doing it, nor do I constantly verbally harangue her to kick the habit.

So disagreement itself cannot constitute *intolerance,* that is, the failure to be tolerant when one ought to be. This is an extremely important trait of tolerance. Simply by disagreeing with a religious belief, public policy or behavioral habit I am not *therefore* automatically acting in a manner that is insensitive or intolerant. It would be inaccurate, not to mention uncharitable, to say that I was. Dissent is not immoral. The moral quality of dissent is determined by the style of its expression and the substance of its conviction, not by the simple fact it is disagreement. So, as philosopher Jay Newman remarks, in the context of tolerance amidst religious diversity, "Tolerating a religious belief . . . does not involve a half-hearted acceptance or endurance of the belief *in itself,* but rather it involves acceptance or endurance of *someone's holding* that belief, that is, of a certain case of believing."[2]

We do not have to agree with people in order to be tolerant, to treat them civilly and with respect. Any suggestion that we do is nothing less than a manipulative call to intellectual stagnation and mental conformity. The demand for acceptance and affirmation—by urging upon dissenters this false tolerance—is itself intolerant because it would require the assent of others who do not wish to give it. It is as such a form of coercion and intellectual imperiousness.

This mistaking tolerance for affirmation was on vivid display in the United Nations' decision to declare 1995 "The Year of Tolerance." In the UN's declaration, tolerance was defined as "respect, acceptance and appreciation of the rich diversity of our world's cultures, our forms of expression and ways of being human."[3] Here the very idea of disagreement, which has to be present before tolerance even becomes a relevant concept, is completely missing. The UN mistook affirmation for tolerance. Without the presence of objection and disapproval, we cannot even get to the work of exercising tolerance. Under the UN's unfortunate misdefinition, fair-minded criticism of a culture's practice, say, Saudi Arabia's denial of female suffrage, qualifies as a narrow-minded disrespect for that nation. In this way the substitution of acceptance for true tolerance leads to conformity and acquiescence to injustice.

But this is not to say, of course, that in every instance we are tolerably disagreeing with someone, we must openly and overtly express our disagreement. Sometimes tolerance is expressed in a prudent and long-suffering silence. The American author and critic Robert Benchley once recounted an uncomfortable moment at a reception by saying, "Drawing on my fine command of language, I said nothing." In some cases toleration is manifest in critical debate and dialogue, in other situations it is best expressed in silence and solicitude.

Principle 2

The practice of tolerance must have limits. Many people think uncritically about tolerance, particularly—ironically—at universities. Bestselling author and longtime University of Chicago professor Alan Bloom famously noted this basic impulse of the contemporary American secular mind. Referring to his long experience with college students, he wrote, "The danger they have been taught to fear . . . is not error but intolerance. . . . There is no enemy other than the man who is not open to everything."[4]

Though American culture today exalts the general idea of tolerance to a kingly place among contemporary values, this is an unwise coronation. Any collection of values that places tolerance at its peak will quickly topple over from the weight of its impossibility.

Tolerance, of course, should not be extended to every person in every circumstance. For example, an individual who, out of a strong desire to be tolerant and nonjudgmental, stands by and watches a heinous assault being committed—doing nothing to stop it or call police when he or she has the ability to do so—could hardly be praised for being tolerant of the beliefs or actions of others, in this case a violent attacker.

In fact, we would normally assign moral culpability to such a person because we know that some actions, and by implication the values from which they spring, ought not be countenanced in any way. As J. Budziszewski notes, "According to our [moral] intuitions, not everything should be tolerated. The duty of tolerance, then, does not take the form 'Tolerate.' Rather it takes the form, 'Tolerate what ought to be tolerated.'

What this shows us is that tolerance is not a mechanical duty, but a duty involving judgment."[5]

We already know this to be true, as our rightfully vigorous judgments against slavery, Jim Crow, the Holocaust and other gross violations of human rights indicate. Tolerance is one value among other important values. It is a virtue the exercise of which depends on a larger moral competence and requires a well-formed character. The classical Western understanding of the unity of the virtues (e.g., courage, honesty, loyalty, diligence) reminds us that the practice of toleration cannot be pre-scinded or removed from a more comprehensive or "thick" conception of the good. Just as a musical note is meaningless separated from the larger melody it is part of or a single word of an oration is unimportant when detached from its context in the speech it is part of, tolerance by itself is incoherent. Since the panoply of human virtues are interdependent, tolerance cannot be understood, practiced or taught in an ethical vacuum. The liberal American habit of "being tolerant" or "teaching tolerance," as though this is a reasonable and realistic solution to our contemporary moral crisis, is as impossible as it is superficial.[6]

So tolerance operates in personal and social relationships in conjunction with other goods; it does not rudely lay atop them, covering over their own distinctive good role and purpose. The very reality of a diversity of moral goods (e.g., innocent people ought not be harmed; we should not abet our friends' self-destructive habits) means that we must be ready to jettison tolerance if necessary to protect them. Simple human decency and concern demand this. So if I awake at night to find my roommate under attack by an intruder, I should come to his aid, and if my friend is an alcoholic and desires me to procure alcohol for her, I should refuse and seek to wisely intervene in her addiction.

That tolerance should not rigidly govern our lives is obvious. Any claim that tolerance should always be practiced is nothing less than an invitation to human brutality, on occasion, and moral relativism, uniformly. And undeniably moral relativism is illogical since it is self-refuting (e.g., the assertion that there are no objective moral truths represents itself as an objective moral truth; therefore if it is true it must also be false, which is nonsense). Neither is moral relativism logical socioculturally. As earlier noted, C. S. Lewis trenchantly showed in the appendix to his book *The Abolition of Man* that across epochs and cultures certain constant values such as respect for parents, benevolence, bravery and honesty in social relations have been consistently affirmed as matters of human obligation and moral duty.[7]

Relativism's appeal in these postmodern times of moral confusion has been chronicled exhaustively.[8] Anyone enamored of relativism need only pause and ask themselves if they have any *moral* expectation that their legal rights be observed or their physical safety be respected. A sliver of honesty on the part of relativists will quickly lead them to acknowledge that indeed they would be outraged by arbitrary arrest by the police or by the vicious brutality of the mugger. The moral relativist can be expected to act like the student-anarchist selling papers advocating social anarchy. A man passed by the student, who called out to him "Anarchy now, read all about it!" The man asked, "How much?" to which the student replied, "Twenty-five cents." The man snatched the paper from the student and walked away. As the student yelled at the man, "Hey, that's twenty-five cents!" the man laughed and said "No it's not. This is your first lesson in anarchy."

Any effort to universalize tolerance, apart from being self-defeating and illogical, is doomed because it would end up giving permission or free rein to those devoted to destroying tolerance. If we tolerate everything, the ethic of tolerance itself is fair game (along with every other good), and we have no grounds on which to proscribe even the most reprehensible conduct. Tolerance cannot be the bottom line or last word to human social arrangements. Tolerance needs limits. Philosopher Karl Popper called this the "paradox of tolerance." His description of this quality of tolerance is especially jolting in the post-9/11 world: "If we extend unlimited tolerance even to those who are intolerant, if we are not prepared to defend a tolerant society against the onslaught of the intolerant, then the tolerant will be destroyed, and tolerance with them."[9]

Principle 3

Tolerance allows for prudent moral criticism and strongly held individual belief. Toleration is not the same as moral silence or moral agnosticism. Someone who never disagrees with anyone about anything for fear of being intolerant even when they know the other person's ideas are incoherent, dubious or flatly untrue, is, well, a coward. Such a person is acting out of a defect in personal character or a capitulation to the cultural force of political correctness, not a sense of friendship or broad-minded humanity.

In fact, true and genuine concern for others—and respect for their dignity as individual and autonomous agents of serious reflection—would seem to drive at prudently pointing out those instances in which they appear to have erred or are plainly in the wrong. Open debate and intellectual confrontation, when performed with respect and sensitivity, is not a sign of intolerance or bigotry but rather it constitutes an overt recognition of the individuality and real moral agency of the person with whom one is dialoguing. If I take seriously the humanity of another person, I will expect of them reasonable, responsible and ethically sound behavior. To harbor such expectations of others is not harsh or unfair. In fact, to expect very little of others in terms of their behavior and character—to have no concern about the ethical direction in which they are forming their character by the habits they are cultivating—is a brutal indifference. We harm others if we do not regard their mental and behavioral habits as relevant and important to their well-being, both now and in their future.

Indeed, even directly confronting people with their own destructive behavioral habits is not a sign of intolerance but, quite the contrary, a mark of true compassion. High behavioral expectations of people are really a sign of respect and concern for them, not indifference and contempt. If you want to help someone, you will honestly and sensitively tell them their mistakes. If you care about somebody, you will consistently hold them to decent ethical standards. If you are compassionate to people, you will not excuse their wrongdoing but fairly name it, and carefully speak to them of the importance of following a tried and true moral code that can bring stability and success to their lives.

The misguided and sentimentalized conception of compassion preeminent in American life today is that nice, tolerant people will allow others to make whatever behavioral choices they wish, without telling them whether what they have done and the habits or tendencies they are thereby forming are right or wrong, personally edifying or personally corrupting. This is not genuine compassion.[10]

Indeed, this confusion of contemporary liberalism has particularly harmed the underclass. Since the 1960s American liberalism has manifested the habit of withholding from the poor, particularly the minority poor, the exhortation toward middle-class or "bourgeoisie" personal values that incline toward socioeconomic mobility, and they have done so in the name of compassionate tolerance, diversity, and the sophisticated recognition of the supposed viability of alternative lifestyles. Meanwhile, the underclass has continued to languish in the swamp of personal irresponsibility.[11] Secular liberalism has replaced the moral vocabulary of Judeo-Christian ethics with the therapeutic slogans of narcissistic culture, in which desires matter more than obligations, intentions more than actions and feelings more than character.[12]

In a long and socially corrosive philosophical journey since the Enlightenment of the eighteenth century, we have moved from a confidence in the wisdom of Western culture's intellectual heritage and Judeo-Christian foundations to a free-floating skepticism about the possibility of knowing objective reality and moral truth. This intellectual devolution has continued since the middle of the twentieth century, and it has manifested in a sneering rebuke of traditional morality and a complacent subjectivism smugly nestled in the obfuscating bushes of "discourse communities," "linguistic paradigms" and "sociocultural contexts." But this nonrealism and jargon of postmodernism, as well as the atomistic commitment to radical individualism it carries, is only the grinding noise of contemporary liberalism's drive to authenticate its contempt for traditional morality and to affirm that faith and ethics is a matter of taste, not truth, and that judgments about right and wrong are only acts of the will, and not public expressions of genuine human knowledge.[13]

Western culture has shifted from a recognition of the fact or phenomenon of pluralism to an ideological conviction that pluralism is itself a proper and normative template for understanding morality and social life.[14] Pluralism or "diversity" has been translated from simply a description of social difference to a value claim about the secular and antitraditional way we are morally obliged to think about ethics and truth. Hence, the misguided yet pervasive view that anyone who really, explicitly believes anything—especially Judeo-Christian values—cannot be tolerant. William Bennett comments at length on this lamentable cultural condition:

> Deep moral convictions are often thought to be antithetical to the spirit of tolerance; in fact, they are not. A very particular and very misguided conception of tolerance holds sway today: the tolerance, rooted in relativism, that proclaims we cannot know right and wrong, that rejects assertions based on inviolable principle, that believes truth is a mere social construction. But this is not tolerance; this is moral exhaustion and sloth. Nor is it even sincere. For what we find in settings where "tolerance" is the chief byword is often something else entirely. College campuses, where the free marketplace of ideas should be flourish most impressively, may be characterized by speech codes, tactics of intimidation, and coerced political conformity.
>
> Properly understood, tolerance means treating people with respect and without malice; it does not require us to dissolve social norms or to weaken our commitment to ancient and honorable beliefs.[15]

Tolerance, then, rightly understood, brings to bear on ethical issues the God-given gifts of human reflection, analysis, moral intuition and far-reaching concern for the well-being of others. The practical wisdom of tolerance in conjunction with our firm moral knowledge leads us *to* humane and discerning judgment, not *away* from it. As one philosopher insightfully and concisely observed, "[Tolerance] is not forbearance from judgment, but the fruit of judgment."[16]

Principle 4

There are important distinctions to be made within the concept of intolerance and between the concepts of intolerance and nontolerance. Aldous Huxley's increasingly prescient novel *Brave New World* depicts a future totalitarian order with a twist: unlike most dystopias in which totalitarianism is enforced by draconian law and an iron fist, Huxley's "World Community" is ordered by government-sponsored hedonistic addictions and tranquilization. In a key scene near the end of the book, John Savage, a rebel against the order, delivers a speech against the government and causes a riot in a "death-conditioning" hospital. The state's police soon arrive armed with "soma" spray (a tranquilizing vapor) and lavish the anesthetic on rioters. One policeman follows the protocol of turning on an anti-riot "Synthetic Music Box," and

> a Voice began to speak. The Voice of Reason, the Voice of Good Feeling. The sound-track roll was unwinding itself in Synthetic Anti-Riot Speech Number Two (Medium Strength). Straight from the depths of a non-existent heart, "My friends, my friends!" said the Voice so pathetically, with a note of infinitely tender reproach that, behind their gas masks, even the policemen's eyes were momentarily dimmed with tears, "what is the meaning of this? Happy and good," the Voice repeated. "At peace, at peace." It trembled, sank into a whisper and momentarily expired. "Oh, I do want to be happy," it began, with a yearning earnestness. "I do so want you to be good! Please, please be good and . . ."
>
> Two minutes later the Voice and the soma vapour had produced their effect. In tears, the [rioters] were kissing and hugging one another—half a dozen twins at a time in comprehensive embrace.[17]

Today we find something akin to mind-numbing soma-spray and Synthetic Anti-Riot Speech Number Two being deployed in public controversy: it is the tranquilizing plea to not be divisive, not to be exclusive, not to be *intolerant*. The miscast charge of intolerance is especially effective in muffling well-intended and fair-minded dissent; it is a veritable reputation ruiner today, first cousin to other frequently misunderstood and wrongly applied taboos in our culture of political correctness, such as racism, sexism, insensitivity and so on. "Be nice, be nice my friends, don't be meanspirited," sounds the Voice of Good Feeling today, "bad people are intolerant, good people are tolerant, be nice, be nice."

Well and good. It is bad to be intolerant, but what exactly is intolerance?

Shades of meaning in intolerance. In *The Revenge of Conscience* J. Budziszewski reminds us that tolerance is an Aristotelian-type virtue. Just as, say, the virtue of courage is midway between fear on the one hand and recklessness on the other, tolerance is situated between its own excess and deficit, between being too tolerant (what Budziszewski calls "softheadedness") and not tolerant enough (what he calls "narrowmindedness"). Budziszewski explains, the "truly tolerant point will always be somewhere between the two endpoints of the continuum, its location depending on the act in question and on the circumstances."[18]

Recognizing that true tolerance is a golden mean leads to a richer understanding of intolerance. Budziszewski continues: "Right away we see that intolerance shows itself in two different ways, for we can err in either of two different directions. One way is by an excess of indulgence—putting up with something we should suppress (softheadedness). . . . The other way that we can err is by a deficiency of indulgence—suppressing what we should put up with (narrow-mindedness)."[19] Softheadedness is a type of intolerance in the sense of wrong toleration, that is, tolerating what ought not be tolerated. It is a mistake in the exercise of tolerance and so qualifies as a type of intolerance. Narrow-mindedness is intolerance in the more straightforward and commonly used sense of not putting up with what you should.

For the purposes of our discussion we will call the excess of toleration (which is softheadedness) "hypertolerance" because it tolerates too much, and we will call the lack of tolerance (which is narrow-mindedness) by its classic term "intolerance."

Intolerance as narrow-mindedness. Let's consider intolerance in the sense of narrow-mindedness first. Intolerance is an immoral deficit of the virtue of tolerance; it is failing to be tolerant when we should. This narrow-minded intolerance has both a political and cultural context. First, to the political.

Politically, to tolerate is to keep lawful. A society that maintains the lawfulness of the distribution and consumption of alcohol, for example, tolerates the sale and consumption of alcohol along with its ill effects and abuses. Conversely, because intolerance is the lack of tolerance, to be intolerant is to proscribe as illegal that which really should be legal. So it may be said that Prohibition of the early twentieth century, which criminalized the sale and use of liquor, was narrow-mindedly intolerant (though certainly well-motivated and correctly wary of the potential harm of alcohol) because it made unlawful activities that for either moral or overridingly pragmatic reasons should not have been criminalized.

Though it is important to note this legitimate political usage of the term *intolerant* (i.e., unjustly criminalizing an activity that ought to be lawful), the term is not widely used in this way in public discussion today. Rather, today the distinctive *cultural* formulation of "intolerance" (in the sense of narrow-minded) is more commonly used—or *misused.*

The cultural misuse of narrow-minded intolerance. To be branded with the cultural sense of intolerance today and its connotation of narrow-mindedness is usually simply the consequence of refusing to enter into the contemporary secularist redefinition of tolerance as the acceptance as true and morally legitimate every nontraditional value claim and personal practice. The new tolerance is of course now mainstreamed in American life. Most citizens sense this new tolerance is a counterfeit. But in their zeal to remake the American ethos into the image of their secular liberal worldview, our cultural elites peddle it openly. For example, recently one dean of a school of education at an elite university said tolerance means "the elevation of all values and beliefs to [a position worthy of equal] respect."[20] Likewise, a U.S. federal judge similarly assured us in a recent opinion that "all faiths are equally valid as religions."[21]

Not even the august U.S. Senate is untouched by this confusion. For example, the 1999 United States Senate Resolution 133, titled "Supporting Religious Tolerance Toward Muslims," reads: "Muslims have been subjected, simply because of their faith, to acts of discrimination and harassment that all too often have led to hate-inspired violence."[22] Of course the outrageous irony of these words, just two years before the bloodbath of Islamist bigotry that occurred on September 11, 2001, is profound. The resolution, sponsored by Republican senator Spencer Abraham of Michigan piously concludes "that any criticism of Islam, though legal, is morally reprehensible."[23] The vague words in the body of Senate Resolution 133 are a classic example of the contemporary doublespeak about tolerance, which, in the name of tolerance, forbids dissent. It reads, "while the Senate respects and upholds the right of individuals to free speech, the Senate acknowledges that individuals and organizations that *foster* such intolerance *create an atmosphere* of hatred and fear that *divides* the nation."[24] Here, criticism equals intolerance. Exactly how criticism ominously "fosters" intolerance and "create[s] an atmosphere" of hatred and fear (by whom?) that "divides" the nation (America is otherwise unified but for the criticism of Islam?) is all left unexplained.

This resolution was part of a concerted campaign to silence critics of militant Islam in the 1990s—critics who had been trying to warn America of the imminent danger posed by Islamist terror worldwide and of Islamic terrorist cells active in America, specifically. Critics—such as Steven Emerson, Dore Gold and Daniel Pipes—whom the resolution tarred as intolerant and divisive, have in fact been vindicated as insightful analysts and thus have been taken seriously since 9/11 and the many Islamist terrorist attacks since.[25] This, even though ethnic-interest pressure organizations such as the Council on American-Islamic Relations (CAIR) still seek, in Daniel Pipes's words, to silence "those who have anything negative to say about militant Islam" by predictably libeling critics as intolerant and divisive.[26]

In the charge of cultural intolerance and narrow-mindedness against critics of CAIR and in the similar refrain indignantly sung by so many political, ethnic, religious and feminist grievance groups all cynically angling for the psychological, moral and political advantage on the playing field of American public opinion, we hear the whir of Huxley's "Synthetic Sound" machine and the purr of the "Voice of Good Feeling," "Be good friends, don't be divisive, be tolerant, be good, be good, dear friends." This strategy of liberal secularism uses the charge of intolerance in the sense of narrow-mindedness in a cultural context to great effect, and although this amounts to no more than an ad hominem attack, it exerts great pressure on the critics. It has a silencing effect on them, and it discourages future criticism.

The sleight-of-hand casuistry found in such reckless and manipulative charges of intolerance is based on a logical fallacy, the fallacy of the false dichotomy. In this case only two positions on a given issue are recognized as legitimate: tolerance or intolerance. For example, make the point in public discussions that militant Islam is hardly a fringe sect of worldwide Islam but has up to 100 million Muslim adherents, and a great many other supporters across the Middle East and Asian lands where Islam predominates. When you have so argued, you likely will be angrily pressed to answer this question: Are you a person who encourages tolerance toward faiths other than your own, or are you prone to make intolerant remarks about another's faith? Choose a side: either keep your silence as a sign of your "tolerance" toward the ideology of Muslim terrorists, or advance your "divisive" and "intolerant" criticism. It is unfortunate—though not surprising, given the way the question is framed—that many just keep silent.

This same rhetorical strategy happens over and over again on topics from same-sex marriage to abortion to affirmative action. About such quashing of opinion, Stephen L. Carter writes: "Nowadays lots of Americans seem reluctant to join public moral conversation, seeming to fear what others might say in return. This is a tragedy. A society that refuses to speak the language of morality is more fearful than free."[27]

Carter's point is well-taken, but we must add that these tactics of intimidation spring overwhelmingly from the left of the political spectrum, not the right, who in the arena of public debate are consistently on the defensive, denying they are homophobic, racist, sexist or otherwise bigoted vis-à-vis the topic at hand.

Hypertolerance. Recall that authentic tolerance is a golden mean between two mistaken extremes, narrow-mindedness and softheadedness. Having discussed legitimate and illegitimate applications of the charge of intolerance in the sense of narrow-mindedness, we will now look at intolerance in the sense of erring on the side of softheaddedness, what we have called "hypertolerance." Hypertolerance is legally permitting that which should not be permitted or praising that which is blameworthy or remaining silent toward an injustice.

For example, early on the morning of September 11, 2001, even before incredulous Californians watched the first flaming Twin Tower collapse, many had retrieved their morning edition of the *Orange County Register* from their lawns and saw its front-page photo and glowing story observing the opening of a new mosque in the county. Post-9/11, such an uncritical panegyric to the romantic mysteries of Islam would be unthinkable. But this story, having gone to press the night before American consciousness changed, was indicative of widespread journalistic efforts to mainstream Islam in America. The irony of this coincidence is that such efforts had included for decades a strained hypertolerance of all things Islam in public forums, perhaps most notoriously in university classes in comparative religion. For a variety of reasons academics everywhere in America, and patently in so-called conservative Orange County, had for decades bent over backward to disabuse religion 101 students of the wild and reckless prejudice that Islam had any connection with terrorism. For professors to privately imagine such a link was pathological; to suggest it in class was banishment; to publish reservations concerning the politically correct lecture litany—*Islam* means "peace"—was academic suicide. Such a critic would certainly be assailed as failing at tolerance.

The photo on the cover of the *Orange County Register* was part of the hypertolerance happy-face approach to Islam that had prevailed in the country. The twisting of tolerance into overindulgence regarding Islam had suppressed commonsense criticism of a genocidal strain of Islam, and thwarted honest public reflection.[28] Once again, the confused conception and application of tolerance as a personal and social virtue damaged our society's ability to critically engage an important matter, in this case, understanding the religion of Islam in all its various manifestations.

To tolerate rightly: Critical tolerance. Given these shades of meaning in intolerance (narrow-minded intolerance of both the political and cultural types, and softheaded hypertolerance), how might we rightly understand the meaning of the positive concept of tolerance? The fact that "critical tolerance" might easily be misconstrued as a contradiction in terms suggests the very need for it today. Because the simple term *tolerance* is wrongly identified with approval so often today, the term *critical tolerance* helpfully returns us to the original meaning of tolerance.

The historic, classic understanding of tolerance is that it may allow an evil or an action generally reviled because its legal suppression would result in an even greater evil. Tolerance has *within itself* then two poles, positive and negative. The positive pole of tolerance is *allowance,* that is, legal permission with no sense of community approval necessarily accompanying this legality. The negative pole within tolerance is *critique*—a critique of the evil that true tolerance recognizes but prudently refuses to criminalize. Therefore our term *critical tolerance* is hardly a contradiction in terms but an expression of the positive and negative aspects inherent within true tolerance itself. Critical tolerance avoids the false dichotomy of the contemporary tolerance-intolerance split (albeit *tolerance* in that sense is misconstrued) and so redeems cultural criticism. Critical tolerance, the true understanding and practice of tolerance, allows us to identify that which is morally wrong, to exercise our moral faculties, but not necessarily accompany this exercise with legal proscription, though certainly allowing for the use of social stigma or other cultural expression of communitarian will.

Indeed, social habits and the ethos they create can be steered and cultivated by means other than the blunt force of law. This is important to remember. Historically American culture preserved its Judeo-Christian flavor through sociocultural vehicles such as stigma, the generally accepted legitimacy of morally imbued voluntary associations like churches and the Boy Scouts, and cinematic and literary affirmations of Judeo-Christian morality.[29] It is a part of the story of our civilization's decline that such nonlegal institutional strategies are increasingly effete in their practical efficacy to resist the cultural scrubbing away of our Judeo-Christian order in favor of secular liberalism.[30]

A recovery of vigorous moral criticism—free from the demagoguery of what might be called the "tolerance card"—is sorely needed today for one obvious reason: to counteract the glib and civilly dangerous dismissal of critics of militant Islam as intolerant by Islamic apologists. Critical tolerance, with respect to this issue, vigorously affirms the First Amendment rights of Muslims in America to freely practice their faith while openly protesting elements of contemporary Islamic rhetoric that are immoral, anti-Semitic, anti-Christian, anti-American, anti-Israel and simply genocidal with regard to these respective religions and nationalities. In this way, critical tolerance shakes its head, though not its fist.

Figure 1 represents the two types of intolerance we have discussed (soft-headed hypertolerance and narrow-minded intolerance) and their relationship to genuine critical tolerance.

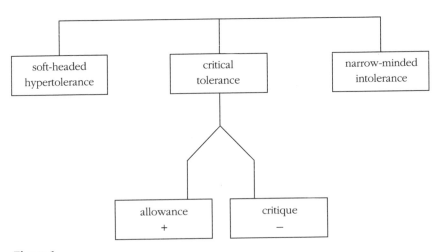

Figure 1

Nontolerance. Having considered the relationship of mistakes in toleration to its authentic practice, what can we say about the straightforward refusal to tolerate? What of the proper criminalization of practices that are justly and properly unlawful, like racial discrimination, theft, battery, forgery and homicide? We would like to suggest the simple and straightforward term *nontolerance* to describe the proper political and cultural attitude toward such deeds.

A society's just proscription of a practice is nontolerance of that practice. To be nontolerant of a practice is to regard it as too bad to allow, as so harmful to an individual person or the fabric of human community that it must necessarily be outlawed. Legal punishment must be given to morally criminal acts to both discourage them and to affirm the minimal ethical vision of a society.

Partial-birth abortions should be seen as a case in point. In this bloody and violent "procedure," also called the D&X (Dilation and Extraction)— the doctor pulls all of the fully developed baby except the head down into the vagina. The doctor then takes a pair of blunt scissors and forces the scissors into the base of the baby's skull, spreading it to enlarge the opening. Using a suction catheter, the doctor then sucks out the brain of the infant human being, killing him or her.[31] A law which forbade this hideous practice would be a good law.* Society's nontolerance of partial-birth abortions would be just.

Thus it is clearer to speak of a law against partial-birth abortions as nontolerant of this evil rather than intolerant of it, since, first, *intolerance* is so often wrongly used the term has lost much of its moral force today but also because *nontolerance* simply denotes refusing to make or keep legal a morally objectionable practice, whereas the word *intolerance*— if construed in the sense of narrow-mindedness, as it usually is—can be taken to denote a failure to be tolerant of that which should be tolerated.

Note, intolerance as a concept has an inward focus. It points our at-

---

*The Physicians' Ad Hoc Coalition for Truth was founded by four doctors specifically for the purpose of exposing the medically fraudulent and true moral nature of partial birth abortion. An article by these four doctors, which appeared early in the debate over this topic, provides a full debunking of partial-birth abortion as a sound medical practice. See Nancy Romer, Pamela Smith, Curtis R. Cook and Joseph L. DeCook, "Partial Birth Abortion Is Bad Medicine," *Wall Street Journal,* September 19, 1996, p. A20. See also the letter to the editor by the same four doctors in the October 14, 1996, edition of the *Wall Street Journal.*

tention inward toward the sentiments of the community or the mind of the individual moral actor who is in the wrong, failing to manifest an intellectual, emotional and psychological orientation of permission toward a practice which should not be outlawed. Conceptually, intolerance directs attention *into* the character of the person or persons, whereas the word *nontolerance* better focuses outward on the character of the deed itself, on the objective moral context external to any of the human actors in the situation. It is the internally directed force of the idea of intolerance—coupled with a frequent disregard for the objective moral status of an external action—that has made it easy for liberal secularists to misappropriate the idea and draft it into the service of their cultural assault on traditional American values in general and on the Judeo-Christian moral tradition in particular.

Principle 5

Tolerance is a moral tool that allows for the construction and maintenance of civic order. " 'Peace, peace,' they say, when there is no peace," cried Jeremiah (Jer 6:14). One meaning of the prophet's cry is that a society's surface appearance of order and peace—its trains running on time, its highways neat and clean—may belie a deeper and insidious social disorder. Remember, images of Iraqis placidly buying and selling in the marketplace, and going to and from work did not hint at the moral disorder of injustice and terror that permeated their society in the shadow of despot Saddam Hussein's sword.

Hussein's winning 100 percent of the votes (not 99 percent but 100 percent!) in the Iraqi 2002 presidential election—each ballot dutifully signed by the Iraqi who cast it—reminds us more of the droning unity and order of the beehive than of the untidy but vital point and counterpoint of human society. This recent Iraqi experience demonstrates once again that the principle of true civic order is not mere outward peace per se, for tyranny can achieve this, but rather what Augustine called the *tranquillitas ordinis*—the peace of a truly just and human order.[32] Augustine's own conception of that was brilliant yet nascent and has seen progressive development throughout history. The American founders built on Augustine's normative vision of the good society by envisioning a *novus ordo seclorum,* a new order of the ages, a truly moral civic order committed to self-government, the charters of which were the Declaration of Independence and the U.S. Constitution of 1787.

We can point to at least four basic ways that the proper practice of toleration supports and enhances civic order.

First, the civic order characteristic of a good republic grants its citizens broad rights to self-determination, a natural liberty they practice in a legal ambience of toleration. Social and political organization is to enhance human lives, not vice versa. Tolerance allows the human person to determine what he or she is, to craft his or her own identity as well as to use his or her economic and personal capital as he or she sees fit. In totalitarian regimes, what a person is and has is ordained by the state. Toleration in a democratic order is an indispensable hedge against this total and inhuman conformity to the Leviathan of overreaching government.[33]

A noteworthy subdivision of this aspect of tolerance is religious toleration. Indeed, the very word *toleration,* as it occurs in the writing of the American founders, consciously intends religious toleration: a full allowance of differences as they pertain to religious confession and worship.[34] Such toleration is not only axiomatic to personal freedom (for what is freedom without liberty of speech and action?) but toleration as religious liberty also has practical national utility. As noted earlier, the wars of religion in seventeenth-century Europe—producing bloody civil disorder, coarsening cultures, weakening nations and draining the public coffers—taught the historically conscious American founders the indispensable practical value of legal religious toleration for civic order.

A second way that toleration supports civic order is to encourage the free exchange of ideas in the construction of public policy. The benefit here is twofold. Governments cannot afford to make reckless policy decisions, and democracies necessarily rely on the free give and take of ideas to produce effective policy—a public dialectic that helps refine the quality of ideas.

This civil conversation requires broad tolerance in the areas of freedom of speech and media, a fact recognized by the preferred position accorded the First Amendment by American courts deliberating matters of Constitutional law. Yet it is unrealistic to imagine that this conversation will never be without tension. The stakes are simply too high—even the fate of the nation—and, on a more humbling note, the pride of debaters is often entwined with the points of view they espouse. Thus rebukes of ideas are taken (and sometimes meant) personally. Yet at its best, civic conversation has about it something of a friendly tension, a commitment to agreeable disagreement, for the sake of the commonweal.

A further benefit to civic order from this free exchange of ideas activated by tolerance is civil peace. A government that intolerantly suppresses dissent dampens citizens' reflectivity, at least, and foments rebellion and sedition, at worst. A tolerant government invites civic order by insuring to the loyal opposition a public voice, thereby mitigating civic alienation and acts of desperation. Thus tolerance, especially in heterogeneous and comprehensively pluralistic cultures like our own, is a moral tool that fosters the construction and maintenance of civic order through dialogue. Genuine tolerance, practiced pervasively and affirmed by a society's central social institutions such as its educational, legal, governmental and journalistic establishments, can foster a cultural ambiance of open-mindedness and civility that allows human reflection and creativity to flourish in a unique and socially transformative way. Politically repressive regimes the world over know this, of course, which is why in them information is tightly controlled and dissent is crushed, lest the dynamo of civic tolerance take root in a society and the brilliance of human inventiveness be unleashed, subverting the forces of dehumanizing dictatorship and totalitarianism.[35]

Third, toleration sustains civic order by promoting cultural criticism, the vigorous analysis—in various venues—of the social values and practices that comprise the daily climate of a nation. Thus a sound ethic of tolerance is a tonic to the body politic. Tolerance does not disallow criticism of persons, practices or institutions but affirms its value, recognizing the primacy of human beings to their social setting. Pseudotolerance (any wrong understanding of tolerance) stifles this freedom of thought and expression by decrying critique as insensitive or divisive. This is a favorite rhetorical strategy of politicians attempting to sneak their particular agenda in under the radar of public critique by shaming their opponents into silence for having had the temerity to express a different opinion. This is the political correctness that pathologizes debate. "Stop being divisive"—or meanspirited or intolerant—"and agree with me," it seems to say.[36]

Fourth, tolerance rightly understood fosters civic order through its willingness not to be tolerant. Some deeds are simply too bad to countenance; true tolerance recognizes this and allows for prudent action, including criminalization. Pseudotolerance, on the other hand, is loathe to either criticize or criminalize its pet projects of social renovation. The limits to true tolerance help foster reflection by always driving us to consider the question, Is this action bad enough to outlaw?

The vitality and dynamic equilibrium of civic order perennially faces real enemies, both external and internal. Now true tolerance has a healthy sense of danger, a vital sense of self-protection analogous to that of living organisms. Tolerance recognizes friends of a society's well-being and predators to the common good. Tolerance does not shirk from exposé, practically heeding the principle popularly attributed to eighteenth-century philosopher Edmund Burke: "All that must happen for evil to triumph is for good men to do nothing." And when criticism is not a sufficient response to an immediate peril to justice and civic order, because that peril is so wrong or dangerous that it cannot be tolerated, tolerance's essential counterpart, nontolerance, urges criminalization. Without this ultimate option the defense of civic order has no teeth.

When pseudotolerance usurps true tolerance, sound judgment can be eclipsed. For example, according to reports, on the morning of September 11, 2001, though the Saudi hijackers circumvented electronic airport alarm systems with their humble weaponry—simple box cutters—bells went off in the heads of security guards who saw them, tripped by the Saudis' suspicious behavior.[37] But the guards failed to act, fearing complaints and lawsuits for "racial profiling," a favorite stratagem of the pseudotolerance squads of the American left, led most often by the American Civil Liberties Union and whatever ethnic interest groups feel aggrieved. Even after the highjackings, various commonsensical and crucial attempts to bolster American security were met by predictable cries of "intolerance!" The review of persons matching the general characteristics of highjackers at airports continues to be consistently miscast by the political left as sinister racial profiling.[38] Similarly, prior to 9/11, investigations into Islamic charities—that were later found to be sending money to Al Qaeda and other terrorists groups—were protested by Arab-American committees as discriminatory and intolerant. So too was

the suspicion of terrorist sponsorship directed at University of South
Florida engineering professor Sami Al-Arian. He was later arrested and
has been charged with supporting terrorist groups.[39]

While the right regard for tolerance and the legal presumption of innocence can themselves sometimes be co-opted by people of bad will
as a cloak for their wrongdoing, pseudotolerance—the suspension of
critical thinking because of the requirements of political correctness or
a confused understanding of tolerance—is uniquely dangerous, especially in times such as these.

Indeed, at this, the halfway point in our delineation of ten positive
principles of tolerance, it should be apparent that tolerance rightly exercised *always* requires vigorous and thoughtful analysis of the situation
at hand. Tolerance is an intellectually demanding art. How remarkably
dissonant this truth is with the contemporary practice of tolerance,
which relies more on the inertia of politically correct habit than on careful moral consideration.

TEN TRUTHS OF
TOLERANCE 2

Tolerance is only complacence when it makes no distinction
between right and wrong.

SARAH PATTON BOYLE

The American mind today has the careless habit of reducing people's very humanity to their conduct. What I do is who I am, and who I am is what I do, the assumption runs, and therefore any disapproval of my conduct—and by implication the moral opinions that inform that conduct—is a cruel rejection of my very self, a denial of my legitimate standing as a member of the human community. It is an unjustified attack on my value and standing as a human being.

This point of view is a quite mistaken exaggeration, and our next component of a proper conception of tolerance attempts to dispel this narcissistic outlook.

Principle 6

Tolerance is rightly applied only to people's conduct and expressions of opinion. To reject an idea is not therefore to reject the person who holds that idea; to disagree with the wisdom or goodness of a person's behavior is not to hate or mistreat that person; to critique a particular value or overall philosophy of life does not necessarily involve denying the humanity or equal standing under the law of those who advocate that value or worldview. A criticism is not the same as an insult.

A primary consequence of our cultural failure to realize this distinction is the hyperpetulance and obscurantism that characterizes our public discourse today. Claims of offense and disrespect fly free and easy, uncon-strained by any serious self-criticism. Yet the counsel of common sense makes clear that citizens do not have a right not to be offended by other people's ideas; they do not have a right not to be criticized respectfully; and their claims to being offended are not self-justifying or self-validating. While certainly politically advantageous in our culture of "victimization," simply asserting a psychic wound at the hands of a conservative's "insen-sitivity" is not a self-validating claim.[1] Nonetheless, because a person's whole humanity is seen as *fully* defined by his or her deeds, people wrongly construe fair-minded challenges to opinions or practices as in-sensitive, intolerant and disrespectful affronts. They mistake the practice of true tolerance as requiring assent to the *morality and truthfulness* of the behavior and ideas being tolerated. It does not. As Josh McDowell and Bob Hostetler rightly say of today's twisted tolerance:

> According to the new tolerance [of today], who I am is inseparable from what I do and think and believe; my identity is wrapped up in my culture and conduct. Therefore, if you express any disagreement with my beliefs, you are disparaging *me!* If you say my behavior is wrong, you're judging *me!* If you criticize my culture, you're criticizing *me!* If you can't accept [that is, affirm as morally legitimate] my lifestyle, you're being intolerant of *me!* . . .
>
> [B]ecause the new tolerance works from the false assumption that "what I do represents who I am," to accept and respect someone, *you must ap-prove and endorse* that person's beliefs, values, and lifestyle. And, if and when you don't, you are considered insensitive, intolerant, and bigoted![2]

The contemporary equation of what I do with who I am, in toto, is a misapprehension of human nature or rather a denial of any essential, transpersonal human essence.[3]

Although the full philosophical story here would take us much too far afield from the discussion at hand, we should say that Western culture's journey from the Enlightenment through Darwinism, biblical higher crit-icism, modernity and now postmodernity has left us with a secularized, instrumental and therefore *diminished* understanding of the human be-ing. We are caught in the grip today of a behavioral, physicalist outlook. "The human animal," as one popular book termed us, is how we under-stand ourselves.[4] In fact, it is not at all uncommon for explicit equations of human worth and animal worth to be announced—and taken seriously—in American public life.*

It should not surprise us then if we are the "thin" people of contemporary secularism—shorn of any objective essence and nonphysical characteristics—that what we *want* and *do* fully defines our very selves.[5] I am defined by my preferences and practices if all I am is a willing animal. The impoverishment of this contemporary view and the amazingly shallow and incomplete account of human existence, personality, relationships, creativity and aspiration it represents should be obvious. It denies the intuitive, classical and ennobling understanding of human beings as intrinsically dignified, bearing the image of God as free and creative personal intelligences. Further, it entails the rejection of a constant and natural moral knowledge as well as the abiding awareness of a Creator, with a persistent yearning for a relationship with him. These are all central components of the Judeo-Christian view of the person, which any strictly behavioralist conception necessarily omits.

The consequences of this omission for the social development of an ethic of toleration are disastrous; it undercuts the enduring, common humanity essential for the free, open and civil critique of the values motivating our behaviors. In contrast, when a transpersonal, intransient, ahistorical understanding of the human person is affirmed, we establish for ourselves the firm footing of community and common identity that we need for vigorous deliberation about the common good.

Principle 7

Tolerance is inconsistent with philosophical indifference. Though certainly the contemporary mind thinks otherwise, toleration and philosophical indifference are not the same thing. To be tolerant and uncaring about the truth or falsity of ideas are not the same thing. It is a widely held if unacknowledged assumption today that the most tolerant people are those who have the least conviction, who have the least confidence

---

*A recent example is the advertising campaign of the animal-rights advocacy group PETA (People for the Ethical Treatment of Animals). Their series of ads, "The Holocaust on Your Plate," morally equates the human suffering endured by the Jewish victims of the Nazi Holocaust with the suffering of slaughtered chickens. For critique of PETA and this campaign, see Dennis Prager, "Burn Families, Barbecue Chickens," May 6, 2003 <www.townhall.com/columnists/dennisprager/dp20030506.shtml>.

in their ability to clarify and understand ethical ideas. The most broadminded are thought to be those who strike a pose of casual indifference to philosophically crucial questions of how we should live, what sort of person we should aim to become and what is truly good. This is a strange intellectual profile to admire. The spirit of our age seems to glorify mystification and perplexity, at least toward concepts connected to the vindication of traditional Judeo-Christian morality (e.g., When does human life begin? What is the proper purpose and scope of human sexuality? Are children better off with a mother and father as opposed to just one parent or two of the same sex?).

But it is not true that to exercise true tolerance we must not care about ideas or find ourselves unable to make distinctions between reasonable ideas and unreasonable ideas, and the relative practical and intellectual justification of disparate values. Real tolerance does not mean we must suspend our critical faculties or embrace an unrealistic homogenization of all values and norms. It does not draft us into the service of an unthinking, mentally totalitarian ethical neutralism, despite the ethos of contemporary liberalism, which generally insists otherwise. To say that toleration requires indifference is essentially to say that toleration requires moral relativism, a view that is plainly incoherent and which nobody really lives as though they believe to be true. After all, can you imagine a man happily agreeing to an order from the IRS that he pay double his rightful tax bill simply because the IRS ordered him to? Such an unfortunate soul would want an explanation and would then seek legal protection, since he believes that governmental agencies ought to be required to consistently follow just laws. Relativism is the temporary refuge of the disingenuous contrarian, and when a commodity or idea she cares about falls prey to its immorality, she will quickly find the arsenal of definite, objective principle and the true understanding of tolerance to which it is inseparably joined.

But beyond this, there is a deeper, psycho-emotional point to be grasped here. The pursuit of truth through intellectual or philosophical effort is a quintessentially human enterprise everyone is called to, particularly Christians.[6] It is a uniquely human endeavor and one that *humanizes* us, helping us to grow as people, as human persons in our spiritual, psychological, emotional, intellectual and social dimensions.[7]

Jacques Maritain, an influential twentieth-century Christian philosopher, once wrote: "Unless one loves the truth, one is not a man."[8] This statement is not merely an epigrammatic flourish but a principle that directs us to look at the very powers that make us distinctively human: the powers of love and intelligence. The human power of love quite naturally seeks the good just as our power of intelligence naturally seeks the truth. As love and intelligence are constitutive of our very being, to forfeit our search for truth is to forfeit nothing less than our very humanity—to effectively renounce being human. When we stop being sincerely concerned about what is good, just and true, we of necessity stop being concerned about human well-being. Yet such pursuits are among our most basic callings, and even in spite of human fallenness they are endeavors we somehow know we should be engaged in. So the statement "unless one loves the truth, one is not a man" is hardly just a line of flowery poetry. Rather, it is a plain description of how human beings look when they are truly acting human, and when they are not.

Principle 8

Tolerance is consistent with a strong confidence in the truthfulness of one's own beliefs and experience. It is widely believed today that anyone with intense convictions ought to be regarded with suspicion. While history certainly is littered with the damage wrought by various fanaticisms and delusions, this assumption of the contemporary mind is yet another incoherence disfiguring our ethic of toleration.

First, the self-refuting nature of this skepticism is important to note. If it is true that we ought always to be suspicious of those with strong beliefs, then surely we ought also to be wary of anyone who insists, "Reject strong beliefs!" Those who strongly distrust anyone with a strong opinion *because* that person holds a strong opinion, are themselves untrustworthy on that basis. The self-defeating nature of this principle disables it as a valid criterion for evaluating the legitimacy of others' convictions.

Further, it shows a moral confusion. After all, we would never reject such strongly worded statements as "Racism is evil!" and "Rape is always wrong!" simply because of the intensity of their pronouncement. Whether they are proper or not is not determined by the certitude of their declaration or the zeal with which they are announced, but rather it is determined by whether they embody sound moral sense and ethical good judgment. Martin Luther King Jr.'s cries for racial equality were not discounted for their passion and conviction, and neither should any ethical or religious claims ever be dismissed on that basis. When any idea or principle is asserted, the primary question which should present itself is, "Is that claim true?" Dismissing claims on grounds other than their having been shown to be false or untenable is fallacious. In fact, today's disinclination to give claims to objective, absolute truth a fair hearing is obscurantist and a version of the genetic fallacy of informal logic (dismissing an assertion because of its source). What is so ironic about this move of the secular establishment is that it is totally blind to the secular absolutism that is so much more powerful in American life today than the Christian traditionalism it frets over in the editorial pages, network television newsrooms and university classrooms it controls. Routinely the secular liberal lobbies such as the American Civil Liberties Union or People for the American Way litigate against an innocuous symbol of America's Christian heritage, like a Christmas crèche or landmark cross.[9]

One recent example is illustrative of this secular assault against Christianity. Grant Park, in Ventura, California, is home to a twenty-six-foot wooden cross on a windswept bluff. Erected in 1912 to replace an earlier cross set in place by Father Junipero Serra, a Franciscan priest responsible for building a string of missions along the California coast in the eighteenth century, the cross became a cultural and physical landmark to the people of the community. But in 2003 a San Francisco attorney, Vince Chhabria, realized that this object somehow constituted an "establishment" of religion, in violation of the First Amendment to the U.S. Constitution. Threatening to sue the city if they did not remove the cross or sell the land, Chhabria has local leaders reviewing their options.[10]

Such episodes are played out regularly all over the country and are emblematic of secular liberal intolerance toward Christianity, rooted in a confused and unreflective suspicion of all holding a vigorous commitment to the truth of their beliefs.

Principle 9

Since tolerance is inevitably connected with disagreement and moral evaluation, it helpfully compels us toward a philosophical confrontation with competing and irreconcilable perspectives about the good. Tolerance amidst the deep pluralism of contemporary life is not only a practical, civil necessity, it is also philosophically useful. It is of course useful in other important ways, but there is a unique intellectual value to tolerance that should be noted.[11]

By placing us under the moral duty of forbearance, that is, the obligation to listen and to watch our neighbors express their opinions and tastes, the ethic of tolerance gives us the reasonable expectation to be given a fair hearing also. Thus the culture of dialogue erected by tolerance well-practiced provides a forum for debate and examination of claims, counterclaims, objections and new arguments. As J. Budziszewski puts this intellectual utility, "What better engine have we for honing truth than to try it against error in a fair fight?"[12] Tolerance gives boundary walls to civic discussion, constructing a clear intellectual playing field in which we as citizens can articulate and pursue our differing visions of ourselves and our lives together. Thus likening tolerance to an engine is apropos because it indicates tolerance should work to drive deliberation forward toward first principles and foundational ideas and assumptions. Tolerance is not passivity of mind; on the contrary, it is activity of deliberation. Of course, this reflective movement in society requires the good faith of disputants to pursue the truth wherever it will lead them, and obviously that is sometimes hard to have.

Nonetheless, the value of tolerance in this regard is noteworthy since it is one of the cardinal confusions of our day that ideas and values— whether expressed as the public will through public policy or held as personal opinions by an individual—can be neutral, which is to say they enjoy a kind of nonideological, nonreligious pedigree. They allegedly descend from no particular worldview source or set of assumptions about personal and social goods, and therefore are to be much preferred to the parochial, hidebound biases of competing values, especially ones with their origins in the now suspicious Judeo-Christian tradition. This purported neutrality is a myth.

The "inevitability of particularity," the unavoidability of specific, value-laden philosophical commitments, directly disproves the assertion of value neutrality.[13] It is simply not logically possible to claim ethical or political knowledge without making a normative, that is a particularistic, claim. "Racism is bad," "Legal equality is good," "Random torture by the secret police is bad," "The rich should pay a higher percentage of their income in taxes than the poor should" are all claims that would be accepted by secular liberalism, the advocates of value neutrality. Yet each of them is a judgmental verdict about, respectively, what people deserve, how law should operate, what people should be protected from, what economic fairness means. We simply cannot make any meaningful claims about ethics, politics, society or religion without being morally or theologically specific, particular and partisan. This is really quite commonsensical, and in our daily lives we all have no difficulty operating in this normative, judgmental way. At the checkout counter we want our full change back; we will not tolerate being shortchanged, even accidentally; at the crosswalk, when we have a green light, we expect to be able to openly walk across the street safely, and if we are prevented from doing so or are struck by a car while doing so, we will believe the driver has done something discourteous or reckless; when standing in line at the post office and a clerk motions for us to come to be served, but the local city council member who just walked in the door cuts in front of us and goes to the clerk for service, we will firmly believe that we have been wronged. These sentiments and many others are rooted in beliefs and commitments that are themselves a part of our particular moral tradition and cultural practice.

If this rootedness and particularity are acknowledged rather than denied, then open and honest discussion can proceed about which values, and the worldviews implied by them, are most reasonable, most practicable, and actually true.

Principle 10

We should always be conscious of the various contexts in which tolerance is exercised. Toleration always takes place within a larger and inevitably moral context. The act of tolerance has, by definition, always been preceded by a series of moral judgments. For example, adultery is wrong, and I will not tolerate it in my life or abet it in the lives of others. But outlawing it seems likely to bring on more problems than it solves, so I maintain that it should not be illegal. Driving drunk is wrong and should be outlawed, but it should not be punishable with lengthy incarceration, unless someone repeatedly does it or injures someone else while doing it, in which case their transgression is greater, and therefore their liberty should be confiscated.

In thinking about the concept of tolerance and its embeddedness in moral calculus, it is helpful to recognize that tolerance has to be applied differently in different contexts. Tolerating someone's expressing a wrong-minded idea is not quite the same intellectual, psychological and emotional act as tolerating your spouse's taste in foreign films that you find dull. Tolerating a change in immigration law you disagree with is not the same as tolerating your Jewish friend's religious practice. We would like to suggest that the legal, social, religious and personal spheres are four distinct areas of human experience in which the act of toleration is expressed, albeit with a unique understanding in each case.[14]

Contexts of Tolerance

Political. Legal or political tolerance involves the de jure or legal protection of the freedom of assembly, speech, religion and other civil rights and liberties that a government chooses to codify. This form of tolerance is "tolerance through law," or the guarantee by law of the privilege to enter into certain activities. Of course, a nation's regime of legal tolerance is only as morally and civilly valuable as the nation's moral character itself. In other words, a nation that restricts religious practice to only one faith, for example, Islam in Saudi Arabia or Iran, does not have a culture of legal tolerance in the religious sphere that is of much use to its citizens who may not embrace Islam.[15] Similarly, the former Taliban government in Afghanistan may have allowed women to leave their homes, but having to do so covered from head to toe in a thick, heavy burkha, and only in the company of a close male relative—and subject to arbitrary beating and detainment by "virtue" police—hardly amounts to civil liberty. So while the mechanism of law can helpfully codify and establish a range of liberty, the specific content and definition of that liberty will vary widely from civilization to civilization.

Social. In the social arena tolerance simply means treating with dignity and respect people with whom we differ politically and culturally. The exercise of social tolerance presupposes an entitlement to decent treatment enjoyed by all people, without regard to their political views or social habits. I will not bomb the Cuban restaurant simply because I do not like Cuban food, nor should I steal the computers from the Republican congressman's office because I disagree with his voting record. Social tolerance is the simple etiquette of public life and is crucial to citizens' quality of life, especially in a pluralistic democracy.

It is the widespread awareness of the necessity of tolerance that makes the charge of intolerance—so often rendered against moral traditionalists as a proxy for real debate—so effective. For example, if the opponent of same-sex marriage can be portrayed by its supporters as personally bigoted and rude, her position will have little credibility with the public mind. Further, to the liberal secularist, the traditionalist's failure to be tolerant also speaks to his unique malevolence. Having no theory of universal human nature, the secularist can only conclude that the socially intolerant traditionalist is an especially deplorable person worthy of great censure. This inevitable posture of the secularist—misconstruing disagreement as bigotry—can easily lead to the unleashing of a corrosive hostility in public life.

On the other hand the traditional Judeo-Christian worldview being advocated in this book has the conceptual resources to attribute intolerance—when it finds the genuine article—to the flaws and weaknesses of general human nature and badly formed human character. This can protect and insulate the larger social order from the unnecessary anger and hostility that can accrue from reckoning one's ideological opponents as uniquely, extraordinarily decadent for their views, as we find secular liberals sometimes doing as they assail the "homophobia" and "misogyny" of moral traditionalists. But secular liberalism—holding only to a belief in the malleability and dynamism of human beings, and in a more or less inevitable progress for secular humanity—has no coherent philosophy of human nature or systematic understanding of character development, and thus has no such socially preservative philosophical means.

In the Christian tradition the unfortunate but universal disposition of people toward unjust intolerance in the social sphere, a hostility toward those who are not "people like us," has been recognized: from the Augustinian dictum *non posse non peccare* (since the Fall we are "not able not to sin") all the way to Reinhold Niebuhr's "Christian Realism" (the persistence of sin in individuals and groups compels a restrained view of sociopolitical possibilities). Christians' philosophical ability to attribute intolerance to a universal trait of people (i.e., their fallenness) rather than a specific ideological defect has a *humanizing* and *safeguarding* effect. It reminds us that we are all prone to such misjudgments and mistakes, and it protects us from demonizing one particular social, ethnic or religious group, and faulting their worldview as the most basic, most primary cause of their intolerance. While this is not to suggest that we do not hold people accountable for bad ideas or bad practices, or that we do not point out such things whenever we see them, it does underline the uniform frailty of human nature and the important fact that all of humanity is under the judgment of sin, and that dangerously false ideas of all kinds can emerge out of that corruption. Thus, for example, Boston University economist Glen Loury has said regarding racism that it is a problem of "sin, not skin."[16] As with other wrong and intolerant attitudes and practices, it is ultimately a failing of human nature, not the special province of any one particular racial group.

Religion. The third context for tolerance deals not only with people's actions but also with their religious beliefs. Tolerance in this context has mistakenly come to be understood as a matter of not making a veridical judgment about the content of any religious beliefs. So, the thinking goes, tolerance does not dispute the truth claims of others but rather accords them the presumption of truthfulness or at least the favor of indifference. But this wrongly assumes that saying nothing to dissuade someone from harmful beliefs (e.g., the practice of clitorectomy or female mutilation among some religious groups) or obviously false beliefs (e.g., the Black Muslims' conviction that white people were created by a mad scientist in a laboratory experiment gone awry) is a kindness.[17]

Yet there is a clear difference between a commitment to tolerance and a philosophical assumption of a uniformity in the truthfulness or harmlessness of belief across all religious traditions. Many writers on religious diversity have virtually entered into the contention that tolerance requires homogeneity of belief and thought. But this is a conceptual confusion. The best of human history indicates an understanding of tolerance based on the recognition of the inherent freedom and dignity of all persons, and their consequent right to be treated accordingly, whether or not they stand in religious agreement with us.[18] The distinctives of faith and practice proper to the various religious traditions need not be whitewashed in order for real religious tolerance to prevail.[19] We can hear, behold and otherwise experience other people's expressions of their religious beliefs without insulting, harming or otherwise attacking them, all the while dissenting from the full metaphysical accuracy and worldview adequacy of their beliefs.

Personal. In the personal context, perhaps more than any other of the contexts discussed, subjectivity rightly prevails. To be in close relationship with someone means to encounter them in the many dimensions of their lives, including their habits of mind, personality and body. In such a relationship we may not agree with or appreciate equally everything we come to know. Indeed some aspects we may find disagreeable or even objectionable. As the old saying goes, "A friend is someone you know very well—but like anyway." In this situation the greater good of maintaining the health and quality of the relationship overrides the distaste we may experience regarding some perhaps ugly attitude or behavior from the other individual: I hate fish, but my wife likes it, so I'll go with her to the seafood restaurant; I don't like country music, but my husband does, so I'll go to the concert with him.

Of course, a moral evaluation is necessary, because if your spouse, friend or colleague, for example, committed an armed robbery or assault of which you are aware, overlooking the moral imperative to hold them accountable to the law for the sake of preserving your relationship would be wrong. On the other hand, calling the police because my friend's DMV registration is overdue or because I saw him jaywalking would also be wrong, because the severity of the offense does not warrant my calling the authorities. Tolerance applied to a personal quirk, matter of taste or minor failing is appropriate and simply the application of common sense. But toleration is not synonymous with turning an ethical blind eye to the serious moral failings of our friends and loved ones, failings either harmful to the community (e.g., theft, battery) or the individual (e.g., self-destructive behavior). Toleration should never become a synonym for carelessness or license.

Consciousness, then, of the contexts of tolerance—legal, social, religious, personal—will help us to see the forest through the trees, as it were, and enable us to prudently practice tolerance in a manner befitting the situation at hand. For recall, tolerance in all of its contexts is never an end in itself but rather an instrument to preserve and accomplish the liberty, civility and individual happiness that a good society aims to secure for its members.

The Task Ahead: The Untwisting of Tolerance

Imagine a coiled telephone cord that is bunched up and tangled into a cumbersome ball. It is hard for you to pull the receiver to your ear without pulling the phone off the table or accidentally unplugging the cord from the phone. But after you patiently let the cord unwind and straighten out, you are able to use the phone much more easily.

Today tolerance has become twisted and knotted like one of those cords. As a result the idea does not work as it should in our society, and citizens on all sides of issues are frustrated about it. What is needed is some cultural untangling, some clear statements about the right meaning and use of tolerance, accompanied by clear debunking of its misuse. We hope this book has contributed to that work.

Our study has indicated that intense religious conviction can be fully compatible with a vigorous ethic of tolerance, and in fact such a moral practice is emphatically *required* and *supported* by the Judeo-Christian tradition. This tradition *uniquely* has the resources to uphold true tolerance and prevent its collapse into an antitraditional, secular intolerance based on an arbitrary selection of untested and ultimately incoherent assertions about human rights and purposes. Despite the official story of secular liberalism, the biblical Christian worldview is an intellectual setting well-suited for the nurturing and application of authentic tolerance, as the record of human civilization these past two millennia indicates.

The effort to fix our broken understanding of tolerance is the only course of action open to our pluralistic civil society, which by its nature depends on the reflective capacities of its citizens to navigate itself through the maze of values, concepts and policies that it may select as ordering ideas. Ultimately, civilizations that fail to choose wisely lead themselves over the cliff of confusion into a sea of destructive strife. The depths of history are littered with such wrecks. May the American experiment in self-government, so well-begun, never so founder.

EPILOGUE

Reflections on Evangelical Christian Witness Today
by Brad Stetson

What we practise, not (save at rare intervals) what we preach, is usually our great contribution to the conversion of others.

C. S. LEWIS

My feeling about people in whose conversion I have been allowed to play a part is always mixed with awe and even fear: such as a boy might feel on first being allowed to fire a rifle. The disproportion between his puny finger on the trigger and the thunder and lightning which follow is alarming. And the seriousness with which the other party takes my words always raises the doubt whether I have taken them seriously enough myself.

C. S. LEWIS

Every age and culture has its own challenges for Christian believers, who know they must bear witness to the truth of the birth, ministry, death, resurrection and return of Jesus Christ. As such challenges go, American Christians living in the first decade of the twenty-first century have it remarkably easy. Yes there are the cultural slights, double standards, insults and erosions of religious liberty, and the seriousness of these difficulties should not be underestimated. But throughout history, and still in many places today, the hardships some Christians face are not the constraint of their religious expressions but the constriction of their very throats. Christians are still murdered, all over the globe, for naming the name of Christ. Just yesterday, I read of a Palestinian Christian, a man who had just come to faith in Christ, who was murdered by Islamists. They quartered his body and mailed the pieces to his family as a warning to them and the community not to convert to Christianity. Such episodes should remind us that the word *persecution*—which evangelicals here are sometimes wont to use to lament their cultural disenfranchisement—has an altogether different meaning for Christians elsewhere.

So what then are American evangelicals to do, at this bank and shoal in time, as they seek to reach their fellow Americans living in the milieu of secular liberalism? I would like to suggest seven vital ideas that must be kept in the front of our minds.

Seven Principles of Personal Evangelism Today

First, as an awareness of what other Christians in other places face suggests, we should embrace and cultivate a deep sense of gratitude regarding all of life. In other words we must count our blessings and name them one by one, in the words of the old spiritual. It is not enough to simply render to God in prayer a general, all-encompassing "thank you" for our blessings. Rather, we should comprehensively reflect and specifically name to God—and one another, when appropriate—the realities, relationships, circumstances and commodities we are thankful for. From his provision for our salvation and relationship with him to our friends and families, to hardships and sufferings, to opportunities for school and work, to food, clothing, shelter and luxuries, we could probably spend quite a long time just in thanksgiving over the details of our lives. As we do this as a regular practice, we develop a deep consciousness of gratitude, a self-pervading awareness of God's hand continually at work in our lives. A personal orientation of habitual gratitude to God brings peace to our lives and a settled confidence that will help us minister to others, including evangelistically.

Inasmuch as we live in an age of ingratitude, where the will to power is exalted as somehow noble and indicative of strength, the warm, sweet aroma of a grateful heart will stand out to people, and in itself speak to them of a better way. And of course a personal disposition of thankfulness sharpens the mind, helping us to understand all manner of things as they really are. As the Reverend William Secker said over a century ago, recognizing the dividends of insight that come from an ingrained personal ethic of gratitude, "A grateful mind is a great mind."

A second principle we must remind ourselves of regularly is that moral excellence must be a reality in our lives. This is not to deny our need for God's grace or the enduring reality of our fallenness, but as a spate of writers in the area of spiritual formation have recently reminded us, we can train in righteousness. Honoring God in our lives does not happen by accident. We can and must plan for it, and practice or "work out" with the spiritual disciplines until we are formed in Christ, a process never truly over for us on this earth, even in the most advanced disciples of Jesus. You can be sure that the non-Christians in your life are watching you to see instances of hypocrisy and moral failing. They may feel, perhaps subconsciously, excused from the claims of Christ or that the gospel is somehow disproved or invalidated by your poor character. Hopefully, such is not the case, but human beings are skilled at making excuses for their own persistence in rejecting God. The deep truth in this tension that every Christian has with those around him, though, is that the nonbelievers in your life are, in their heart of hearts, secretly hoping you will show them a better way. They want you to show them the heart of Christ because there is within them, too, a subtle and perhaps unacknowledged yearning to know their Creator, and to be made right with him. Through moral excellence we can help create an interpersonal and social environment that inclines the ears of those around us to the voice of God's Spirit, speaking to them in those still, silent moments when sleep is elusive and the mirror of the soul unfogged by the day's business. As Charles Spurgeon once said, "A Christian should be a striking likeness of Jesus Christ. . . . We should be pictures of Christ."

Third, in the churning soul of the unregenerate person is a commitment to self-justification. It is as though self-justification is the default position of the human soul. We find it easy to convince ourselves we are not so bad; we can take care of ourselves; we don't need a savior. Americans today are probably self-sufficient if not affluent in their own lives, and they have been exposed to basic themes of Christianity through American culture. So they feel they already know about it, their cultural acquaintance serving as a kind of inoculation against genuine Christianity—thus the penchant for self-justification is especially strong. This shell can be hard to pierce, but knowing it is there and knowing its composition is helpful in understanding the psychology of the non-Christian.

Self-justification is a psycho-emotional, intellectual and spiritual quality that manifests itself in many ways, including New Age eccentricities (recall G. K. Chesterton's quip: "When people stop believing in God they don't believe in nothing, they believe in anything"), an essentially religious devotion to politics, a workaholic pursuit of career advancement, and moral relativism.

This latter is an exercise in psychological self-protection. If there are no objective moral duties, the relativist subconsciously reasons, then nothing I do can be wrong. Therefore nothing is wrong with me. No one can demonstrate to me that what I have done or hope to do is improper.

Moral relativism is a specious way of acquitting ourself at the bar of conscience. Our natural moral sense and the Holy Spirit tell us we fall short of the good, but rather than accept that about ourselves and hopefully find our way to the foot of the cross in repentance, we rationalize our misbehavior. Indeed, E. Michael Jones in *Degenerate Moderns* has perceptively described much of the intellectual edifice of modernity (the life and thought of Sigmund Freud, Margaret Mead, Alfred Kinsey and other prophets of contemporary secularism) as self-justification for sexual misbehavior specifically.[1] Relativism in this context is especially appealing to people because it allows them to continue practicing or pursuing sexual activities the Judeo-Christian ethic regards as morally wrong. Relativism licenses them, in their minds, to believe that the Judeo-Christian ethic is wrong, not their particular sexual predilection. In our culture today, where human sexuality in its many expressions is emphasized and cultivated, this absolution provided by normlessness is very useful (for a while, anyway, until the spiritual, moral, psychological and perhaps physical consequences expose the folly of such thinking).

A psychological self-deceit very similar to this takes place regarding tolerance, and it helps explain our contemporary confusion over the idea. If I manifest a total tolerance (that is, no standards of behavior) toward others, then I cannot be a hypocrite regarding my own failings since I made no judgments about others. By redefining tolerance as affirmation of others' behavioral choices, whatever they may be, I loose myself from any moral standards of conduct that I may fail to keep. So it psychologically pays not to judge others, because then I do not have to judge myself or accept the legitimacy of someone else's judgment of me. This contour of the contemporary mind corrupts true tolerance for the sake of self-justification, and turns the idea into a means by which I can demonstrate to myself and those around me that I am a broad-minded, compassionate, nonjudgmental and morally consistent person. I can never be a hypocrite, because I have not placed others under any standards of conduct.[2] This narcissistic attitude partly explains why the debased pseudotolerance of today is so attractive and so widely practiced. On the streets of secular society today, we are unlikely to get in trouble for being too tolerant.

Although this mechanism enjoys widespread use in the minds of contemporary Americans, it is misguided for three reasons. First, my wrong-doing is not made right simply by the fact that neither I nor those around me *think* that it is wrong. Second, this psychological self-deceit is just a way of trying to fake out our conscience. But it is a hopeless effort. Our awareness of our wrongdoing stays with us even if we deny we have done wrong, and even if we deny others—who have acted as we have—are guilty of any wrongdoing. Our moral sense is hard-wired into our consciousness; we cannot truly get rid of it. Deep down, even the worst tyrants, sadists or sociopaths know they are practicing wrongdoing. Third, judging oneself—or accepting reasonable criticisms of oneself from others—is not an activity that should be avoided. Such an exercise is no less than the path to moral progress and character development. Of course we should admit to ourselves our genuine wrongdoing, and of course we should, in sensitive, wise and patient ways, appropriately offer constructive criticism to those we care about regarding their own ethical shortcomings. That is proper compassion. Ignoring problems that need to be fixed is not a very effective method of care taking, either for our own souls or the souls of others.

A fourth issue regarding the contemporary mind is the fundamentally angry character of life today. Many people, it seems, go through their daily lives with an at-ready supply of rage. This rage might be unleashed at the slightest provocation: a long red light, a pedestrian in the cross-walk, being put on hold when calling the pharmacy, a glare from a stranger on the street, a long checkout line at the supermarket. The particular circumstance that brings to the surface the swirling brew of rage is irrelevant. The problem people face in embracing the gospel message is circumventing this roadblock of rage. People live with anger every moment of every day, like a malevolent conjoined twin, and it becomes an integral part of their self-understanding. Many people wrongly understand anger as empowering and its expression as a demonstration of strength. Thus, they think, to leave their anger is to become weak and vulnerable. This is an objectively false sentiment, but given the character of contemporary life it is understandable why those long joined with anger might feel this way. The believer must find a way, first through personal example, to show others that true strength lies in rest not rage, peace not petulance, patience not pride, forgiveness not fury.

Fifth, we should remember that deeds, not words, are the most effective tools for evangelism. The old saying "I can't hear your words, because your deeds are speaking too loudly" illustrates the natural human revulsion we feel when people hypocritically tell us to believe or do one thing and then act contrary to what they have just prescribed. It is a simple but important truth of human psychology that we must earn the right to a serious hearing from people when the topic is serious. Preaching the cross affects people much more deeply when we have shown in deeds that we care for them. If we show someone that their well-being matters to us, and we demonstrate in our conduct before them our own unconditional commitment in Christ, then our words of witness will hold more weight. God can much more effectively use what we say if we, as ambassadors of Christ, have represented our Master well. The old slogan is true: people don't care what you know, until they know that you care.

How then do we go about developing within ourselves genuine concern for the acquaintance, colleague or neighbor God has brought into our lives? The primary means is by praying for that person. With a specific, sustained, focused practice of prayer regarding a particular person, God will develop within us an authentic concern for that person. We will start to care about that individual's life and circumstances. This real sense of connection to the person will naturally lead to acts of civility, kindness and service that make it clear that you are a person of integrity, and this is a naturally attractive quality to people today.

Sixth, Christian apologists must remember that overwhelmingly people in contemporary American society reject the gospel for spiritual, psychological and emotional reasons, not for intellectual ones. Few non-Christians have conducted any kind of comprehensive review of the historical, textual, philosophical or psychological evidences for the truth of Christianity. There are internal, nonrational barriers to Christian commitment, always ultimately including the individual will itself. Unresolved anger at our parents' failures, unfulfilled hopes and dreams as well as just plain busyness and lack of reflection can all conspire to lock non-Christians into habits of unbelief.[3] So while rational apologetics of an evidential or presuppositional sort are of course important, we should not confine ourselves to those lines of argument alone in reaching out to people. Instead we need to be ready to meet people where they are—personally, psychologically, intellectually—and *comprehensively* communicate to them the all-surpassing and perfect love of Christ, which is the master key that alone can release people from the prison of patterned unbelief.

We are trying to reach *human beings,* not machines. Humans are not purely rational creatures who will simply audit the evidence before them and on that ground alone make a personal and profound commitment. Human beings carry with them a lot of *pain.* There is a galaxy of hurt swirling around inside the psyche of everyone we meet, and it is this suffering and the grief, anxiety, anger, hate and fear it yields that bind so many non-Christians to the ultimately frustrating outlook on life that they have embraced.

In just one summer at a local café I frequented, I met three people (all non-Christians, I would later come to find out) who were experiencing intense pain in their lives. All of these people were friendly, intelligent individuals who outwardly appeared like everyone else, but each was experiencing a powerful and unique pain. This locked them into patterns of thinking and feeling that were preventing them from understanding God's love, and from accepting how it could change their lives. William, a high school counselor, was a recovering alcoholic. Years earlier, driven to homelessness by alcohol, he had been left to die in a snow bank by his own father. Monica, an unemployed thirty-five-year-old mother of three young children, was enduring a nasty divorce proceeding. She had just been evicted from her apartment because, she was told, her kids were too loud for the neighbors. Steven, an engineer, was living alone in a trailer park. His wife, whom he had divorced two years ago, was threatening to move out of state with their two young daughters, whom he already saw infrequently. For these individuals the pain and frustration of their lives was front and center in their consciousness; it was all they could see. Any effort to speak to them of the possibility of a peace that surpasses all human understanding (Phil 4:7) would have to start right where they were at.

This all underscores again the imperative of showing through our character and conduct that it matters to us how people fare in their daily lives. Emotion, though rightly discounted as a governing principle of knowledge or ethics, is nonetheless the currency of our time. Those who wish to do "existential business" must learn to responsibly and sensitively trade with it.

Last, the Christian engaged in personal evangelism in these politically acrimonious and ideologically charged times must emphasize that the decision to come to faith in Christ is utterly apolitical and is essentially *personal.* The decision of faith is made primarily *because it is true* and only secondarily for one's own or society's benefit. Embracing the Lord of life involves a decision and then a journey of *ultimate spiritual and moral commitment,* which far exceeds in scope and depth any obligations of national citizenship, membership in a political party, social movement or participation in some other cause or organization. The kingdom of God radically transcends our loyalty to human institutions, ideologies and personalities. Emphasis of this truth demonstrates important wisdom, but it also has practical implications for our evangelism. There are no doubt many people in these polarized times who shrink at the prospect of Christian commitment because they feel that they would then become "one of those," whatever *those* may be: a member of the "religious right," a "fundamentalist," a "Jesus freak," a "right-wing extremist." The question, What will the neighbors think? weighs heavily on people's minds in matters religious, too, and it is the task of the believer to emphasize the utter singularity of Christian commitment. We must distinguish humble, genuine faith in Christ from national, political, social and ideological commitments, and from various public examples of those who associate themselves with Christian faith but who have engaged in political or social causes in sometimes unappealing ways.

Yet Christianity is an all-encompassing faith that pervades all of our life and being. Thus there are inferences about myriad subjects (ethics, psychology, politics) to be drawn from Bible-based Christian commitment, and certainly not all of those inferences on any given subject will necessarily have equal cogency. Christians have a duty to vigorously strive to believe and advocate values consistent with biblical faith.

The Opportunity Now

Not only should the Christian nurture an outlook conducive to effective personal witness, but the believer should also seize opportunities for the public witness to good moral order.

These present times, in all their complexity, should be regarded by evangelical Christians as a chance to be in the vanguard of articulating and practicing true tolerance toward a pluralistic culture in desperate need of it. As people explicitly committed to the distinctive truthfulness of their own particular religious creed, evangelicals uniquely offend today's dominant secular sensibilities and thus present a direct challenge to its relentlessly homogenizing force and its abduction of tolerance into its service. By asserting a clear philosophy of tolerance, this cognitive minority secures both for itself and others a fair hearing.

Evangelical Christians should also take the lead in this vital civic endeavor because its pursuit is intrinsically right. By asserting a clear philosophy of tolerance they serve the common good and evince an unassailable interest in it. This is because true tolerance by definition is a two-way street: it can never be manipulated to serve partisan interests of any kind, and its advocacy and observation only furthers and enhances civil rights and civil dialogue. Thus any outlook or worldview that urges the commonweal toward an authentic social ethic of tolerance can only be regarded by others of goodwill as politically humane and responsible. Furthermore, vying for a right understanding of tolerance debunks the pretensions of today's pseudotolerance, exposing it as the partisan tool it is and warning of its devolution into intolerance of every out-group, particularly those with religious commitments and traditional moral convictions.

So the confusions of our age amount to a forum for the clarion expression of a personal and social Christian ethic as well as the declaration of the gospel account of human experience and destiny. This is how believers should regard their social setting today, a context which, like all else, is ultimately superintended by the absolutely sovereign and loving God. Christians must also remember that the results and success of their personal, social, political or evangelistic strivings are not up to them. The liberty of genuine tolerance ever reminds us that people make their own decisions. Christians are never responsible for the formation of others' convictions; they are only responsible for living lives of integrity in Christ and faithfully and wisely proclaiming the Christian message in the many contexts of their lives.

And Remember

While Christians are called to love neither the world nor anything in the world (1 Jn 2:15), they are also called to be "rooted and established in love" (Eph 3:17), to "let [their] gentleness be evident to all" (Phil 4:5), and to allow their love to "increase and overflow . . . for everyone" (1 Thess 3:12). Thus disciples of Jesus must make an important distinction between ideas and the people who hold them. We must oppose with great intensity the values, sentiments and idea structures (the "noosphere," or mental atmosphere) that are corrupt and corrupting to human persons and their communities, but at the same time we must never permit that antipathy to infiltrate our attitude toward or treatment of those who hold such ideas. This unfortunately is not a principle that has received sufficient attention in evangelical circles. Too often moral revulsion, political opposition and philosophical dispute have become translated into personal hostility and alienation. However sharp and piercing the sounds of the culture wars may become, followers of Christ must always be vigilantly on guard against their own hearts being hardened toward others because of ideological difference.

Christian philosopher Dallas Willard summarized the matter well when speaking of how Christians should relate to their non-Christian neighbors: "If it is true that our ways will at some point part for eternity, I shall love them none the less for it. And the best gift I can give them is always *the character and power of Christ in me and in others who really trust him.*"[4]

SELECT
BIBLIOGRAPHY

Since books that are concentrated exclusively on toleration are curiously relatively rare, this bibliography is focused on them. Books marked with an asterisk (*) are written from an explicitly Christian perspective.

Bollinger, Lee. *The Tolerant Society: Freedom of Speech and Extremist Speech in America*. Oxford: Oxford University Press, 1986.

*Budziszewski, J. *True Tolerance: Liberalism and the Necessity of Judgment*. New Brunswick, N.J.: Transaction, 1992.

*Conyers, A. J. *The Long Truce*. Dallas, Tex.: Spence, 2001.

Fotion, Nick, and Gerard Elfstrom. *Toleration*. Tuscaloosa: University of Alabama Press, 1992.

*Gaede, S. D. *When Tolerance Is No Virtue*. Downers Grove, Ill.: InterVarsity Press, 1993.

Gilson, Étienne. *Dogmatism and Tolerance*. New Brunswick, N.J.: Rutgers University Press, 1952.

Heyd, David, ed. *Toleration: An Elusive Virtue*. Princeton, N.J.: Princeton University Press, 1996.

Horton, John, ed. *Liberalism, Multiculturalism and Toleration*. London: Macmillan, 1993.

———, and Susan Mendus, eds. *Aspects of Tolerance*. London: Methuen, 1985.

King, Preston. *Toleration*. London: Allen & Unwin, 1976.

Levine, Alan, ed. *Early Modern Skepticism and the Origins of Toleration*. Lanham, Md.: Lexington Books, 1999.

*Locke, John. *A Letter Concerning Toleration*. 1689; reprint, Amherst, N.Y.: Prometheus Books, 1990.

*McDowell, Josh, and Bob Hostetler. *The New Tolerance*. Wheaton, Ill.: Tyndale, 1998.

Mendus, Susan. *Toleration and the Limits of Liberalism*. London: Macmillan, 1989.

———, ed. *Justifying Toleration*. Cambridge: Cambridge University Press, 1988.

———. *The Politics of Toleration in Modern Life*. Durham, N.C.: Duke University Press, 2000.

Mendus, Susan, and David Edwards, eds. *On Toleration*. Oxford: Oxford University Press, 1990.

Newman, Jay. *Foundations of Religious Tolerance*. Toronto: University of Toronto Press, 1982.

*Taylor, Daniel. *Is God Intolerant?* Wheaton, Ill.: Tyndale, 2003.

Tinder, Glenn. *Tolerance: Toward a New Civility*. Amherst: University of Massachusetts Press, 1976.

———. *Tolerance and Community*. Columbia: University of Missouri Press, 1995.

Walzer, Michael. *On Toleration*. New Haven, Conn.: Yale University Press, 1997.

Weissberg, Robert. *Political Tolerance*. Thousand Oaks, Calif.: Sage, 1998.

Wolff, Robert Paul, et al. *A Critique of Pure Tolerance*. Boston: Beacon, 1965.

Zagorin, Perez. *How the Idea of Religious Toleration Came to the West*. Princeton, N.J.: Princeton University Press, 2003.

Notes

Chapter 1

[1]Dinesh D'Souza, *Illiberal Education* (New York: Free Press, 1991).

[2]Dinesh D'Souza, *What's So Great About America?* (Washington, D.C.: Regnery, 2002), p. 27.

[3]Ibid., p. 50.

[4]See Thomas G. West, *Vindicating the Founders: Race, Sex, Class and Justice in the Origins of America* (Lanham, Md.: Rowman & Littlefield, 1997), for further discussion of similar themes.

[5]Klaus K. Klostermaier, *A Survey of Hinduism* (Albany, N.Y.: State University of New York Press, 1994), p. 343.

[6]Ibid., p. 344.

[7]For description of this genocidal clash in Rwanda, see Michael Barnett, *Eyewitness to a Genocide* (Ithaca, N.Y.: Cornell University Press, 2003). On the political and social dysfunctions of sub-Sahara Africa generally, see Keith Richburg, *Out of America* (New York: Basic Books, 1997). See pp. 90-99 in Richburg's book for a compelling description of the Hutu-Tutsi conflict.

[8]James Redfield, *The Celestine Prophecy* (New York: Warner Books, 1994). For a critical analysis of the religious and political themes of Redfield's novel, see Brad Stetson and Joseph G. Conti, "Pulp Theology," in *Social Justice Review* 91, nos. 5-6 (2000). The remarkable commercial success of Redfield's fiction would be surpassed a decade later by Dan Brown's fantasy *The Da Vinci Code: A Novel* (New York: Doubleday, 2003), which likewise rejects historic Christianity. Helpful critiques of Brown's influential work are Darrell L. Bock, *Breaking the Da Vinci Code* (Nashville: Thomas Nelson, 2004); Erwin Lutzer, *The Da Vinci Deception* (Wheaton, Ill.: Tyndale House, 2004); and Ben Witherington III, *The Gospel Code* (Downers Grove, Ill.: InterVarsity Press, 2004).

[9]See Muriel Porter Weaver, *The Aztecs, Maya, and their Predecessors: Archaeology of Meso-America*, 2nd ed. (San Diego, Calif.: Academic Press, 1981), pp. 516-17.

[10]"Saudi Telethon Host Calls for Enslaving Jewish Women," April 26, 2002 <www.national review.com/document/document042602.asp>.

[11]Charles Krauthammer, "A Violent Religion?" December 6, 2002 <www.townhall.com /columnists/Charles Krauthammer/ck20021206.shtml>.

[12]David Harsanyi, "Fatwa: Coming to a Country Near You," December 6, 2002

[13]See Art Moore, "Sudan Jihad Forces Islam on Christians," March 4, 2002 <www.worldnet-daily.com/news/article.asp?ARTICLE...ID=26672>; "Islamists Burn to Death Christian Pastor, Family," June 4, 2003 <www.worldnetdaily.com/news/article.asp?ARTICLE...ID=32897>. See also the report by William L. Saunders Jr. and Yuri G. Mantilla, "Human Dignity Denied: Slavery, Genocide, and Crimes Against Humanity in Sudan," available from the Family Research Council at <www.frc.org/index.cfm?I=IS01K1&f=wuo4l11>.

[14]Paul Kelso, "Channel 4 Exposes Saudi Police Torture," *The Guardian*, March 5, 2002 <www.guardian.co.uk/saudi/story/0,11599,662104,00.html>.

[15]"Muslim Mobs Burn Christian Homes," April 28, 2004 <www.worldnetdaily.com/news/article.asp?ARTICLE...ID=38239>. See also J. P. Zmirak, "Victims of Islamic 'Tolerance,' " May 2, 2002 <www.frontpagemag.com/articles/ReadArticle.asp?ID=1580>.

[16]D'Souza, *What's So Great About America?* p. 50.

[17]Russell Kirk, *The Roots of American Order* (Washington, D.C.: Regnery Gateway, 1991), p. 6.

[18]Michael Novak, *On Two Wings: Humble Faith and Common Sense at the American Founding* (San Francisco: Encounter Books, 2002), p. 89.

Chapter 2

[1]Michael Novak, *On Two Wings: Humble Faith and Common Sense at the American Founding* (San Francisco: Encounter Books, 2002), pp. 5-24, for the role of what Novak calls "Jewish Metaphysics" in the American founding.

[2]See ibid., p. 5 for Novak's description of this clipping of the wing of faith.

[3]A. J. Conyers, *The Long Truce: How Toleration Made the World Safe for Power and Profit* (Dallas: Spence, 2001), p. 33.

[4]Dennis Prager and Joseph Telushkin, *The Nine Questions People Ask About Judaism* (New York: Simon & Schuster, 1986), p. 30.

[5]Ibid., p. 96.

[6]Ibid., p. 58.

[7]Russell Kirk, *The Roots of American Order* (Washington, D.C.: Regnery Gateway, 1991), p. 24.

[8]For vivid description of the American civil rights movement and Dr. King's work in particular, see Taylor Branch's Pulitzer-Prize-winning history, *Parting the Waters: American in the King Years 1954-63* (New York: Simon & Schuster, 1988).

[9]Conyers, *Long Truce*, pp. 30-31. On the general contributions of Judaism to Western civilization as a whole, see Thomas Cahill, *The Gifts of the Jews* (New York: Doubleday, 1998).

[10]Helpful treatments of natural law include J. Budziszewski, *Written On the Heart* (Downers Grove, Ill.: InterVarsity Press, 1997); J. Budziszewski, *What We Can't Not Know* (Dallas: Spence, 2003); Edward B. McLean, ed., *New Perspectives on Natural Law* (Wilmington, Del.: ISI Books, 2000); Alexander P. d'Entreves, *Natural Law* (London: Hutchinson University Library, 1951); Heinrich A. Rommen, *The Natural Law: A Study in Legal and Social History and Philosophy* (Indianapolis: Liberty Fund, 1998).

[11]See, e.g., Deut 30:11-14; Rom 2:14-15.

[12]See C. S. Lewis, "Illustrations of the Tao," *The Abolition of Man* (New York: Macmillan, 1965).

[13]Kirk, *Roots of American Order*, p. 37.

[14]See Jacques Maritain, *Moral Philosophy: An Historical and Critical Survey of the Great Systems* (New York: Charles Scribner's, 1964), chap. 1.

[15]See Søren Kierkegaard, *The Concept of Irony, With Continual Reference to Socrates*, trans. Howard V. Hong and Edna H. Hong (Princeton, N.J.: Princeton University Press, 1992).

[16]Mortimer Adler, *Ten Philosophical Mistakes* (New York: Macmillan, 1985), p. 142.

[17]On abortion as an index for other political views, see Kristen Luker, *Abortion and the Politics of Motherhood* (Berkeley: University of California Press, 1984).

[18]Edmund Burke, quoted in Thomas Sowell, *A Conflict of Visions* (New York: William Morrow, 1987), p. 16.

[19]William Godwin, quoted in Sowell, *Conflict of Visions*, p. 16.

[20]Martin Luther King Jr., "Letter From Birmingham Jail," in *Why We Can't Wait* (New York: Mentor Books, 1964), p. 82.

[21]Conyers, *Long Truce,* pp. 226-27 (italics in original).

[22]Cicero, quoted in Kirk, *The Roots of American Order,* p. 108.

[23]Kirk, *Roots of American Order,* p. 125.

Chapter 3

[1]J. Budziszewski, *True Tolerance* (New Brunswick, N.J.: Transaction, 1992), p. 289.

[2]A. J. Conyers, *The Long Truce* (Dallas: Spence, 2001), p. 244.

[3]Vincent Carroll and David Shiflett, *Christianity on Trial: Arguments Against Anti-Religious Bigotry* (San Francisco: Encounter Books, 2001), p. 145.

[4]Ibid., pp. 145-46.

[5]Ibid., p. 145.

[6]Nick Fotion and Gerard Elfstrom, *Toleration* (Tuscaloosa: University of Alabama Press, 1992), p. 76.

[7]Ibid.

[8]C. S. Lewis, "Equality," *Present Concerns: Essays by C. S. Lewis,* ed. Walter Hooper (San Diego: Harcourt Brace Jovanovich, 1987), p. 17.

[9]Jacques Barzun, *From Dawn to Decadence* (New York: HarperPerennial, 2000), p. 429.

[10]Voltaire, quoted in Will and Ariel Durant, *The Age of Voltaire* (New York: MJF Books, 1992), p. 753.

[11]Russell Kirk, *The Roots of American Order* (Washington, D.C.: Regnery Gateway, 1991), p. 29.

[12]James Madison, quoted in *The Federalist,* ed. Jacob E. Cooke (Middletown, Conn.: Wesleyan University Press, 1961), p. 349.

[13]Thomas Sowell, *A Conflict of Visions* (New York: William Morrow, 1987), p. 33.

[14]Martin Luther, quoted in R. E. O. White, *Christian Ethics* (Atlanta: John Knox Press, 1981), p. 225.

[15]White, *Christian Ethics,* p. 224.

[16]Budziszewski, *True Tolerance,* p. 273

[17]John Calvin, quoted in A. James Reichley, *Faith in Politics* (Washington, D.C.: Brookings Institution Press, 2002), pp. 34-35.

[18]Fotion and Elfstrom, *Toleration,* p. 77.

[19]Budziszewski, *True Tolerance,* p. 291.

[20]Ibid.

[21]Ibid., p. 292.

[22]Ibid.

[23]R. Emmett Tyrell, "The Dark Sage," *The American Spectator,* November-December 2002, p. 53.

[24]Carroll and Shiflett, *Christianity on Trial,* p. 94.

Chapter 4

[1]James C. Livingston, *Modern Christian Thought: From the Enlightenment to Vatican II* (New York: Macmillan, 1971), p. 1.

[2]Maurice Cranston, "John Locke and the Case for Toleration," in *On Toleration,* ed. Susan Mendus and David Edwards (Oxford: Clarendon, 1987), p. 102. For helpful descriptions and summaries of Locke's thought, see James Tully, *An Approach to Political Philosophy: Locke in Contexts* (Cambridge: Cambridge University Press, 1993), and C. B. Macpherson, *Possessive Individualism: Hobbes to Locke* (Oxford: Oxford University Press, 1962).

[3]John Locke, *A Letter Concerning Toleration* (Amherst, N.Y.: Prometheus Books, 1990), p. 13.

[4]Ibid., p. 17.

[5]Cranston, "John Locke and the Case for Toleration," p. 119.

[6]Locke, *Letter Concerning Toleration,* pp. 17, 42.

[7]Roger Kimball, "Mill, Stephen, and the Nature of Freedom," in *The Betrayal of Liberalism,* ed. Hilton Kramer and Roger Kimball (Chicago: Ivan R. Dee, 1999), p. 51.

[8]Robert H. Bork, *Slouching Towards Gomorrah* (New York: Regan Books, 1996), p. 17.

[9]For an overall description of Mill's thought see Wendy Donner, *The Liberal Self: John Stuart Mill's Moral and Political Philosophy* (Ithaca, N.Y.: Cornell University Press, 1991), and Neil Thornton, *The Problem of Liberalism in the Thought of John Stuart Mill* (New York: Garland, 1987).

[10]See John Stuart Mill, *On Liberty* (Chicago: Henry Regnery, 1955), pp. 75-76.

[11]Maurice Cowling, quoted in Kimball, "Mill, Stephen, and the Nature of Freedom," p. 44.

[12]Kimball, "Mill, Stephen, and the Nature of Freedom," p. 58.

[13]Ibid.

[14]For a helpful discussion of the path to religious toleration in colonial America, see Mark A. Noll, *The Old Religion in a New World: The History of North American Christianity* (Grand Rapids: Eerdmans, 2002), pp. 74-91.

[15]George Will, *With a Happy Eye, But . . . America and the World 1997-2002* (New York: Free Press, 2002), p. 150.

[16]Dinesh D'Souza, *What's So Great About America?* (Washington, D.C.: Regnery, 2002), p. 90.

[17]The most influential articulation of the "elective affinity" between Calvinist Christianity and capitalism in the new nation is Max Weber, *The Protestant Ethic and the Spirit of Capitalism* (New York: Charles Scribner's, 1958).

[18]D'Souza, *What's So Great About America?* p. 94.

[19]Winthrop S. Hudson and John Corrigan, *Religion in America,* 6th ed. (Upper Saddle River, N.J.: Prentice Hall, 1999), p. 113.

[20]Ibid., p. 103.

[21]Ibid.

[22]John Mark Terry, *Evangelism: A Concise History* (Nashville: Broadman & Holman, 1994), p. 123.

[23]Michael Novak, *On Two Wings* (San Francisco: Encounter Books, 2002), p. 1.

[24]For a survey of the contributions of Christianity to human societies through the centuries, see Alvin J. Schmidt, *Under the Influence: How Christianity Transformed Civilization* (Grand Rapids: Zondervan, 2001), and Rodney Stark, *For the Glory of God* (Princeton, N.J.: Princeton University Press, 2003).

[25]John Adams, quoted in Novak, *Two Wings,* p. 14.

[26]"Religion and morality are indispensable supports" to good government, said Washington, quoted in Novak, *Two Wings,* p. 71.

[27]John Adams, quoted in Novak, *Two Wings,* p. 71 (italics in original).

Chapter 5

[1]The Declaration of Independence and the Bill of Rights have served this purpose historically, though an encroaching statism is progressively stunting these natural rights. On this trend see part one of Robert Bork, *Slouching Towards Gomorrah: Modern Liberalism and American Decline* (New York: HarperCollins, 1996); James Bovard, *Lost Rights: The Destruction of American Liberty* (New York: St. Martin's, 1994); and Aaron Wildavsky, *The Rise of Radical Egalitarianism* (Washington, D.C.: American University Press, 1991). On the social need for public truths see Os Guinness, *Time for Truth* (Grand Rapids: Baker, 2000); Charles Drew, *A Public Faith* (Colorado Springs: NavPress, 2000); Richard John Neuhaus, ed., *Virtue: Public & Private* (Grand Rapids: Eerdmans, 1986); Richard John Neuhaus, *America Against Itself* (Notre Dame,

Ind.: University of Notre Dame Press, 1992), Amitai Etzioni, ed., *New Communitarian Thinking* (Charlottesville: University Press of Virginia, 1995), chaps. 8-10; Lynne Cheney, *Telling the Truth* (New York: Simon & Schuster, 1995). On the personal need for truth see for example J. I. Packer and Thomas Howard, *Christianity: The True Humanism* (Waco, Tex.: Word, 1985); Francis Schaeffer, *The God Who Is There,* 2nd ed. (Downers Grove, Ill.: InterVarsity Press, 1998); Jacques Maritain, *The Peasant of the Garonne* (New York: Holt, Rinehart & Winston, 1968).

[2]On the essential nature of personal and intellectual virtue for the reliable acquisition of knowledge generally, see W. Jay Wood, *Epistemology* (Downers Grove, Ill.: InterVarsity Press, 1998).

[3]On the spiritual nature and usefulness of doubt, see the reflections of Os Guinness, *On Doubt* (Downers Grove, Ill.: InterVarsity Press, 1976); on God's superintendence of all truth, see Arthur Holmes, *All Truth Is God's Truth* (Downers Grove, Ill.: InterVarsity Press, 1983).

[4]These themes touch on the current controversy over the "openness" of God, and the extent of God's foreknowledge and its compatibility with human free will. The literature on this debate is already vast, but for representative views see Clark Pinnock et al., *The Openness of God: A Biblical Challenge to the Traditional Understanding of God* (Downers Grove, Ill.: InterVarsity Press, 1994); James K. Beilby and Paul R. Eddy, eds., *Divine Foreknowledge: 4 Views* (Downers Grove, Ill.: InterVarsity Press, 2001); William Lane Craig, *The Only Wise God: The Compatibility of Divine Foreknowledge and Human Freedom* (Grand Rapids: Baker, 1987). For an excellent and concise summary and critique of openness theology, see Timothy George, "What God Knows," *First Things,* June-July 2003, pp. 7-9.

[5]For a philosophically rigorous discussion of the nature and function of truth in both personal and intellectual life—as well as the intrinsic value of truthfulness for human development—see Bernard Williams, *Truth and Truthfulness* (Princeton, N.J.: Princeton University Press, 2003).

[6]Richard John Neuhaus, "Encountered by the Truth," *First Things,* October 1998, pp. 82-83. For further discussion on Christian humility in the context of Christian apologetics, see Douglas Groothuis, *Christianity That Counts: Being a Christian in a Non-Christian World* (Grand Rapids: Baker, 1995), pp. 63-65, and Daniel Taylor, *The Myth of Certainty* (Downers Grove, Ill.: InterVarsity Press, 1992). For interesting reflection on the experiences of philosophers and theologians from a variety of traditions seeking knowledge of God through various Christian and non-Christian avenues, see Kenneth Cragg, *Troubled by Truth: Biographies in the Presence of Mystery* (Cleveland: Pilgrim Press, 1992).

[7]For penetrating discussion on the centrality of anger today and the implications of this reality, see Dallas Willard, *The Divine Conspiracy* (San Francisco: HarperSanFrancisco, 1998), pp. 147-55. On the destructive social effects of anger—seen, for example, in the near tripling of the violent crime rate since 1960, the commission of about twenty thousand murders annually in the United States, the more than doubling of the divorce rate since 1960, the tripling of the teen suicide rate since 1960, and the persistence of over one million abortions committed every year along with an out of wedlock birth rate of about one-third of all births (and double that among black Americans) see William J. Bennett, *The Index of Leading Cultural Indicators* (New York: Simon & Schuster, 1999). On murder specifically and the individual and social trauma it produces, see Brad Stetson, *Living Victims, Stolen Lives: Parents of Murdered Children Speak to America* (Amityville, N.Y.: Baywood, 2003).

[8]Dallas Willard, *Renovation of the Heart* (Colorado Springs: NavPress, 2002), p. 78.

[9]On these themes see Dean Merrill, *Sinners in the Hands of An Angry Church* (Grand Rapids: Zondervan, 1997), and Cal Thomas and Ed Dobson, *Blinded by Might* (Grand Rapids: Zondervan, 1999).

[10]See for example Mt 10:39; 18:3-4; Jn 12:24-25; 1Cor 1:18—2:5. For entertaining but insightful meditation on Christian paradoxes, see Robert L. Short, *The Gospel According to Peanuts* (New York: Bantam, 1965). Martyred twentieth-century missionary Jim Elliot's saying, "He is no fool who gives what he cannot keep to gain what he cannot lose," well captures this paradoxical essence. For his timeless story see Elisabeth Elliot, *Shadow of the Almighty* (New York: Harper & Row, 1979).

[11]Dallas Willard, "Language, Being, God and the Three Stages of Theistic Evidence," in *Does God Exist? The Great Debate*, ed. J. P. Moreland and Kai Nielsen (Nashville: Thomas Nelson, 1990), p. 216 (italics in original).

[12]This survey draws on the remarks of Peter Kreeft and Ronald K. Tacelli, *Handbook of Christian Apologetics* (Downers Grove, Ill.: InterVarsity Press, 1994), pp. 364-66. For an insightful examination of the concept of truth in contemporary American culture, see Douglas Groothuis, *Truth Decay: Defending Christianity Against the Challenges of Postmodernism* (Downers Grove, Ill.: InterVarsity Press, 2000).

[13]Oceans of ink have been spilled debunking the pretensions of relativism to intellectual seriousness. For a handy overview of the inconsistencies and internal contradictions of relativism, especially as they relate to Christian truth claims, see Paul Copan, *"True For You, But Not For Me": Defeating the Slogans That Leave Christians Speechless* (Minneapolis: Bethany House, 1998).

[14]G. K. Chesterton, quoted in Peter Kreeft and Ronald Tacelli, *Handbook of Christian Apologetics* (Downers Grove, Ill.: InterVarsity Press, 1994), p. 365.

[15]For commentary on pragmatism and its impact on American social evolution, see William Marnell, *Man-made Morals: Four Philosophies That Shaped America* (New York: Doubleday, 1968), pp. 264-385. See also the introduction by Joseph Blau in William James, *Pragmatism and Other Essays* (New York: Washington Square Press, 1963).

[16]Valuable critique of scientism, the moral values it presupposes and its inability to within itself justify its own aims, goals and values is found, for example, in J. P. Moreland, *Scaling the Secular City* (Grand Rapids: Baker, 1987, pp. 197-200), and Huston Smith, *Why Religion Matters: The Fate of the Human Spirit in an Age of Disbelief* (San Francisco: HarperSanFrancisco, 2001).

[17]For detailed criticisms of the coherence approach to truth, see J. P. Moreland and William Lane Craig, *Philosophical Foundations for a Christian Worldview* (Downers Grove, Ill.: InterVarsity Press, 2003), pp. 142-44.

[18]Ibid., pp. 135-42, and Groothuis, *Truth Decay*, pp. 86-92 for a defense of the correspondence view.

[19]Feminist writers today are the most active proponents of emotivism, which flies under various contemporary banners, such as "somatic epistemology" and "women's ways of knowing." For examples of feminist epistemology, see for example, Beverly Wildung Harrison, *Our Right to Choose* (Boston: Beacon, 1983); Linda Alcoff and Elizabeth Potter, eds., *Feminist Epistemologies* (New York: Routledge, 1992); Alison M. Jaggar and Susan R. Bordo, eds., *Gender/Body/Knowledge: Feminist Reconstructions of Being and Knowing* (New Brunswick, N.J.: Rutgers University Press, 1989). For some valuable criticisms of academic and popular feminism, which is now the dominant and controlling outlook regarding gender, sexuality and male-female relations in our country, see Christina Hoff Sommers, *Who Stole Feminism?* (New York: Simon & Schuster, 1994); *The War Against Boys* (New York: Simon & Schuster, 2000); Daphne Patai and Noretta Koertge, *Professing Feminism: Cautionary Tales from the Strange World of Women's Studies* (New York: Basic Books, 1994); Carolyn Graglia, *Domestic Tranquility: A Brief Against Feminism* (Dallas: Spence, 1998); Phyllis Schlafly, *Feminist Fantasies* (Dallas: Spence, 2003). A concise critique of feminism in Christianity specifically is found in Leslie

Zeigler, "Christianity or Feminism?" in *Unapologetic Apologetics,* ed. William Dembski and Jay Wesley Richards (Downers Grove, Ill.: InterVarsity Press, 2001), pp. 179-86. A statement of an evangelical Christian feminism is found in Rebecca Merrill Groothuis, *Good News for Women* (Grand Rapids: Baker, 1997).

[20]See note 13 in chap. eleven for some useful descriptions and critiques. See also J. Budziszewski, *How to Stay Christian at College* (Colorado Springs: NavPress, 1999), pp. 45-49; Dallas Willard, "The Unhinging of the American Mind: Derrida as Pretext," in *European Philosophy and the American Academy,* ed. Barry Smith (Lasalle, Ill.: Open Court, 1994); D. A. Carson, *The Gagging of God: Christianity Confronts Pluralism* (Grand Rapids: Baker, 1996), esp. pp. 93-140; Millard Erickson, *Postmodernizing the Faith: Evangelical Responses to the Challenge of Postmodernism* (Grand Rapids: Baker, 1998). For a clear and concise delineation of postmodern theory's most prominent schools and argumentative thrusts, see John McGowan, *Postmodernism and Its Critics* (Ithaca, N.Y.: Cornell University Press, 1991), especially pp. ix-xi.

[21]For a well-conducted and balanced discussion of how an awareness of subjectivity can be incorporated into orthodox Christian faith, see C. Stephen Evans, *Subjectivity and Religious Belief* (Washington, D.C.: University Press of America, 1978), especially pp. 201-14.

[22]Budziszewski, *How to Stay Christian at College,* p. 45 (emphasis in the original).

[23]On the necessity of social institutions providing meaning and purpose to people's lives, see Peter Berger and Richard John Neuhaus, eds., *To Empower People: From State to Civil Society* (Washington, D.C.: AEI Press, 1996). See also Robert Wuthnow, *Meaning and Moral Order* (Berkeley: University of California Press, 1987).

[24]For a sustained critique of the postmodernist orientation toward truth, see Millard J. Erickson, *Truth Or Consequences: The Perils and Promise of Postmodernism* (Downers Grove, Ill.: InterVarsity Press, 2001).

Chapter 6

[1]On this approach as the prevailing practice of American life, see Robert Bellah et al., *Habits of the Heart: Individualism and Commitment in American Life* (New York: Harper & Row, 1985).

[2]On "plausibility structures," see Peter Berger, *A Rumor of Angels: Modern Society and the Rediscovery of the Supernatural* (New York: Doubleday, 1969), pp. 38-42.

[3]For defenses of philosophical realism, see Étienne Gilson, *From Aristotle to Darwin and Back Again* (Notre Dame, Ind.: University of Notre Dame Press, 1984), and J. P. Moreland, *Universals* (Montreal: McGill-Queen's University Press, 2001).

[4]For a critique of multiculturalism as a principle of social order, see Alvin J. Schmidt, *The Menace of Multiculturalism: Trojan Horse in America* (Westport, Conn.: Praeger, 1997), and Arthur M. Schlesinger Jr., *The Disuniting of America* (New York: W. W. Norton, 1991). On the differing utility of various cultural values to socioeconomic mobility and prospects for individual success in a democratic capitalist setting, see Lawrence Harrison, *Who Prospers? How Cultural Values Shape Economic and Political Success* (New York: Basic Books, 1992), and Lawrence Harrison and Samuel Huntington, eds., *Culture Matters: How Values Shape Human Progress* (New York: Basic Books, 2000).

[5]For stimulating discussion along these lines, see James Emery White, *Embracing the Mysterious God: Loving the God We Don't Understand* (Downers Grove, Ill.: InterVarsity Press, 2003).

[6]For reflection on the inevitability of probability as the basis of religious commitment, see the classic study by Edward John Carnell, *Introduction to Christian Apologetics* (Grand Rapids: Eerdmans, 1948), pp. 113-14.

[7]On the rational probability of the resurrection see Gary Habermas and Antony Flew, *Did Jesus Rise from the Dead?: The Resurrection Debate* (San Francisco: Harper & Row, 1987); *Jesus' Resurrection: Fact or Figment?* ed. Paul Copan and Ronald K. Tacelli (Downers Grove, Ill.: InterVarsity Press, 2000). See also Gary Habermas, *The Risen Jesus and Future Hope* (Lanham, Md.: Rowman & Littlefield, 2003).

[8]See also Mk 16:15-18; Lk 24:47-48; Acts 1:8.

[9]For example, Acts 16:31; Rom 10:13. Questions of election and predestination, though obviously important, are beyond the scope and purview of this study. For stimulating discussion, see David Basinger et al., *Predestination and Free Will: Four Views of Divine Sovereignty and Human Freedom* (Downers Grove, Ill.: InterVarsity Press, 1986).

[10]Ian Markhan, *Plurality and Christian Ethics* (Cambridge: Cambridge University Press, 1994), pt. 4. For review and commentary on Markham's project as well as some challenging observations, see Richard John Neuhaus, "Truth and Tolerance," *First Things,* October 1994, pp. 74-78. For a popular statement of many of the same themes presented by Markham and Neuhaus, see David Couchman, "Tolerance: A Strange Reversal?" at <www.facingthechallenge.org/tolerance.htm>.

[11]For a helpful discussion of the biblical view of truth, see chap. three of Douglas Groothuis's *Truth Decay* (Downers Grove, Ill.: InterVarsity Press, 2000).

Chapter 7

[1]See James Davison Hunter, *Culture Wars* (New York: Basic Books, 1991), pp. 67-134.

[2]See David T. Koyzis, *Political Visions & Illusions: A Survey & Christian Critique of Contemporary Ideologies* (Downers Grove, Ill.: InterVarsity Press, 2003) for a valuable typology of political views today.

[3]Robert H. Bork, *Slouching Towards Gomorrah: Modern Liberalism and American Decline* (New York: HarperCollins, 1996), p. 5.

[4]For a provocative discussion of the extent and harmfulness of unbridled judicial activism, see the symposium "The End of Democracy? The Judicial Usurpation of Politics," *First Things,* November 1996, pp. 18-42, and "The End of Democracy? A Discussion Continued," *First Things,* January 1997, pp. 19-28.

[5]Bork, *Slouching Towards Gomorrah,* pp. 7-9.

[6]Ibid., p. 9.

[7]See Thomas Sowell, *The Vision of the Anointed: Self-Congratulation as a Basis for Social Policy* (New York: Basic Books, 1995), esp. chaps. 1-2, for basic outlines of the mindset and operating methods of those politicians, policy-makers and bureaucrats who justify their positions on the basis of their own surety of their superior motives.

[8]Francis Canavan, *The Pluralist Game: Pluralism, Liberalism and the Moral Conscience* (Lanham, Md.: Rowman & Littlefield, 1995).

[9]See ibid., pp. 63-81; 93-104.

[10]See part two of William Watkins, *The New Absolutes* (Minneapolis: Bethany House, 1996) for an examination of some of these values and how they are defended by secular liberals.

[11]For excellent discussion of the compatibility of moral traditionalism with a vigorous participation and defense of free market capitalism, see Richard John Neuhaus, *Doing Well and Doing Good: The Challenge to the Christian Capitalist* (New York: Doubleday, 1992).

[12]Daniel Taylor makes this general point in *Is God Intolerant?* (Wheaton, Ill.: Tyndale, 2003), pp. 53-55.

[13]See Paul Johnson's *Intellectuals* (New York: HarperPerennial, 1990). See also Irving Kristol, "The Adversary Culture of Intellectuals," in *Neo-Conservatism: The Autobiography of an Idea*

(New York: Free Press, 1995); Thomas Sowell, *Knowledge and Decisions* (New York: Basic Books, 1981); and Thomas Sowell, *The Vision of the Anointed* (New York: Basic Books, 1996).

[14]Christopher Lasch, *The Revolt of the Elites and the Betrayal of Democracy* (New York: W. W. Norton, 1995), p. 215. For reflection on how American society as a whole manages to contain many religious believers and to be much more religious than Europe yet still continue to secularize, see Wilfred M. McClay, "Two Concepts of Secularism," *Wilson Quarterly,* summer 2000.

[15]This shorn and isolated conception of the person is what underlies the late John Rawl's singularly influential *A Theory of Justice* (Cambridge, Mass.: Harvard University Press, 1971). For a powerful critique of this theory of the person see Michael Sandel, *Liberalism and the Limits of Justice* (Cambridge: Cambridge University Press, 1982) and Brian Crowley, *The Self, the Individual and the Community* (Oxford: Oxford University Press, 1987).

[16]See Willard Gaylin and Bruce Jennings, *The Perversion of Autonomy* (New York: Free Press, 1996) for a helpful contemporary discussion of the inherent link between individual and communal quality of life.

[17]Mary Ann Glendon, *Rights Talk* (New York: Free Press, 1991), pp. x, 14.

[18]City University of New York Religious Identification Survey, January 9, 2002 <www .christianitytoday.com/ct/2002/100/33.0.html>. This same survey noted the percentage of self-identifying Christians (of all kinds) in the United States dropped during the 1990s from 86 to 77 percent.

[19]"Number of Unchurched Adults Has Nearly Doubled Since 1991," May 4, 2004 <www.barna.org/Flexpage.aspx?Page=BarnaUpdateNarrow&BarnaUpdateID=163>.

[20]*The Confessions of St. Augustine* 4.1, trans. F. J. Sheed (Kansas City: Sheed & Ward, 1970), p. 51.

Chapter 8

[1]See C. S. Lewis, *Mere Christianity* (New York: Macmillan, 1960). See also John R. W. Stott, *Basic Christianity* (Downers Grove, Ill.: InterVarsity Press, 1986).

[2]Valuable sources include Millard J. Erickson, *The Evangelical Mind and Heart* (Grand Rapids: Baker, 1993); James Davison Hunter, *American Evangelicalism* (New Brunswick, N.J.: Rutgers University Press, 1983); Kenneth S. Kantzer and Carl F. H. Henry, *Evangelical Affirmations* (Grand Rapids: Zondervan, 1990); George Marsden, *Fundamentalism and American Culture* (New York: Oxford University Press, 1980); Mark Noll, *The Scandal of the Evangelical Mind* (Grand Rapids: Eerdmans, 1994); Robert Wuthnow, *The Struggle for America's Soul: Evangelicals, Liberals & Secularism* (Grand Rapids: Eerdmans, 1989).

[3]This list is directly based on Alister McGrath's work, with slight emendations. See his book *A Passion for Truth: The Intellectual Coherence of Evangelicalism* (Downers Grove, Ill.: InterVarsity Press, 1996), p. 22.

[4]George Barna, "People's Faith Flavor Influences How They See Themselves," August 26, 2002 <www.barna.org.FlexPage.aspx?Page=BarnaUpdate&BarnaUpdateID=119>.

[5]Nicholas D. Kristof, "God, Satan and the Media," *New York Times,* March 4, 2003 <www .nytimes.com/2003/03/04/opinion/04KRIS.html>; and "Evangelicals Prefer That States Outlaw Gay 'Marriage,'" *Washington Times,* April 14, 2004 <www.washtimes.com/national/ 20040414-123951-2597r.htm>.

[6]The deep connection between Protestant theology and individualism, and its role in the rise of American capitalism, has been classically analyzed by Max Weber in *The Protestant Ethic and The Spirit of Capitalism* (New York: Charles Scribner's Sons, 1958).

[7]See Erwin Lutzer, *Christ Among Other Gods* (Chicago: Moody Press, 1994), pp. 31-39, for discussion of these various distinctions between the Christian and secular worldviews.

[8]See Brad Stetson, "Nights of the Living Dead," *Christianity Today,* February 4, 2002.

[9]See Harold Netland, *Dissonant Voices: Religious Pluralism and the Question of Truth* (Grand Rapids: Eerdmans, 1991), p. 308.

[10]See, for example, Noll, *Scandal of the Evangelical Mind,* and David F. Wells, *No Place for Truth: Or, Whatever Happened to Evangelical Theology?* (Grand Rapids: Eerdmans, 1993).

[11]For examples on the growing emphasis on intellectual rigor among evangelicals, see J. P. Moreland, *Love Your God with All Your Mind* (Colorado Springs: NavPress, 1997); and James Sire, *Habits of the Mind* (Downers Grove, Ill.: InterVarsity Press, 2000). For an example of the diffusion of classic Christian spirituality to the evangelical popular readership, see the best-selling book—even by secular measures—by Rick Warren, *The Purpose-Driven Life* (Grand Rapids: Zondervan, 2003).

[12]Andre Codrescu, speaking on "All Things Considered," National Public Radio, December 19, 1995, cited by Daniel Taylor, *Is God Intolerant?* (Wheaton, Ill.: Tyndale House, 2003), p. 56. Apparently the liberal devotion to diversity does not include the views of Southern Baptists.

[13]This point is made by Taylor in *Is God Intolerant?* p. 57.

[14]This general point is made by Michael Peterson et al., *Reason and Religious Belief* (New York: Oxford University Press, 1991), p. 221. Regarding the charge of anti-Semitism sometimes directed against Christian evangelism and the contention of the necessity of faith in Jesus Christ, see the essay by Jewish ethicist Dennis Prager arguing that Christian evangelism and its exclusivist views on salvation are not intolerant, "A Jew Defends Evangelical Christians," October 23, 2002 <www.townhall.com/columnists/dennisprager/dp20021023.shtml>.

[15]See John Hick, *An Interpretation of Religion* (New Haven, Conn.: Yale University Press, 1989).

[16]On diversity, see Frederick Lynch, *The Diversity Machine* (New York: Free Press, 1997); and on multiculturalism see Alvin Schmidt, *The Menace of Multiculturalism* (Westport, Conn.: Praeger, 1997).

[17]Part of the discussion that follows is draws from Dallas Willard, "Being a Christian in a Pluralistic Society," found at <www.dwillard.org/articles/artview.asp?artID=17>.

Chapter 9

[1]Bernard Goldberg, *Bias* (Washington D.C.: Regnery, 2002), p. 126.

[2] Randy Dotinga, "Newsroom Conservatives Are a Rare Breed," *Christian Science Monitor,* June 3, 2004 <www.csmonitor.com/2004/0603/p02s01-usgn.html>.

[3]Hugh Hewitt, "L.A. Times Fighting Liberal Bias?" June 4, 2003 <www.worldnetdaily.com /news/article.asp?ARTICLE...ID=32889> (emphasis added).

[4]Goldberg, *Bias,* p. 181.

[5]Rod Dreher, "God in the Newsroom," March 7, 2003 <www.nationalreview.com/dreher /dreher030703.asp>

[6]Dan Seligman, "Without Fear, Favor or . . . Offensiveness," November 19, 2001 <www .coloringthenews.com/html/review_wsj.html>.

[7]For further critique of the intellectual and spiritual implications of this climate, see C. John Sommerville, *How the News Makes Us Dumb* (Downers Grove, Ill.: InterVarsity Press, 1999).

[8]See Carl Campanile, "School's Out," *New York Post,* July 28, 2003, p. 3.

[9]For helpful discussion of this topic, see Stanton L. Jones and Mark A. Yarhouse, *Homosexuality: The Use of Scientific Research in the Church's Moral Debate* (Downers Grove, Ill.: InterVarsity Press, 2000).

[10]Peter Hong, "Lesbian Sues Over Physician's Refusal to Do Insemination," *Los Angeles Times,* February 18, 2003, p. B6.

[11]Julie Foster, "California Schools' New Homosexual Curriculum," December 26, 2000

<www.worldnetdaily.com/news/article.asp?ARTICLE...ID21132> (italics in original).

[12]Campaign for California Families, April 21, 2003 <www.savecalifornia.com/press/newsreleases/release.cfm?nrid=PR030421A>.

[13]"Nickelodeon to Air Special on Gay Parents Despite Protests," June 18, 2002 <www.cnn.com/2002/SHOWBIZ/TV06/17/gay.parents.ap/>.

[14]"2 Gay Men Are Wed in Canada After Ruling," *Los Angeles Times,* June 11, 2003, p. A13.

[15]Mandi Steele, "College Profs Steeped in Postmodernism," July 5, 2002 <www.worldnetdaily.com/news/article.asp?ARTICLE...ID28173>. On the practical consequences for society of such teaching within the halls of academe, see Heather MacDonald, *The Burden of Bad Ideas: How Modern Intellectuals Misshape Our Society* (Chicago: Ivan R. Dee, 2001).

[16]William J. Bennett, "Teaching September 11," *Wall Street Journal,* September 10, 2002 <http://online.wsj.com/article/0,,SB1031622250819825115.djm,00.html>.

[17]Tammy Bruce, *The New Thought Police* (Roseville, Calif.: Prima, 2001), p. 212.

[18]Alan Charles Kors and Harvey A. Silverglate, *The Shadow University* (New York: Free Press, 1998), pp. 165-66.

[19]Charles Colson, "Like It or Not: Cardinal Arinze at Georgetown," June 4, 2003 <www.townhall.com/columnists/chuckcolson/cc20030604.shtml>.

[20]Cited in Josh McDowell and Bob Hostetler, *The New Tolerance* (Wheaton, Ill.: Tyndale House, 1998), p. 110.

[21]William Kristol, editor of the *Weekly Standard,* asserted on "FoxNews with Tony Snow," Fox News, March 22, 2003, that he had received an e-mail from this student informing him of this class policy.

[22]J. D. Hayworth, "Hate Speech at Columbia is Academic," April 9, 2003 <www.townhall.com/columnists/GuestColumns/Hayworth20030409.shtml>.

[23]"Campus Leftists Attack Ad on Black Reparations," March 8, 2001 <www.newsmax.com/archives/articles/2001/3/7/221937.shtml>.

[24]Pamela Ferdinand, "Free Speech Debate Splits Brown," *Washington Post,* March 21, 2001, p. A3.

[25]See John Cise, "Copies of California Patriot Stolen; Publication Staff Allegedly Harassed," *Daily Californian,* February 27, 2002 <www.dailycal.org/particle.php?id=7838>; Ellen Sorokin, "Berkeley Conservatives Tell of Death Threats for Criticism," *Washington Times,* March 5, 2002 <www.washingtontimes.com/national/20020305-21028866.htm>.

[26]"Berkeley Demonstrators Block Speech by Former Israeli Prime Minister," *Sacramento Bee,* November 29, 2000 <www.sacbee.com/news/calreport.calrep_story.cgi?N20.html>.

[27]Tammy Bruce, *The Death of Right and Wrong* (Roseville, Calif.: Prima, 2003), p. 161.

[28]Diane Ravitch, "Cut on the Bias," *Wall Street Journal,* July 1, 2003, p. A10. See also "A Glossary of Banned Words, Usages, Stereotypes and Topics," in Diane Ravitch's book *The Language Police* (New York: Alfred A. Knopf, 2003), pp. 171-202.

[29]"Center for the Study of Popular Culture Releases Poll Conducted at Ivy League Universities," January 9, 2003 <www.serve.com/Lincolnheritage2/Articles/The_Address_Article_Search/Address_Articles_since_1997/Address_1997_Education/University_classroom_and_polit/university_classroom_and_polit.html>. See also Lee Bockhorn, "The Ivy League Left," January 17, 2002 <www.theweeklystandard.com/Content/Public/Articles/000/000/000/790qheqq.asp>; and Frank Luntz, "Inside the Mind of an Ivy League Professor," August 30, 2002 <www.frontpagemag.com/articles/ReadArticle.asp?ID=2642>.

[30]Anne Cumming, "Professor: UNC Lacks Political Pluralism," *Greeley Tribune,* February 25, 2002 <www.greeleytrib.com/apps/pbcs.dll/article?aID=/20020217/NEWS/102170013&rs=2>.

[31]See Kathleen Maclay, "Researchers Help Define What Makes a Political Conservative," *UC Berkeley News,* July 22, 2003 <www.berkeley.edu/news/media/releases/2003/07/22_politics.shtml>.

[32]Alan Charles Kors, "The Assault upon Liberty and Dignity," March 13, 1998 <www.newsmax .com/articles/?a=1999/7/30/103757>.

[33]Herbert Marcuse, quoted in Roger Kimball, *The Long March: How the Cultural Revolution of the 1960s Changed America* (San Francisco: Encounter, 2000), p. 170. For Marcuse's complete essay see Robert Paul Wolff et al., *A Critique of Pure Tolerance* (Boston: Beacon Press, 1965).

[34]Kimball, *Long March*, p. 170.

[35]Ibid., p. 171.

[36]Hilton Kramer and Roger Kimball, "Introduction: The Betrayal of Liberalism," in *The Betrayal of Liberalism*, ed. Hilton Kramer and Roger Kimball (Chicago: Ivan R. Dee, 1999), p. 15.

[37]John O'Sullivan, "The Moral Consequences of Impatience," in *The Betrayal of Liberalism*, ed. Hilton Kramer and Roger Kimball (Chicago: Ivan R. Dee, 1999), p. 222. On the sleight of hand of liberal tolerance, see also Francis J. Beckwith, "Deconstructing Liberal Tolerance," *Christian Research Journal* 22, no. 3 (1991): <www.equip.org/free/DL104.pdf>.

Chapter 10

[1]Ann Coulter, *Slander* (New York: Crown, 2002), p. 167.

[2]Marvin Olasky, "Anti-Christian Bigotry," *World,* April 27, 2002 <www.worldmag.com /displayarticle.cfm?id=5954>.

[3]Ibid.

[4]Charles Colson, "The Last Acceptable Prejudice," June 11, 2003 <www.townhall.com /columnists/chuckcolson/cc20030611.shtml>.

[5]Bill Moyers, "Commentary," November 8, 2002 <www.pbs.org/now/commentary /moyers15.html>. On Moyers see also Stephen F. Hayes, "PBS' Televangelist," *Weekly Standard*, February 25, 2002, pp. 18-23.

[6]Richard John Neuhaus, "Fare Thee Well, Tony Lewis," *First Things,* March 2002, pp. 73-74.

[7]Bernard Goldberg, *Bias* (Washington D.C.: Regnery, 2002), p. 127.

[8]Diane Alden, "Christianity Under Siege, Part 1: The Stones Cry Out," January 3, 2002 <www.newsmax.com/commentmax/get.pl?a=2002/1/3/044554>.

[9]In fact, the sizable secularist constituency of the Democrat party has been identified as an "anti-Christian fundamentalist" motivated voter. For detailed discussion of the growing strength of the secularist vote and its devotion to the Democrats, see Louis Bolce and Gerald De Maio, "Our Secularist Democratic Party," *The Public Interest,* fall 2002, pp. 3-20. For commentary on this phenomenon, see Claudia Winkler, "The Party of Unbelievers," *Weekly Standard,* January 8, 2003; and David Brooks, "A Matter of Faith," *New York Times,* June 22, 2004, p. A23.

[10]John Leo, "Tufts Evangelicals Are Punished for Acting on Their Beliefs," May 9, 2000 <www.jewishworldreview.com/cols/leo050900.asp>.

[11]Ibid.

[12]"Briefs/North America," *Christianity Today,* March 2003, p. 23.

[13]John Leo, "Anti-Discrimination Policies Threaten First Amendment Rights," January 10, 2003 <www.jewishworldreview.com/cols/leo011003.asp>.

[14]John Leo, "Hold That Conscience," *U.S. News & World Report,* March 26, 2001, p. 13.

[15]"Judge: Woman Free to Wear Cross to Work," June 26, 2003 <www.worldnetdaily.com/news /article.asp?ARTICLE...ID=33263>.

[16]Richard Foot, "Christian Values Often a Disguise for Intolerance: Supreme Court Judge," November 10, 2000 <www.nationalpost.com/news/story.html?f=/stories/20001110/364301.html>.

[17]Randall Palmer, "Religious Hatred?" May 16, 2002 <www.abcnews.go.com/sections/world/>.

[18]Tomas Dixon, " 'Hate Speech' Law Could Chill Sermons," *Christianity Today,* August 5, 2002, pp. 22-23.

[19]Jerry Falwell, "ABC Bleeps Out Jesus," June 1, 2002 <www.worldnetdaily.com/news /article.asp?ARTICLE...ID=27817>.

[20]" 'Jesus' Banned From Brick Walkway," July 23, 2003 <www.worldnetdaily>. Correctly discerning the political realities of today and the substantial secularization of the Democratic Party, Mildred Tong, the mother who purchased the brick, remarked, "Chicago . . . I knew it was liberal and filled with Democrats and whatever, but I didn't know it would come down to this, that we couldn't profess our faith."

[21]"Quotation Marks," *Christianity Today,* April 2003, p. 23.

[22]"Columbine Memorial Tiles May Not Carry Religious Messages," January 27, 2003 <www .baptiststandard.com/2003/1_27/pages/columbine.html>.

[23]Jon Dougherty, "Ban on Christmas Leads to Court Fight," December 10, 2002 <www .worldnetdaily.com/newsarticle.asp?ARTICLE...ID=29942>.

[24]Matt Pyeatt, "ACLU Demands California School to Drop 'God Bless America' Display," October 15, 2001 <www.cnsnews.com/Culture/Archive/200110/CUL20011015a.html>.

[25]"Celine Dion Song Banned: 'Too Christian' for School," June 8, 2003 <www.wnd.com/news /article.asp?ARTICLE...ID=32973>. Dion's song is titled "The Prayer Lyrics," which is found in the album *These Are Special Times,* released by Sony in 1998.

[26]"Biblical Verses Removed from Grand Canyon," July 16, 2003 <http://story.news.yahoo .com/news?tmpl=story&cid=857&ncid=757&e=10&u=/nm/20030715/od_uk_nm/oukoe_life _grandcanyon>. After complaints from outraged citizens in Arizona and beyond, the plaques were replaced, again overlooking the Grand Canyon.

[27]Dennis Prager, "Taliban Come to Los Angeles," June 8, 2004 <www.townhall.com/columnists/ dennisprager/dp20040608.shtml>. See also "Hundreds Protest City's Plan to Negotiate With ACLU Over County Seal," June 8, 2004 <www.nbc4tv/politics/3395668/detail.html>.

[28]"Help the ACLU of Utah Find the Last Ten Commandments Monument on Government Property in Utah," August 5, 2003 <www.acluutah.org/10comandAA.htm>.

[29]The definitive book on this longstanding secular war is Richard John Neuhaus's *The Naked Public Square* (Grand Rapids: Zondervan, 1984). For a clear understanding of the indispensable role of religion in the founding and continuing life of the nation, see Os Guinness, *The Great Experiment: Faith and Freedom in America* (Colorado Springs: NavPress, 2001). See also Michael Novak, *On Two Wings* (San Francisco: Encounter, 2002).

Chapter 11

[1]Maurice Cranston, "Toleration," in *The Encyclopedia of Philosophy,* ed. Paul Johnson (New York: Macmillan, 1967), 8:143.

[2]Jay Newman, *Foundations of Religious Tolerance* (Toronto: University of Toronto Press, 1982), p. 8 (emphasis in original).

[3]UN declaration on tolerance, quoted in Daniel Taylor, *Is God Intolerant?* (Minneapolis: Bethany House, 2003), p. 48.

[4]Alan Bloom, *The Closing of the American Mind* (New York: Simon & Schuster, 1987), pp. 25, 27.

[5]J. Budziszewski, "Tolerance and Natural Law," *Revue Generale de Droit* 29, no. 2 (1998): 234.

[6]See J. Budziszewski, *The Revenge of Conscience: Politics and the Fall of Man* (Dallas: Spence, 1999), pp. 46-49 for helpful discussion along these lines.

[7]See C. S. Lewis, "Illustrations of the Tao," in *The Abolition of Man* (New York: Macmillan, 1947).

[8]For critiques of moral relativism see Francis Beckwith and Gregory Koukl, *Relativism: Feet Firmly Planted in Mid-Air* (Grand Rapids: Baker, 1998); Paul Copan, *"True For You, But Not For Me"* (Minneapolis: Bethany House, 1998), parts 1-2; Gertrude Himmelfarb, *One Nation, Two Cultures* (New York: Vintage, 2001); Peter Kreeft and Ronald K. Tacelli, *Handbook of Christian Apologetics* (Downers Grove, Ill.: InterVarsity Press, 1994), pp. 362-83; Dennis Mc-Callum, ed., *The Death of Truth* (Minneapolis: Bethany House, 1996); J. P. Moreland, *Scaling the Secular City* (Grand Rapids: Baker, 1987), pp. 240-48.

[9]Karl Popper, *The Open Society and Its Enemies* (London: Routledge & Kegan Paul), 1966), 1:265.

[10]On the personal and social destructiveness of this false compassion, see Marvin Olasky, *The Tragedy of American Compassion* (Washington, D.C.: Regnery, 1992).

[11]For reflection on this cultural phenomenon, what novelist Tom Wolfe christened "Radical Chic" in his 1970 cultural meditation of that name, see Myron Magnet, *The Dream and the Nightmare: The Sixties' Legacy to the Underclass* (New York: William Morrow, 1993). See also Gertrude Himmelfarb, *The Demoralization of Society: From Victorian Virtues to Modern Values* (New York: Alfred A. Knopf, 1995); Charles Murray, *Losing Ground* (New York: Basic Books, 1984); and Roger Kimball, *The Long March: How the Cultural Revolution of the 1960s Changed America* (San Francisco: Encounter Books, 2000). For fascinating integration of the "Radical Chic" mentality to the perverse loathing of America manifested by some segments of American liberalism following the 9/11 terrorist attacks, see Shelby Steele, "Radical Sheik," *Wall Street Journal,* December 10, 2001, p. A18.

[12]For a classic study of American narcissism, see Christopher Lasch, *The Culture of Narcissism* (New York: W. W. Norton, 1979).

[13]The following works provide a critical understanding of the main analytical thrusts of post-modernism: Matei Calinescu, *Five Faces of Modernity* (Durham, N.C.: Duke University Press, 1987); Terry Eagleton, *The Ideology of the Aesthetic* (Oxford: Blackwell, 1990); Ernest Gellner, *Postmodernism, Reason and Religion* (New York: Routledge, 1992); Stanley Grenz, *A Primer on Postmodernism* (Grand Rapids: Eerdmans, 1994); Douglas Groothuis, *Truth Decay* (Downers Grove, Ill.: InterVarsity Press, 2000); Kevin Hart, *The Trespass of the Sign* (Cambridge: Cambridge University Press, 1989); David Harvey, *The Condition of Postmodernity* (Oxford: Blackwell, 1989); McCallum, *Death of Truth;* John McGowan, *Postmodernism and Its Critics* (Ithaca, N.Y.: Cornell University Press, 1991); Alister McGrath, *A Passion for Truth* (Downers Grove, Ill.: InterVarsity Press, 1996), chap. 4; John Murphy, *Postmodern Social Analysis and Criticism* (New York: Greenwood, 1989); Gene Edward Veith Jr., *Postmodern Times: A Christian Guide to Contemporary Thought and Culture* (Wheaton, Ill.: Crossway, 1994).

[14]For analysis see Ian Markham, *Plurality and Christian Ethics* (New York: Cambridge University Press, 1994.), esp. pts. 3-4.

[15]William J. Bennett, *The Broken Hearth* (New York: Doubleday, 2001), p. 138.

[16]J. Budziszewski, *True Tolerance: Liberalism and the Necessity of Judgment* (New Brunswick, N.J.: Transaction, 1992), p. 7.

[17]Aldous Huxley, *Brave New World* (New York: HarperPerennial, 1998), pp. 214-15.

[18]Budziszewski, *Revenge of Conscience,* p. 45.

[19]Ibid., p. 44.

[20]Quoted in Josh McDowell and Bob Hostetler, *The New Tolerance* (Wheaton, Ill.: Tyndale House, 1998), p. 19.

[21]Ibid., p. 19.

[22]Senate Resolution 133, quoted in Daniel Pipes, *Militant Islam Reaches America* (New York: W. W. Norton, 2002), p. 175.

[23]Ibid., p. 176.

[24]Ibid.

[25]Perhaps the most prophetic of the many critics of radical Wahhabist Islam, the strain of Islam that most aggressively and directly seeks to kill Christians, Jews and all Americans, is Steven Emerson. See his book *American Jihad* (New York: Free Press, 2002), and the video of the same name that resulted in his famous banishment from the supremely "tolerant" airwaves of National Public Radio. On the intellectual underpinnings of Islamic terror and never-ending jihad against Israel, America, and the West in general, see Paul Berman, "The Philosopher of Islamic Terror," *New York Times Magazine,* March 23, 2003, accessed online at <www .nytimes.com/2003/03/23/magazine/23GURU.html>.

[26]Pipes, *Militant Islam Reaches America,* p. 177.

[27]Stephen L. Carter, *Civility* (New York: Free Press, 1998), p. 213.

[28]For helpful background and analysis of what Daniel Pipes has so rightly called "Islamofascism," the murderous Islam of Osama bin Laden's ilk, see Bernard Lewis, *Islam and the West* (New York: Oxford University Press, 1993); and his *What Went Wrong: Approaches to the Modern History of the Middle East* (New York: Oxford University Press, 2002); Robert Spencer, *Islam Unveiled* (San Francisco: Encounter, 2002); Robert Spencer, *Onward Muslim Soldiers: How Jihad Still Threatens America and the West* (Washington, D.C.: Regnery, 2003); and Dinesh D'Souza, *What's So Great About America?* (Washington, D.C.: Regnery, 2002).

[29]For a classic statement of the socially preservative work of voluntary associations, also known as "mediating institutions," see Richard John Neuhaus and Peter Berger, *To Empower People,* 2nd ed. (Washington, D.C.: American Enterprise Institute Press, 1996).

[30]For helpful social history in this regard, see Gertrude Himmelfarb, *The Re-Moralization of Society* (New York: Alfred A. Knopf, 1995); Christopher Lasch, *The True and Only Heaven* (New York: W. W. Norton, 1991); Christopher Lasch, *The Revolt of the Elites and the Betrayal of Democracy* (New York: W. W. Norton, 1995); Christopher Lasch, *The Culture of Narcissism* (New York: W. W. Norton, 1979); Jacques Barzun, *From Dawn to Decadence* (New York: Harper-Collins, 2000); John W. Whitehead, *Grasping for the Wind: The Search for Meaning in the 20th Century* (Grand Rapids: Zondervan, 2001).

[31]See Nat Hentoff, "No Limit on 'Choice?' Here's the Ugly Result," *Los Angeles Times,* July 26, 1993, p. B7.

[32]See Augustine's *The City of God* for classical reflections on the good society. George Weigel's *Tranquillitas Ordinis* (New York: Oxford University Press, 1998) pursues many of Augustine's themes for a contemporary audience.

[33]For a record of the inhumanity and horror of communist, totalitarian governments in recent history see Stephane Courtois et al., *The Black Book of Communism,* ed. Mark Kramer, trans. Jonathan Murphy (Cambridge, Mass.: Harvard University Press, 1999).

[34]See Newman's *Foundations of Religious Tolerance* for a survey of the topic. See as well Harold Netland, *Dissonant Voices* (Grand Rapids: Eerdmans, 1991), pp. 306-14, for helpful discussion on religious toleration.

[35]For an account of how the creative moral vision of dissident writer Aleksandr Solzhenitsyn contributed to the demise of the former Soviet Union, see Os Guinness, ed., *Character Counts* (Grand Rapids: Baker, 1999), pp. 135-60.

[36]For legions of examples of this favorite tactic of the political left in America today, see Ann Coulter, *Slander* (New York: Crown, 2002); Larry Elder, *The Ten Things You Can't Say in America* (New York: St. Martin's, 2000); and Tammy Bruce, *The New Thought Police* (Roseville, Calif.: Prima, 2001).

[37]See John Perrazo, "The ACLU's War Against National Security," October 8, 2003

<www.frontpagemag.com/Articles/ReadArticle.asp?ID=10209>.

[38]For discussion of these charges and the many troubling absurdities surrounding airport security as well as larger questions of immigration security and policy, see Michelle Malkin, *Invasion* (Washington, D.C.: Regnery, 2002).

[39]At this date Al-Arian's trial is pending. Regarding the cases of Al-Arian and Islamic charities, see Emerson, *American Jihad*.

Chapter 12

[1]For studies of American's exaltation of the victim and his whine, see Larry Elder, *Showdown* (New York: St. Martin's, 2002), chap. 5; Robert Hughes, *Culture of Complaint* (New York: Warner Books, 1994); Charles Sykes, *A Nation of Victims: The Decay of the American Character* (New York: St. Martin's, 1992).

[2]Josh McDowell and Bob Hostetler, *The New Tolerance* (Wheaton, Ill.: Tyndale House, 1998), pp. 40, 42.

[3]Helpful surveys of the study of human nature are Leslie Stevenson's books *The Study of Human Nature* (New York: Oxford University Press, 1981) and *Seven Theories of Human Nature* (New York: Oxford University Press, 1974). For a discussion and defense of the classical view of human nature and essence, see part one of J. P. Moreland and Scott B. Rae, *Body & Soul: Human Nature & the Crisis in Ethics* (Downers Grove, Ill.: InterVarsity Press, 2000).

[4]See Phil Donahue, *The Human Animal* (New York: Simon & Schuster, 1985).

[5]For critique of this view see J. Budziszewski, *The Resurrection of Nature: Political Theory and the Human Character* (Ithaca, N.Y.: Cornell University Press, 1986); Brian Crowley, *The Self, the Individual, and the Community* (New York: Oxford University Press, 1987); Raymond Denehy, *Reason and Dignity* (Washington, D.C.: University Press of America, 1981); Michael Sandel, *Liberalism and the Limits of Justice* (Cambridge: Cambridge University Press, 1982); Charles Taylor, *Sources of the Self* (Cambridge, Mass.: Harvard University Press, 1989); Glenn Tinder, *Against Fate: An Essay in Personal Dignity* (Notre Dame, Ind.: University of Notre Dame Press, 1981). For articulation of the classical Christian understanding of the human person and human nature see J. P. Moreland and David Ciocchi, eds., *Christian Perspectives on Being Human* (Grand Rapids: Baker, 1993); Moreland and Rae, *Body and Soul*.

[6]For fascinating discussion along these lines, see Nancy B. Barcus, *Developing a Christian Mind* (Downers Grove, Ill.: InterVarsity Press, 1977); J. P. Moreland, *Love Your God with All Your Mind* (Colorado Springs: NavPress, 1997); and James Sire, *Habits of the Mind: Intellectual Life as a Christian Calling* (Downers Grove, Ill.: InterVarsity Press, 2000).

[7]For summary of the composition of the human person, and in particular the relationship of the soul to all the other parts of the human person and the role each part can play in a fruitful and continually growing life of true discipleship to Jesus, see Dallas Willard, *Renovation of the Heart* (Colorado Springs: NavPress, 2002).

[8]Jacques Maritain, *The Peasant of the Garonne* (New York: Holt, Rinehart & Winston, 1968), p. 85.

[9]For penetrating discussion of what he frankly calls the anti-American philosophy underpinning the work of such organizations, see David Horowitz, "People Against the American Way," May 13, 2003 <www.frontpagemag.com/Articles/ReadArticle.asp?ID=7783>. For book-length critique of the psychology and quasi-religious motivation of the American left, see Horowitz's illuminating study, *The Politics of Bad Faith: The Radical Assault on America's Future* (New York: Free Press, 1998).

[10]See "Churchgoers Hold Vigil For Landmark," May 5, 2003 <www.thetrenchcoat.com/archives/2003/05/05cross-to-bear-ii/>.

[11]For discussion of other practical applications of tolerance, see Andre Comte-Sponville, *A Small Treatise on the Great Virtues* (New York: Henry Holt, 2001), pp. 157-72.

[12]J. Budziszewski, *The Revenge of Conscience: Politics and the Fall of Man* (Dallas: Spence, 1999), p. 44.

[13]On the inevitability of particularity see the important work, Roy A. Clouser, *The Myth of Religious Neutrality: An Essay on the Hidden Role of Religious Belief in Theories* (Notre Dame, Ind.: University of Notre Dame Press, 1991).

[14]Reflection on these areas of tolerance is based in part on the discussion conducted by Harold Netland in *Dissonant Voices: Religious Pluralism and the Question of Truth* (Grand Rapids: Eerdmans, 1991), pp. 305-14.

[15]On the nature of Islam in Saudi Arabia specifically, see Dore Gold, *Hatred's Kingdom* (Washington, D.C.: Regnery, 2003). For helpful summaries of varieties of Islamic theology and politics—especially with reference to the causes and consequences of the attacks of 9/11—see John Ankerberg and John Weldon, *Fast Facts on Islam* (Eugene, Ore.: Harvest House, 2001).

[16]See Loury's valuable reflections in his book *One by One from the Inside Out: Essays and Reviews on Race and Responsibility in America* (New York: Free Press, 1995).

[17]The best source for understanding the racist theology of the Nation of Islam is still Malcolm X with Alex Haley, *The Autobiography of Malcolm X* (New York: Ballantine, 1973). See also James Cone, *Martin & Malcolm & America* (Maryknoll, N.Y.: Orbis, 1992), pp. 154-66. Cone's book is notable for its brilliant comparison and contrast of Malcolm X's and Martin Luther King Jr.'s personal, theological and political differences.

[18]For development of this general theme, see George Carey, "Tolerating Religion," in *The Politics of Toleration in Modern Life,* ed. Susan Mendus (Durham, N.C.: Duke University Press, 2000), pp. 45-63.

[19]Writers most representative of the drive for regarding all religions as more-or-less true, an approach to the study of religion known now as "religious pluralism," are John Hick and the late Wilfred Cantwell Smith. Representative of their works are John Hick, *An Interpretation of Religion* (New Haven, Conn.: Yale University Press, 1989), and *A Christian Theology of Religions: The Rainbow of Faiths* (Louisville, Ky.: Westminster John Knox, 1995); and Wilfred Cantwell Smith, *Towards a World Theology* (Philadelphia: Westminster Press, 1981). For critique of this movement, see Netland, *Dissonant Voices,* and his *Encountering Religious Pluralism* (Downers Grove, Ill.: InterVarsity Press, 2002); Dennis L. Okholm and Timothy R. Phillips, eds., *More Than One Way? Four Views on Salvation in a Pluralistic World* (Grand Rapids: Zondervan, 1995); Brad Stetson, *Pluralism and Particularity in Religious Belief* (Westport, Conn.: Praeger, 1994).

Epilogue

[1]See E. Michael Jones, *Degenerate Moderns: Modernity as Rationalized Sexual Misbehavior* (San Francisco: Ignatius Press, 1993).

[2]Excellent reflection on the moral dynamics of hypocrisy is found in James S. Spiegel, *Hypocrisy: Moral Fraud and Other Vices* (Grand Rapids: Baker, 1999).

[3]For representative discussion of this reality, see Paul C. Vitz, *Faith of the Fatherless: The Psychology of Atheism* (Dallas: Spence, 1999).

[4]Dallas Willard, *Renovation of the Heart: Putting On the Character of Christ* (Colorado Springs: NavPress, 2002), p. 255 (italics in original).

Index